My # 1 917 353 4491

My voice mail +1 917 353 6245

3333

02/9614 1113   Vincent voice mail

Vladimira

02/ 4143 4286 (H)

02/7117 1416 (cell)

Lorann
02/2311230

Praguewalks

This is the
Henry Holt Walks Series,
which originated with
PARISWALKS *by Alison and Sonia Landes.*
Other titles in the series include:

LONDONWALKS *by Anton Powell*
JERUSALEMWALKS *by Nitza Rosovsky*
ROMEWALKS *by Anya M. Shetterly*
VIENNAWALKS *by J. Sydney Jones*
RUSSIAWALKS *by David and Valeria Matlock*
VENICEWALKS *by Chas Carner and Alessandro Giannatasio*
BARCELONAWALKS *by George Semler*
BEIJINGWALKS *by Don J. Cohn and Zhang Jingqing*
NEW YORKWALKS *by The 92nd Street Y*
MADRIDWALKS *by George Semler*
BERLINWALKS *by Peter Fritzsche and Karen Hewitt*
FLORENCEWALKS *by Anne Holler*

PRAGUEWALKS

Ivana Edwards

Photographs by
Ivana Edwards

An Owl Book

Henry Holt and Company • New York

Henry Holt and Company, Inc.
Publishers since 1866
115 West 18th Street
New York, New York 10011

Henry Holt® is a registered
trademark of Henry Holt and Company, Inc.

Published in Canada by Fitzhenry & Whiteside Ltd.,
195 Allstate Parkway, Markham, Ontario L3R 4T8.

Library of Congress Cataloging-in-Publication Data
Edwards, Ivana.
Praguewalks/Ivana Edwards; photographs by Ivana Edwards.—
1st Owl Book ed.
p.   cm.—(Henry Holt walks series)
"An Owl Book."
Includes index.
1. Prague (Czech Republic)—Guidebooks.   2. Prague (Czech
Republic)—Tours.   I. Title.   II. Title: Prague walks.
III. Series.
DB2607.E38   1994   93–30358
914.37'120443—dc20   CIP

ISBN 0-8050-2360-7

Henry Holt books are available for special promotions
and premiums. For details contact:
Director, Special Markets.

First Owl Book Edition—1994

Designed by Claire Naylon Vaccaro
Maps by Jeffrey L. Ward

Printed in the United States of America
All first editions are printed on acid-free paper. ∞

1   3   5   7   9   10   8   6   4   2

To my uncle
Otakar Marek,
in memoriam

Contents

Acknowledgments

My aunt Naďa Marková gets first thanks for cheerful assistance too extensive and varied to mention. My deepest gratitude goes to my father, Sam Edwards, and my stepmother, Martina, who, despite heavy schedules of their own, played a major role in expediting and easing my sojourns in Prague over the past year, and made possible the writing of this book. Many thanks are due to Luboš Mayer, for his help and chauffeuring; to Magda Mrázová and Jaroslava Mrázová for their support; to Zdeněk Lukeš, Dobroslav Líbal, the staff at the Pragensis branch of the Prague Municipal Library, Hana Krejčová at the Klementinum, and all those who provided their time and expertise. Not to be forgotten is Pavla Bartaková, who generously shared her cherished library with me. Much appreciation is due to my editor, Theresa Burns, for her unfailing enthusiasm, good humor, and sound guidance. Thanks also to Fifi Oscard for delivering this project to my door, and to my agent, Ed Knappman. And not least, to Dan Stracuzza for his support and conscientious processing and printing of my photographs.

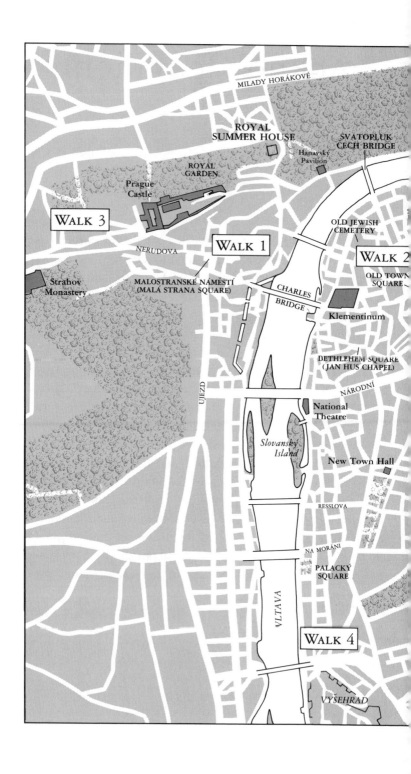

MILADY HORÁKOVÉ

ROYAL
SUMMER HOUSE

SVATOPLUK
CECH BRIDGE

Hanavský
Pavilion

ROYAL
GARDEN

Prague
Castle

WALK 3

OLD JEWISH
CEMETERY

NERUDOVA

WALK 1

WALK 2

Strahov
Monastery

OLD TOWN
SQUARE

MALOSTRANSKÉ NÁMĚSTÍ
(MALÁ STRANA SQUARE)

CHARLES
BRIDGE

Klementinum

BETHLEHEM SQUARE
(JAN HUS CHAPEL)

NÁRODNÍ

UJEZD

National
Theatre

Slovanský
Island

New Town Hall

RESSLOVA

NA MORÁNI

PALACKÝ
SQUARE

VLTAVA

WALK 4

VYŠEHRAD

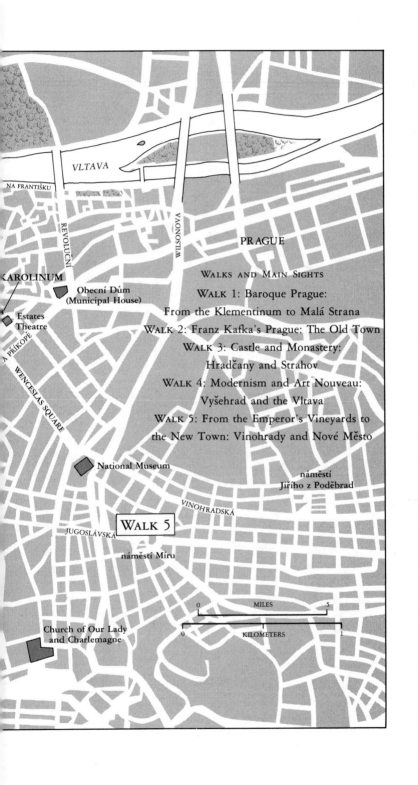

PRAGUE

WALKS AND MAIN SIGHTS

WALK 1: Baroque Prague:
From the Klementinum to Malá Strana
WALK 2: Franz Kafka's Prague: The Old Town
WALK 3: Castle and Monastery:
Hradčany and Strahov
WALK 4: Modernism and Art Nouveau:
Vyšehrad and the Vltava
WALK 5: From the Emperor's Vineyards to
the New Town: Vinohrady and Nové Město

VLTAVA

NA FRANTIŠKU

REVOLUČNÍ

WILSONOVA

KAROLINUM

Obecní Dům
(Municipal House)

Estates
Theatre

A PŘÍKOPĚ

WENCESLAS SQUARE

National Museum

náměstí
Jiřího z Poděbrad

VINOHRADSKÁ

WALK 5

JUGOSLÁVSKÁ

náměstí Míru

Church of Our Lady
and Charlemagne

MILES
0   5

KILOMETERS
0   1

Introduction

You, dear traveler about to embark on your journey, will be in exquisite company: nearly a thousand years' worth of continental romantics and realists have feasted their eyes on the ancient capital of Bohemia and reported back in no uncertain terms. Thomas Mann called Prague one of the most magical cities on earth: "In her old beauty she surpasses much of what is Italian." It is not hard to see what he meant, for in its hilly, deeply curving river-valley setting Prague seems to have been built for the crown of a city. As French architect Jean Nouvel has noted, "All residents opening their windows here have the impression they live in a castle."

Prague is one of those cities that profoundly score the face of Europe, but here the feeling of eternity has hardly changed (though much else has). It is the ultimate nostalgia trip for those who resonate to the grandeur, the sweep, and, yes, the pathos of history.

In the last few years, visitors have been joined by returning natives, on whom it instantly dawns that the Prague they are seeing is actually more extraordinary and

Charles Bridge and the Old Town

redolent of the past than the Prague of their youthful memories, the legends, or the hype. There are so many "returning to Prague" stories . . . so many have left, so many have returned . . . and so many dreamed of returning before time caught up with them.

My own returning occurred in the summer of 1964, in what proved to be an unexpected, sharply personal revelation that had a lot to do with identity, taking place as it did at the time of a precarious coming-of-age. On the last leg of my first European tour I arrived at Prague's old Ruzyně Airport, then reminiscent of a World War II airplane hangar, to an overwhelming royal reception, as the first member of my family to go back more than a decade. (My parents had bundled me up and departed in the face of the dooming Communist makeover in which my father had no intention of participating.) I recall a torrent of red roses, endless posing for my uncle's manic camera, and being excitedly fussed over by relatives, including battling grandmothers, who enveloped me in warm affection and curiosity.

Once I was in the city, shadowed by my devoted entourage that seldom left me alone, my eyes and expectations took a while to adjust to the shades of yellow that seemed to predominate—or was it the opalescence of light, especially before dusk, and the aureate view of Prague Castle (known as the Hrad) from the Old Town side of the river, that made it seem so? *Zlatá Praha,* golden Prague . . . the description is said to come from the copper roofing—long since dismantled—that Emperor Charles IV ordered for the Castle when he was renovating it. But these were the dreary gray days of the early sixties, and the famous Prague gold was less in evidence than it is today, when many buildings and coats-of-arms and hundreds of gold-whiskered tops of spires seem freshly gilded. It didn't take long, then as now, to see and feel beyond the surface to the otherworldly depths, to be transported back through hundreds of years of history, and farther back still into the Middle Ages, along meandering cobblestoned lanes with little hand-cut squares of granite embedded in the sidewalks in simple geometrical patterns.

Despite my delight in discovery, it was impossible to escape the presence of the ruling Communist government that shrouded everyday life like rusty chain mail, suffocating the natural vitality of a nation. Disregarding the pall as much as I could, I stopped at my family's landmarks and started to feel a pungent blend of pleasure and melancholy flowing through my veins, suffusing my brain. The sense of incalculable loss hit me hardest when my uncle took me to the top of the Gothic Bridge Tower on the Malá Strana side. This instantly became my favorite view of the city—the panoply spread below is enchanting, but there is something tangible and irrepressible about rooftops when you are so close to them, yet far enough to take them all in at once.

While those memories can't fail to linger in thinking about a lost generation, Prague is a different city today. In November 1989, the day we had all been dreaming about and praying for finally dawned as the oppressors gave way. Their time was up and they knew it. Prague Castle, as conspicuous as a compass to align oneself by, used to look phantasmagoric. Long the seat of Kafkaesque power (the Hapsburgs were entrenched for three hundred years), it seemed to brood like a despised, all-seeing warden over the whole city. The atmosphere could be so unsettling, some travelers probably aborted their stay. Back home they would shake their heads at the intensity and poignancy of it all. This went on for more than forty years (fifty years if you count the Nazi occupation). Now the Hrad is home to a democratically elected government and a president who is also a voice of conscience to the whole world, Václav Havel.

Just as Paris is France—almost anything of real consequence that happens in the country begins there— Prague *is* the Czech lands. This was also true in the former Czechoslovakia, which helps explain why the Slovaks felt they had to separate: they no longer wanted to be dominated by Prague. Today, with its 1.25 million people, 497 square kilometers, and 10 districts, a stranger will find a city seething with post-Communist impatience, anxiety, and sometimes confused expectations and behavior. The invincible urge is to forget the past and quickly forge a future. Ironically, most of what visitors want to see—monuments, palaces, gardens, art, architecture—is old, but everything else promises, in time, to be new. A new society, emerging from synthetic isolation and cultural oblivion, is abuilding.

It is often said that Prague is preserved more by love than by law. And this seems true; Praguers are surrounded by the past at every turn in one of the world's largest and best-preserved historic centers. (In 1992 Prague was named to the United Nations UNESCO World Heritage List of sites "considered to be of such exceptional interest and such universal value that their protection is the responsibility of all mankind.") They may occasionally grumble about the inconvenience of the eternal maintenance of old structures and the inevitable frailties of their great age, yet the majority wouldn't change anything and instinctively understand that here is something too special to tamper with. For the gift of Prague is sheer beauty—the haunting, as well as haunted, kind, possessed by only a few world-class cities simultaneously blessed and cursed with centuries-deep layers of tumultuous, polemical pasts and visionary, urbanistically astute rulers.

The rising and falling topography is what makes Prague one of the most stunning cities ever built and sets it apart from, indeed above, the flat-terrained beauty contestants in the "most ravishing" sweepstakes—on a continent where ancient loveliness is not exactly in short supply. Like Rome, Prague rises on and around seven thickly wooded hills. The variety of terrain provides superb, changeless vistas from vantage points throughout the city; one of the most filmed, photographed, sketched, painted, sculpted, and etched is that from Charles Bridge looking up at the Castle crowning the bluff.

But there are other, much less familiar views that are known only to native Praguers or longtime residents. Several of these naturally place in the center of the picture the axis of the city's historic core: the river Vltava, with its eight islands and sixteen bridges. Others offer unexpected panoramic perspectives on Prague's fabled red roofs and spires. Still others help to expose the enigmatic byways of the city's inner life and complex history at cobblestone level, through its streets, squares, and neighborhoods, its gardens, cemeteries, and memorials.

It is the purpose of this book to steer you beyond and away from the usual two- or three-day whirlwind tourist itineraries—the Royal Road through the Old Town to Prague Castle and St. Vitus Cathedral, and the glitzier Wenceslas Square/Na příkopě shopping, hotel, and entertainment scene—that constitute the basic Prague walks, the centerpieces of anyone's stay. That doesn't mean you should avoid them, of course. You could hardly miss them anyway—it would be like going to Manhattan for the first time and managing to skip Fifth Avenue. The first three walks in this book will pass through or skirt the glorious inevitables. The last two will take you to districts where Praguers live and while away their recreational hours, and also introduce you to art and architecture that you will find nowhere else in Europe.

A word about Praguers. Some long-term (meaning since the 1989 revolution) expatriates, as well as other visitors, have noted that they find the city and its people unfathomable. They can't understand why Praguers seem to want to flee from the past, intent on putting it behind them, preferring even to disown it. But the Praguers' attitude toward history is not surprising. The Czech experience with Communism is an ongoing national trauma and probably impossible for anyone who did not live through it to empathize with fully. It is something social historians and psychologists will have to sort out. Suffice

Malá Strana rooftops

it to say that a new life lies ahead for all and that many middle-aged and older Czechs (the young are largely fearless) are coping silently, feeling their way, with a degree of bravado when confronted by Western lifestyles and attitudes that may mystify observers. They care terribly what you think, yet will usually not express such feelings. For visitors it is usually best to restrain criticism and unsolicited advice lest it be viewed as patronizing. However, I do not hesitate to advise that this rule does not apply to establishments where you are paying a good price and getting less than what you were led to believe you could expect.

Though the thousands of Americans in residence at this writing might belie the fact, Prague is still novel territory for many North Americans. Even some Western Europeans are newly discovering it now that most of Central and Eastern Europe are free. And so one unique and timely attraction of Prague is that it offers a chance to witness the unfolding of its rebirth and return to the continental mainstream of which it had previously been a part. Until the Velvet Revolution of 1989, when the monstrous concrete slab of Communism was finally lifted and Czechs and Slovaks could breathe freely again, Praguers were all too aware that their magnificent city, their tragic heroine, was all they had. Today visitors can participate with them in rebuilding the country, in reinventing the city, and in helping Praguers catch up with the waning twentieth century just by being there and being open to the experience of getting to know the people.

Something bizarre ended, something perhaps unimaginable today even to those who lived through it, and something new started. Prague is now a place of epochal opportunity, a new frontier, making it more exciting for the foreseeable future than its well-settled and perhaps jaded Western European counterparts.

Welcome to Prague.

Information
and Advice

The enduring wonder of the glories of Prague against all odds, homegrown and imported, from the distant past and the recent past, heightens the sense of awe the visitor feels in this city. But despite the history, the consensus is that the best is yet to come as the country re-creates itself. In the years since the 1989 revolution there has been more of everything—tourists, taxis, restaurants, hotels, nightclubs, stores, concerts. And, yes, more crime and sleaze—two categories that were news to Czechs accustomed to police-state repression but that won't impress in the slightest the majority of urban-dwelling Westerners who think they've seen it all. In 1992 it all seemed to take off, commercially speaking. As of this writing, mass tourism is a rapidly evolving industry in the Czech Republic, most highly developed in the capital, which has always seen many more visitors than the rest of the country. Free-market rules are being improvised every day as fledgling, though enthusiastic and hard-

Sightseeing on Charles Bridge

working, entrepreneurs try their wings, so be prepared to run into occasional awkward behavior and service, which can manifest itself in a variety of ways, from apathy and sheer ineptness to outright profligacy.

Though it should not deter you, any negative aspects are at their worst in June, July, and August, when the city is overrun by tourists (you'll have the same problem between Christmas and *Silvestr* [New Year's]). The government bureaucracy is a conspicuous cause of soul-numbing frustration, and I strongly recommend that you avoid dealing with any state agency if possible. This is, after all, Kafka country. Contrary to any tombstone you may have seen, the world of the author of *The Trial*, in which the hero is hounded for an unnamed crime, not only still lives but flourishes—to the despair of all who must entangle themselves in it. This also goes for the government-run tourist information bureau, PIS (Pražská Informační Služba). Don't bother trying to phone, for instance; PIS's single line is permanently busy. You will have to go there in person (they are located in central Prague on Na příkopě 20, not far from Wenceslas Square). Just don't expect the most up-to-date information or answers to all your reasonable questions. This also applies to the usually helpful American Hospitality Center (run by Czechs), located on the ground floor of Provaznická 1, just behind the Můstek metro station; they're friendly and do have CNN and decent pizza, but they too have been known to give incorrect information.

So what is the unknowing traveler to do? Just be patient and perhaps somewhat less demanding than you might be elsewhere. By all means make your needs known, but realize that across-the-board efficiency has not yet arrived here. You will, however, run into many people who are trying hard, and an incipient, linear "Germanic" temperament characterized by extreme efficiency bodes well, at least for some Praguers. It is safe to say that Czechs are generally sensitive—perhaps oversensitive is more accurate—eager to please, and anxious to catch up with the Western modus operandi from which they were isolated for so long. By the time this book is published, standards will undoubtedly be much better established in the more tourist-frequented districts. In farther-flung areas, the management may be slower at figuring things out. Depending on whether you are in a hurry, that may or may not bother you; your experiences will simply be an even more authentic throwback to the past.

VISAS AND TRAVEL

To anyone who remembers the annoying prerevolutionary formalities, wherein you were obligated to exchange a certain amount of foreign currency into Czech crowns along with getting your visa stamped, travel to the Czech Republic is now a breeze and as simple as visiting any European nation. American citizens do not need visas for stays of less than thirty days—just grab your valid passport and go. Canadian citizens, however, do need visas (in retaliation for Canadian government requirements of Czech visitors), which cost $49 Canadian. Apply at your local consulate (in Montreal: 1305 Pine Avenue West) or to the embassy in Ottawa (50 Rideau Terrace, Ottawa, Ontario, K1M 2A1). Visas may also be obtained at major border crossings and at the airport upon payment of the fee and completion of the application form.

The most convenient air service to Prague is via ČSA, Czechoslovak Airlines, which offers nonstop flights on comfortable Airbus 310/300 planes from New York, from Montreal, from Chicago via Montreal, and from Toronto via Montreal. The trip is seven hours or so from New York and the service is professional in business and economy classes. Ruzyně Airport, an expanding facility about twenty kilometers west of the city, is a fast fifteen-minute drive from the center. Public buses (Nos. 119 and 254) depart from the main terminal every half hour and will connect you with the metro at the Dejvická station. ČSA operates a shuttle bus to its central city terminal on Revoluční Street, also connected to the Dejvická metro station. Taxis are also readily available at the main terminal: the fare should be no more than $10 to the center on the meter, but be sure to confirm this with any prospective cabdriver. If you have a valid international driver's license, car rentals from agencies such as Pragocar are also available. If you're arriving by train at the Central Railway Station (Hlavní nádraží) on Wilsonova, you can also catch the ČSA shuttle bus, a taxi, or the metro (Red Line C).

TO READ

Arming yourself with reading matter of substance before departure is challenging, because as of this writing there is little nonfiction in print in North America, or in English, specifically about Prague. You might find Joseph Wechsberg's discursive, anecdotal, and affectionate 1971 *Prague the Mystical City* in a library, but the author ends with the Soviet invasion of 1968. Francis Dvornik's *The Slavs in European History and Civilization* (1962) does have most of the facts of the Czech and Slovak past (from the thirteenth century to the eighteenth century only), though it is presented in a pedestrian, academic style, which is also true of the *The United States, Revolutionary Russia and the Rise of Czechoslovakia*, by Betty Miller Unterberger. For rectification of this unfortunate state of affairs, readers who want a substantial social and cultural history of this famous city will have to wait a few more years. Your best bet in the meantime, short of learning to read Czech, is to find some memoirs, such as Heda Margolius Kovály's *Under a Cruel Star*, an extremely moving retelling of the horrific early Communist period. Alan Levy's 1972 *Rowboat to Prague*, about the late sixties, is a pleasure, and has been reissued by Second Chance Press. Fiction is a much better option: the earlier short stories and novels of Milan Kundera, such as *The Joke* and *The Book of Laughter and Forgetting*; anything by Ivan Klíma; Josef Škvorecký's *The Cowards* and *Dvořák in Love*, for example; Bohumil Hrabal's *I Served the King of England*; and Jiří Weil's grueling *Life with a Star*. Another favorite is Marcia Davenport's *The Valley of Decision*, although it is actually more about Pittsburgh. In a similar category is Jan Novak's *The Willys Dream Kit*, partly set in the American Midwest. And anything by Václav Havel, the president of the Czech Republic, a world-famous essayist and playwright, is especially prophetic and inspiring.

CLIMATE

Prague's climate is officially described as maritime. The weather is somewhat tempered by not-too-distant encircling mountains, which means it doesn't rain that much, but seasonal extremes in temperature are typical. In fact, the weather will remind Americans of their own Northeast. If you don't thrive at extremes, avoid July and August—it's *hot* (temperatures often climb into the 80s Fahrenheit, though averaging in the 70s). Ditto for the post-Christmas to New Year's celebrations—it's cold (the range is 25–34). Competition from your fellow travelers is stiff during these two periods as well; it's often too much for the fragile service sector to handle. Western Europeans especially come here then, and Praguers vanish to their country retreats.

The best months to visit Prague are April, when it's still sweater weather (the range is 48–56), and May, for glorious skies—the most clarity you'll see all year. This is also lilac weather and the time of blossoming horse chestnut trees—you'll see their frothy blooms all over town. June starts to heat up and get smoggy (the range is 56–72). February is cold and gray, but at least it's not January, and there are plenty of snug and cheerful venues *indoors*; March is nearly twice as sunny (33–45). September is excellent (52–68), and the crowds begin to thin out noticeably. October starts to get chilly (43–54), but it's still pleasant if you don't mind packing accordingly. Rainfall is heaviest in July, but you'll see few heavy or persistent downpours; the thirstiest month is February. Always remember to bring a lightweight folding umbrella in spring, summer, or fall.

MONEY

The currency in the Czech Republic is the "crown" (*koruna*, abbreviated *Kč*), each of which breaks up into 100 "hellers" (*haléře*). As of this writing the rate is about 27 Kč to the U.S. dollar, and 44 Kč to the British pound. The best exchange rates are at banks, though Prague is full of conveniently located money-changing bureaus charging high commission rates. If you change more money than you need, major banks will buy back whatever you want to sell for dollars or common European currencies. Changing money on the street for black-market rates is a relic of the past, because the rate is hardly better and it is, as ever, risky. Cash advances are available on major credit cards at the Živnostenská Bank (tel. 22 43 46) at 20 Na příkopě, where you can also most easily exchange Czech crowns or any other common currency for U.S. dollars. Hours are Monday to Friday from 8:00 A.M. to 12:45 P.M. and from 1:15 to 6:00 P.M.; Saturdays from 8:00 A.M. to 12:00 noon. Among its branches in the center of town, Komerční Bank has an exchange office at the Central Railway Station open from 8:00 A.M. to 6:00 P.M. Monday to Friday. And the American Express office at 56 Wenceslas Square (tel. 257 528) also provides banking services.

There are two price scales operating in the Czech Republic—one for Czechs who are dependent on the local economy and are paid in crowns, and one for visitors and foreign businesspeople who are generally charged prices similar to those in Western Europe. For example, a hotel room rate for a foreigner might be $220, while the same room would cost a local citizen only 750 Kč. As market forces take over, the economy gains strength, and salaries rise, these two price scales will merge uniformly. In fact, this is already happening, and it is making life difficult for average Praguers on low salaries or fixed incomes and for those who have no foreign currency.

Here are some general price ranges. Cup of coffee: 15–25 Kč; half-liter of beer: 10–20 Kč (low end), 50 Kč (high end); local brand small bottle of mineral water: 10–15 Kč; an English-language newspaper: 25 Kč; restaurant dinner for one: 80–160 Kč (low end), 350–800 Kč (high end); movie ticket: 20–30 Kč.

ACCOMMODATIONS

A hotel shortage exists during peak season (May to October), but a number of projects under way in this hot-growth market should ease the situation in the near future. Of Prague's existing approximately seventy-five hotels, only about fifteen are in the four- and five-star slots. Five-star hotels include the Palace, the Intercontinental (recommended only for the view), the Esplanade, and the Hyatt International Praha in the Dejvice district. Room rates in these average $250 per night. There are a number of large, ultra-modern, soulless (and expensive) new hotels catering primarily to the foreign business trade, such as the Panorama, the Forum, and the Atrium (788 rooms), but I don't recommend them if atmosphere and location matter to you—you might as well be in Atlanta, Georgia. By the time you read this, there will be others, including a Four Seasons on the riverbank and a Ritz Carlton, equally well situated.

One of the few hotels in the Old Town (Staré Město), that is, Prague 1, is the small, comfortable Ungelt on Štupartská Street, a few steps from the Old Town Square. Reasonably priced is the President (next to the dismal-looking Intercontinental) on the riverbank, with about as much charm as its neighbor. And then there is the small-ish, truly inimitable art nouveau Grand Hotel Evropa on Wenceslas Square, which will not be tampered with too much in the future, I hope. It is said to be hard to get reservations there, but drop-ins sometimes get lucky. Also on Wenceslas Square is the four-star Ambassador, an old favorite with a cozy, bustling lobby; rooms usually must be booked well in advance. In Malá Strana a good choice is the tiny Hotel U Páva, but it's expensive. Your options at lower prices improve if you don't mind staying outside the city center. No need to renounce convenience; just ask for something near a subway or streetcar line.

Another alternative for budget travelers is to try one of several accommodation agencies that will refer you to a private home or apartment. This has become a popular and reasonable option and is highly recommended not only for the price, but because you get a chance to meet the locals, away from the usual tourism hustle. Adventurous travel is surely not about situating yourself in lodgings that specialize in your class and nationality. (Access to a refrigerator is only occasionally a possibility in these places.) One such agency (this is not a comprehensive list) is Top Tour at Rybná 3 in the Old Town (Prague 1), which can also find space in hostels; another is Alltours on Vodičkova 15 (tel. 235 12 31 or 235 55 94); and a third is Pragotur at U Obecního Domu 2, Prague 1 (tel. 232 22 05). The former state travel agency, Čedok, which has a number of conveniently situated offices (for accommodations, try to go to the one at Panská 5, Prague 1, tel. 2127 552 55), can also steer you to housing. If you'd prefer to book a higher-priced hotel before you leave home, you can do it through Čedok in New York at 10 East 40th Street (tel. 212-689-9720, toll free 800-800-8891, fax 212-481-0597). The American Hospitality Center has an accommodations office near the Old Town

Square at Melantrichova 8 (tel. 26 77 70). Prague Suites offers a higher-priced option for long- or short-term stays (tel. 26 93 84). Finally, if you're arriving by train, the Central Railway Station (Hlavní nádraží) has Ave Ltd. (tel. 236 2560), Wilsonova 8, on the second level, a computerized service that locates accommodations, and they're open late: till 2:00 A.M. from May to September, and till 10:30 P.M. from October to April.

An agency that specializes in what it calls bed-and-breakfast facilities is Tourtip Viviane at Cukrovarnická 22, 162 00 Prague 6, Střešovice (tel. 35 23 13 or 31 24 142, fax 31 24 123). It offers accommodations in three categories, ranging from suites in private homes to rooms in pensions. IBV Bed and Breakfast Systems operates out of Silver Spring, Maryland, and provides a similar service (tel. 301-942-3770, fax 301-933-0024).

TRANSPORTATION

Humankind has yet to invent a more pleasant form of locomotion than the streetcar, at least in Prague. It is an unexpectedly efficient system, far preferable to the local smelly buses that, mercifully, serve mainly the outskirts of the city. Free of exhaust fumes, lurching less, and competing less with traffic, the electric red-and-cream-colored trams (many have been transformed into sparkling mobile advertising billboards) provide one of the best ways to see the city if you want to get off your feet—excluding rush hour, of course. Just board anywhere in the center and ride around. You can always go back in the opposite direction on the same route or get off where you choose. One of the best routes is the No. 17, which rumbles serenely along the Vltava River, or the equally scenic No. 22, which plies the rails up to Prague Castle. The trip is like an unbelievably cheap (4 Kč, about 15 cents U.S.), leisurely sightseeing tour of the city each time. On weekends and holidays there's a historic tram, No. 91, that stops at most of the city's major sights, though not the Castle. This tram has meticulously spiffed-up vintage cars with highly varnished wooden seats and moldings, somewhat larger windows, and conductors in gray woolen uniforms that are also a throwback to the past. (Tickets for the historic tram are 10 Kč for adults and 5 Kč for children.) Able-bodied persons rarely sit for long on crowded cars: a cane-armed pensioner is sure to nudge you off your seat with fierce, unmistakable entitlement.

When the weather is good and the distance short, I prefer the streetcar to the subway, especially if I have to transfer from one underground subway line to another. Otherwise, getting around on the clean, comfortable (upholstered seats), streamlined metro is a snap. It runs from 5:00 A.M. to midnight every day including weekends at intervals of one to ten minutes. Three intersecting lines—Green Line A, Yellow Line B, and Red Line C—will take you almost anywhere you are likely to want to go in the city.

Like buses and streetcars, the subway is on the honor system, and if you are caught in a spot check without a validated ticket, the fine is 200 Kč. A single ticket costs 4 Kč, and one-day passes, as well as two-, three-, and five-day passes, are available. If you are staying longer than a week, consider buying a one-month pass for 120 Kč. These passes, called *časova síťová jízdenka*, available at central bus and subway stations (look for signs saying "DP" or "Předprodej Jízdenek") as well as at some newsstands, called *tabak*, are the best deal going, price-wise. They also eliminate fumbling for change and are valid on the whole system—metro, streetcars, and buses. They are sold in the foyers of subway stations Anděl, Dejvická, Háje, Hradčanská, I.P. Pavlova, Kačerov, Můstek, Nádraží Holešovice, Náměstí Míru, Národní třída, Nové Butovice, and Želivského. You need a passport-sized photo to get one. Single tickets, identical in appearance for the entire network, must be validated before boarding and are good for one ride only, unlike the long-term passes, which are for unlimited travel.

Taxi fares are straightforward if you can find an honest driver (and some do exist). Since the revolution, the number of cabs has more than tripled, and taxi wars—at the expense of foreign visitors—have broken out. Locals tend not to take cabs, so the unscrupulous exploit tourists. The worst "criminal" taxis cruise Wenceslas Square and the Charles Bridge area. When the meter is turned on, a price of 6 Kč should register, with a 10-Kč increase per kilometer, and one Kč for every minute at rest. The rate window in the upper right-hand corner of the meter should show a "1" for Prague city limits. Higher numbers are illegal and will cause the fare to jump rapidly, so check this on entering the cab. Meters have been known to be tampered with, so it's advisable to ask the fare in advance, as well as asking how much the driver charges per kilometer. And make sure the meter is in full view; if it isn't, and the identification number is not clearly visible, don't enter. In case of trouble, note the license plate number and the name of the cab company, if there is one, and don't forget to ask for a receipt if you want to pursue a complaint (tel. 232 3171). When all is functioning properly, taxis are quite cheap—unless you take a hotel cab. Though more reliable, they are several times as expensive. You can order a taxi on the phone. In fact, phoning for a cab is a hedge against thievery, because the company has a reputation to uphold. It often happens, however, that the meter will have been turned on when the call came in. One of the most reliable companies is Czech Taxi Praha (tel. 202 929 or 202 952–9).

ENTERTAINMENT

Prague is famous for its lively and reasonably priced theater scene. Yes, it's usually in Czech, but at the historic Stavovské (Estates) Theater, formerly known as the Tyl and the Nostic, they provide inexpensive headsets with simultaneous live English translation. With more English speakers now in residence, struggling, small-scale English-

Lamppost at the Estates Theater

language theater companies are springing up, so check the weekly *Prague Post* newspaper listings. Jazz may be heard at numerous clubs around town, one of the best and least expensive (20 Kč) being **Malostranská Beseda** in the Malá Strana Town Hall (Malostranské náměstí), upstairs. The music is eclectic, everything from jazz to rock to bluegrass. The club **Reduta**, on Národní Třída at no. 21, is also a jazz hot spot; another is the **Euro Club** (formerly the Press Jazz Club), at Opletalova 5 off Wenceslas Square; the largest venue in the city for everything from big bands to modern jazz to blues, the **Euro** opens at 10:00 P.M. There's a cover charge of 50 Kč (students 25 Kč), and it has a restaurant and bar that open at 10:00 A.M. If it's rock music you want, hop next door to the **Rock Café** for reliable live entertainment, reasonable prices, and industrial decor. A hot disco is the spacious **Radost**, at Bělehradská 120, in the New Town (oddly enough, this place also presents poetry readings on Sundays at 6:00 P.M.—in English!).

Opera is featured at the **National Theater** (Národní divadlo), heavy on the Czech repertoire, of course, but if you love Janáček, what better place to hear one of his several masterpieces? Not to speak of Dvořák or Smetana or Martinů or Mozart. . . . In May the annual Prague Spring Music Festival has a full slate of performances all over the city. But you don't have to wait until spring: Prague is full of music at all times, including in the churches, an old tradition (one of Mozart's organ recitals was given at the Strahov Monastery church in Hradčany). The churches with the most extensive year-round music programs are St. Nicholas in Malá Strana, St. Nicholas in the Old Town Square, St. James (Sv. Jakub) on Malá Štupartská in the Old Town, and St. Giles (Sv. Jiljí) on Husova 8, also in the Old Town. The secret (as of this writing) to obtaining good, non-tourist-priced seats is either to have a Czech friend buy them for you or, for the Prague Spring Festival, to go directly to the Festival offices at Hellichova 8 in Malá Strana. (Prague Spring tickets go fast and should be ordered by the end of March.) Ticket agencies are convenient but will impose sizable surcharges. There are numerous movie theaters and American films to choose from all over town, but you will find many films are dubbed, an unfortunate custom here.

Many Czech rock entertainers have European reputations. Among the top performers are: Půlnoc (avant-garde rock of the sixties and seventies), Vladimír Mišík and Etc. (folk rock), Mňága a Ždorp (folk and rock), Tři Sestry (near punk), Nerez (jazz pop), Žlutý Pes (southern-style rock), Laura a Její Tygři (eclectic, including Latin rhythms and blues), David Koller (hard rock), Shalom (Jewish techno-pop), Janek Ledecký (rock-pop). For jazz, look for Jiří Stivín, Emil Viklický, and Tony Ackerman and Martin Kratochvíl.

FOOD

For the gastronomically inclined, the revolution has been tasted in Prague restaurants as much as in the corridors of power at the Castle. The dining scene is in continuing, often unpredictable flux, the result of inexperience and experimentation. Still, it is a significant improvement on what used to prevail when the government ran the kitchens of the city's restaurants and tried to run the minds of their customers and employees. The good news is that new restaurants are legion, and several are actually shooting for creativity and are serving a far greater variety of cuisines. A few are worth searching out by anyone who cares about food—and who cares about prices. In general, restaurants are far more expensive than they used to be, and the ingredients and cooking are far better, with fresh fruit and vegetables often available, but service still leaves much to be desired, though this too is rapidly improving. Under Communism the waiter's attitude was that the customer was sitting at his table to provide the waiter with a salary, and surliness was taken for granted. This is less often the case now, though waiters (along with cabdrivers) are often still viewed by Praguers as a local scourge. Some establishments that take credit cards will charge *you* the transaction fee, usually about 5 percent, which is customarily the vendor's responsibility in the West. And around holiday periods, such as Christmas and New Year's, all too many restaurants, and even cafés and bars, close shop, leaving hungry tourists stranded or just plain locked out of the overcrowded eateries that remain. Why this should be is mystifying (and especially annoying in the Old Town, where tourists congregate) but probably has something to do with the work ethic not being fully restored yet; some (vacationing) Prague restaurateurs appear to be slow in adjusting to the seasonal demands of their business. On the other hand, it is also possible to be pleasantly surprised by thoughtful and cheerful staff—if the place is not overcrowded.

Despite the new choices, for urban Westerners the range of restaurants is still somewhat limited; it's expanding daily, though, and extremes already appear entrenched. For example, U Malířů (At the Painter's), in Malá Strana, probably one of the most expensive restaurants in Europe, bills itself as the first private foreign restaurant in Czechoslovakia. It used to be a cozy, simple place where students hung out and talked long into the night. In 1990 the management presented brand-new pink damask tablecloths. Otherwise it looks very much unchanged, with the same decoratively painted vaulted ceilings and dark wood wainscoting. And yet everything is changed. It serves quite delicious, though not cutting edge, French food. The prices? Well, as they say about yachts, if you have to ask, you probably can't afford it: thirty dollars U.S. for even a superlative bowl of consomme? But do not despair: elsewhere, reasonably priced meals can be found, and new, ambitious establishments are springing up all the time. As ever, you simply have to know where to go, and so I've listed some good bets in the restaurant section at the back of this book.

As for what to eat, the truth is that Czech cooking is not at its best in the average restaurant (someone—a foreigner—once described it as nursery food in grown-up helpings). But it can be simply wonderful at home, so if you are invited to the home of somebody who knows how to cook from fresh ingredients, you'll probably be in for a treat. For example, the delicate fruit dumplings (*ovocné* or *jahodové knedlíky*), a Czech specialty that should be made with fresh strawberries or plums or other fresh fruit, are almost never found in restaurants. Those that offer them usually use canned fruit.

You may have heard that Czech cooking is heavy on meat and starches, and just plain heavy. I am not going to disabuse you entirely of that notion, but please note that meat, especially the ubiquitous pork (*vepřové*), which can be the tastiest meat around, is a genuine pleasure if it is skillfully cooked and roasted. The dumplings (knedlíky) made of potatoes or bread and wheat flour that usually accompany meat dishes—along with cabbage or sauerkraut—are only really tasty when they are soaked in gravy. Decent Wiener schnitzel is available, and smoked meats, another Czech specialty, are usually excellent. Prague ham is a renowned delicacy. Also look for *Uherský salám*, a peppery Hungarian salami, which is preferred by connoisseurs. With rye bread and some sliced pickles you have a classic Prague snack. Another popular traditional fast food is *párky* (*horké párky* translates as "hot dogs"), frankfurters often sold in pairs on the street, on railway platforms, at soccer matches—wherever crowds gather. Game, including venison, was a favorite prerevolutionary option and is still popular.

There's no getting around the fact that on the whole vegetarians and cholesterol watchers are going to be frustrated in the capital of the country with one of the highest levels of meat consumption in the world, unless they stick to salads and eat in restaurants that don't concentrate on traditional Czech food. This is entirely possible as newer, more sophisticated eateries crop up. As Czechs travel and sample the foods and cooking of other countries, something that was impossible for most of them during the Communist era, they are becoming more health-conscious and aware of the possibilities and uses of new or little-known ingredients. They are a sensitive people, anxious to catch up with what they missed and to raise standards to those of the rest of the continent. The process is well under way, accelerated, no doubt, by a healthy profit motive.

An option for some vegetarians is freshwater fish, such as trout and carp, from the well-stocked ponds of southern Bohemia. Fried carp is a traditional Christmas Eve dish. Soups (*polévky*) are often nourishing and filling, especially if you're on a budget. The most common soup is *hovezí vývar*, a beef broth usually made with vegetables. Don't hesitate to send it back if it has a sour odor, an indication of its having been reheated once too often. Vegetarians may prefer *bramboračka*, a potato soup often flavored with mushrooms, or a cream-of-mushroom soup (*žampionové krém*) of velvety texture and deep, woodsy mushroom flavor. In winter, salads and fresh vegetables can still be scarce. The rest of the year most establishments (especially those that take credit cards) have some fresh or frozen vegetables on hand. Also improving is the availability of a greater selection of greens, beyond butter leaf lettuce (*hlávkový salát*) in season only and more often than not used solely as a garnish by the non–vegetable-eating Czechs. Good-quality whole-grain breads and rolls are also a postrevolutionary novelty. Vegetarians in Prague gravitate to the **Country Life** restaurant on Vodičkova and Jungmannova (see page 253).

Among other Czech specialties, try *svíčková*, a roast beef dish (using a filet mignon cut of meat) served with a rich vegetable-based cream sauce and bread dumplings. This is always accompanied by a lingonberry (European cranberry) preserve for a sweet-and-sour combination, and often, at least in restaurants, a somewhat redundant dollop of whipped cream. The national Czech dish is roast pork, the generous cracklings ideally a golden brown and sprinkled with caraway seeds; the pork is served with bread dumplings and cabbage, either white or red. Roast duck or goose served with sauerkraut is another traditional treat. Instead of the usual dumplings, try *bramborák*, spicy, garlicky potato pancakes.

The most ubiquitous desserts (*moučníky*) are crepe-type pancakes called *palačinky*—good with chocolate or fruit and whipped cream—ice cream and fruit parfaits, and *lívance*, which are blueberries on a crumpetlike base—with whipped cream, of course. Pastries will rarely remind you of Vienna or Paris, but they have their occasional charms. One of my favorites is *věnečky*, a fluted *pâte aux choux* pastry ring filled with a mildly alcoholic egg-yolk pastry cream. *Koláče*, formed as yeast buns or strip cake and shallowly filled with *tvaroh* (the curds of a creamy cheese similar to farmer's cheese) or plum jam (*povidla*), can be delicious.

The fruit dumplings mentioned above, by the way, are supposed to be served with a generous sprinkling of *tvaroh* or poppy seeds, followed by an equally generous topping of confectioner's sugar, over which is poured plenty of melted butter. When your fork bites into the warm, tender, *delicate*, fresh-fruit–filled dumpling and the juices run out to mingle with the melting *tvaroh*, sugar, and butter, well, your taste buds will go wild. At least that is how it is done in my family—a frankly good, if sinful, indulgence.

Assorted rip-offs are not unusual on the restaurant scene. Watch out for hidden charges at the more expensive establishments, such as bowls of olives, salads, nuts, or appetizers that appear on the table. You will often be charged for them if you eat them. Another coverup can be the cover charge, not always clearly stated on the menu. If you're using a credit card, check the amount and the date for accuracy to avoid scams, but these are unusual. Most new restaurants are trying to build a reputation and will act accordingly.

Tipping varies with the type of restaurant and the

clientele. In the more expensive places 10 to 15 percent is expected, but in cheaper ones, less frequented by foreigners, a few crowns used to be enough, or rounding off to the nearest whole number, and that's still what most Czechs tip. If the service has been especially effortful, you might want to add another 8 or 10 percent. A number of restaurants are adding automatic service charges of 15 to 20 percent to the bill.

For American-style fast-food lovers, there are now five McDonald's in Prague. By the time this book is in print, there will inevitably be other such eateries.

Comestibles Glossary

apple	*jablko*
bacon	*slanina*
beef	*hovězí*
beer	*pivo*
bread	*chléb*
breakfast	*snídaně*
butter	*máslo*
chicken	*kuře*
cream	*smetana*
cucumber	*okurka*
dinner	*večeře*
egg	*vejce*
fat	*tuk*
lemon	*citron*
lunch	*oběd*
meat	*maso*
milk	*mléko*
mineral water	*minerálka*
oatmeal	*ovesné vločky*
oil	*olej*
onion	*cibule*
orange	*pomeranč*
pepper	*pepř*
pork	*vepřové*

potatoes	*brambory*
rice	*rýže*
salad	*salát*
salt	*sůl*
sugar	*cukr*
tomato	*rajče*
turkey	*krocan*
veal	*telecí*
vinegar	*ocet*
water	*voda*

DRINK

Taverns, beer halls (*pivnice*), wine cellars (*vinárny*), and cafés (*kavárny*) have historically been places where average Praguers all but *lived*, not just where they drank a particular brew. With small, overcrowded apartments and little incentive for either profit or advancement, few actually worked during the Communist period: "We pretend to work and they pretend to pay us," as the saying went. Informal drinking establishments were an extension of the living room, centers of social and cultural life. (This was also true in Franz Kafka's day—late-nineteenth, early-twentieth century—though the lower middle classes had much less leisure time.) Some preferred their drink in the rougher, noisier, simpler (but no less smoky) surroundings of the *pivnice*, while others were attracted to the marginally fussier socialist café—the clientele, of course, changed the atmosphere accordingly.

The grand old café is no longer what it was. Under Communism turn-of-the-century-style café life all but died out, relegated to proletarian establishments long on dreariness and cheap aluminum cutlery, and short on serendipity and sheer sybaritic distraction, no longer places where you could spend the whole day reading the newspapers provided. Few cafés except for those at the Grand Hotel Evropa and at the Obecní Dům on náměstí

Republiky still harbor intimations of the festive buzz, the warmth and sociability, that was possible amid the grandeur.

As for literary cafés like the Arco, Franz Kafka's hangout, where the clientele was particular and the highlights of Prague culture were conceived, written, drawn, and discussed—their activity was supplanted by the beer-swilling pubs (most of which also serve food) and cafés of a different, popular genre. In these places talk was often necessarily circumspect during the Communist decades; prying ears were dangerous. The pub scene is still going strong, of course, though for many Praguers it too is veering toward the unrecognizable, especially in terms of price. Numerous pubs in the city center have been gentrified and now seem to cater mainly to tourists.

Czech beer (*pivo*) is a widely exported national emblem and the perfect accompaniment to traditional Czech food, both for taste and for digestive reasons. For many Czechs it's the only sane thirst quencher, and anyone who's ever downed a cold mug on a hot, parched day knows what that means. So here's some beer lore.

The year of the earliest recorded recipe for beer in Bohemia is said to be 1088; the recipe was found on a church wall in Vyšehrad, the citadel settlement on the river that we will explore on Walk 4. The brewing method for pilsner, the best-known Bohemian beer and the original lager, was discovered in 1842 in Pilsen (Plzeň). It's a fine-filtration (also called bottom-fermenting) process that screens out the particles that make normal beer dark, turns it golden, and improves the flavor. It is said that the Germans copied the system and made it famous. Today Pilsen is a generic name, despite the best efforts—seventy-five years' worth—of the original brewery in Pilsen to trademark the name. Brands of beer in this small country run into the hundreds. Outside the Czech Republic you will most likely find Pilsner Urquell as the only authentic Pilsen-made beer.

Besides Pilsner Urquell, other excellent local brands

are Branik, Velké Popovice, and Gambrinus. Note that beers are classified by degree, depending on the sugar content rather than the alcohol content, although the more sugar, the more alcohol. A 12-degree beer (*dvanáctka*) contains 2.5 to 3.5 percent alcohol. The strongest beers, called *ležák*, can go up to 20 degrees. Generally, two kinds of beer are served in pubs: light (*světlé*) and dark (*černé*). If you can't make up your mind, try ordering a half-and-half, called *řezané*, which means "cut" beer. Storage and pouring ability are important to preserving the taste and quality of the beer. Connoisseurs watch for temperature. Czech beer should be cold—that's why it's served in mugs with handles—and the foamy head should be thick, leaving rings as it diminishes in the glass. To order, pub etiquette mandates you place a coaster (commonly found in the center of the table) in front of you, which tells the waiter you would like a beer. But before you sit down at what looks like an empty spot, ask the others at the table if the place is free: *"Je tu volno?"*

A recommended pub is **U Fleků** in the New Town, Křemencova 9 (take metro line B to Národní Třída), because it's the last one that still brews its own beer—a classic black variety—on the premises, serves hot food, and has a huge outdoor courtyard in the summer. The waiters speak German here because this place attracts German tourists, but even if you don't speak Czech *or* German, you will still meet lots of fellow travelers.

The Czech wine industry is small and is largely for local consumption. But as vineyards are being restituted to their original owners and are privatized, the potential of Czech wine making grows apace. Some of the best young white wines come from South Moravia and are starting to be exported; several are exceedingly agreeable, dry, and reportedly don't cause allergic reactions among some people who are prone to them (perhaps because they don't contain sulfites). Some of the better-known white varieties include Ryzlink Rýnský (muscat bouquet), Rulandské Bílé (a semidry burgundy), and Müller Thurgau (also with a muscat bouquet). Silvan has a rich green color and a soft bouquet. Among the better reds are Ludmilla, from the Bohemian Mělník area, and the wines of the Valtice area, also part of Moravia. In addition, watch for Rulandské Červené, a high-quality red burgundy, and Vavřinecké, with a bouquet of dried plums. As for spirits, the best known is Becherovka, an intensely herbal liqueur that may at first seem a touch medicinal, though it becomes quite smooth and pleasing when you get used to it.

Mineral-water drinkers have lots to choose from, but the favored brand is the excellent local Mattoni. And imported spring waters are increasingly available in several grocery stores.

Na zdraví! (To your health!)

HEALTH

Medical care is best obtained at the modern **Diplomatic Health Center for Foreigners**, located at Na homolce 724, Prague 5 (tel. 5292 21 46, or 5292 21 91 after normal working hours). The clinic offers twenty-four-hour emergency services, gynecology, and dental services with English-speaking doctors. Generally they demand a minimum 1,000-Kč (about $35) deposit except for emergencies. (Don't forget to bring your passport.) During the week you can also go to the Fakultní Poliklinika, Karlovo náměstí 28, 2nd floor, open Monday 7:15 A.M. to 5:00 P.M., Tuesday to Thursday, 7:15 A.M. to 3:45 P.M., and Friday, 7:15 A.M. to 2:30 P.M.

Pharmacies (*lékárny*) are centrally located, including one opposite the Main Post Office and a beautiful, historic one on Male náměstí, just off the Old Town Square. The most centrally located twenty-four-hour emergency pharmacy is at no. 7 Na příkopě (tel. 22 00 81-2). There's a network of others in the individual districts, such as Malá Strana: Moskevská (tel. 72 44 766); and

Door at Schonborn Palace, Malá Strana

Vinohrady: Ječná 1 (tel. 26 71 81). Don't try to buy contact-lens supplies in pharmacies; only optical stores (*oční optika*) selling eyeglass frames stock them. (For the information of trivia mavens, the soft contact lens is a Czech invention developed with the United States.)

EMERGENCIES

Since the pace of life in Prague hardly seems frenzied, it is easy to be lulled into complacency about crime. Fortunately, it is largely confined to petty thievery. Be warned that Prague (along with Warsaw, Milan, and Rome) is among the top four pickpocket draws in Europe, according to a 1993 U.S. State Department report. These nimble-fingered types operate in most tourist-congested areas and on crowded public transportation. Prague police are used to dealing with visitors and will be helpful, but they don't usually speak English, so try your embassy if you can't communicate with them. Your hotel is, of course, the first place to turn for assistance, but here are some useful telephone numbers.

Emergency medical aid	155
Police	158
Fire	150
Automobile breakdown	154
Airport	334 3314
Taxi	20 29 51, 20 39 41 (twenty-four hours)
Lost or stolen credit cards	236 66 88 (Visa or Diner's Club) 239 235 (MasterCard)
American Express	235 24 68 or 257 528 (office hours) 235 74 00 (after hours)

TELEPHONE AND MAIL

Communications headquarters is the Main Post Office (Hlavní Pošta) on Jindřišská Street, just off Wenceslas Square. It is open twenty-four hours a day. You can receive mail there through Poste Restante at window 28; mail should be addressed "Poste Restante, Jindřišská 14, 110 000 Praha 1." Stamps can be bought here, at large hotels, *tabaks*, souvenir shops, and often from postcard vendors (but only with the cards). The post office is also the cheapest place from which to send faxes. The American Express office also provides client mail services: the mailing address is Wenceslas Square 56, 11326-1 Prague, Czech Republic.

If long-distance phone calls cannot be booked from

your hotel, they can be made from the telephone center located to the left off the Main Post Office entrance hall. After hours you can also call from the telegram room on your right. It makes sense, however, to call collect as often as possible rather than pay for long-distance calls; the price difference is almost two to one. To reverse the charges, dial 0132 and say *"Na účet volaného."*

To place an international call, dial 00 + country code + local code and number. The country code for the United States and Canada is 1; for the United Kingdom it's 44.

Pay phones are located throughout the city center— under arcades and especially in subway stations. Local calls generally cost 1 Kč via the orange or yellow boxes. There are also gray boxes that take only 5-Kč coins. You can contact English-speaking operators by dialing 0149. The procedure for dialing is explained through pictures on all phones: generally, the trick is to understand that you don't drop the coin in the slot until you have dialed and have been connected to your party. Those are the older phones, and there are not that many left in the center of town. They are being replaced by new card phones. You can buy a card at the Main Post Office or at newsstands and shops showing a yellow and blue sign. To make the call, pick up the receiver, insert the card, and dial.

Above all, be patient with the overtaxed phone system. It's the only historical thing in Prague that will drive you crazy if you let it. Note that as of this writing the entire phone system is being updated and many numbers are being changed.

MUSEUMS

Prague was once the home of a matchless art collection, that of the Hapsburg emperor Rudolf II (1552–1612). As head of the very large Holy Roman Empire, he had his pick of masterpieces, but more importantly he had a superb eye for quality and let nothing stand in the way of an acquisition once he had set his mind and heart on it. Experts estimate that if the works had remained together, Prague would today be richer in art than any other metropolis on earth. Unfortunately the emperor's lavish hoard was dispersed during the Thirty Years' War and scattered around Europe. Though this was an incalculable loss, Prague still has an abundance of art scattered in castles, palaces, convents, and other venues all over town. Much of it is being reorganized and moved to other locations as the cultural world continues to reform itself following the great economic and social changes of the new Czech Republic. All information here and throughout the walks is as current as possible.

St. George's Convent (Klášter sv. Jiří), in the courtyard behind the apse of St. Vitus Cathedral, houses Czech art dating from the Middle Ages to the waning of the rococo, much of it little known outside the country. The convent features an exceptional collection of the mid-fourteenth-century "beautiful style," focusing on artists who combine the gentle, cushy humanism of Italy with the cold, brittle exactitude of the Netherlands. Not to be missed under any circumstances are the six unique, intensely powerful images by Master Theodoric, Charles IV's court painter, the grand master of the beautiful style (more of his work is at Karlštejn Castle outside Prague). Hours: Tuesday through Sunday, 10:00 A.M. to 6:00 P.M.

The **National Gallery**'s Sternberg Palace collections are located near the entrance to the Castle. They are home to the celebrated Dürer *Feast of the Rose Garlands*, a number of key Lucas Cranachs, and some great works by Canaletto, Rubens, Jan Gossaert, Rembrandt, and Pieter Breughel the Elder, among others. Hours: Tuesday through Sunday, 10:00 A.M. to 6:00 P.M.

The **Art Gallery of Prague Castle** has what's left of Rudolf II's fabulous collection (Vienna's Kunsthistorisches Museum has some of it, as does almost every major museum in Europe), as well as Italian, German, Flemish, and Czech baroque paintings by Rubens, Tin-

Mother and Child over Ovocný trh (Fruit Market) portal

toretto, Titian, Veronese, and others. Hours: Tuesday through Sunday, 9:00 A.M. to 5:00 P.M.

The **St. Vitus Cathedral Treasury** in the eighteenth-century Chapel of the Holy Rood (second courtyard of Prague Castle) has a brilliant array of the goldsmith's art, plus pieces in silver, enamel, and crystal. Don't miss the bronze monstrances and reliquaries dating from the eleventh century. Hours: Tuesday through Sunday, 9:00 A.M. to 5:00 P.M.

The **Loretto Treasure** is covered in Walk 3. Hours: Tuesday through Sunday, 9:00 A.M. to 12:00 noon, and 1:00 P.M. to 5:00 P.M.

The thirteenth-century **Convent of St. Agnes of Bohemia**, in the Old Town at 17 U Milosrdných Street, is Prague's oldest Gothic building and features Czech art of the nineteenth-century, plus changing temporary exhibitions. Hours: Tuesday through Sunday, 10:00 A.M. to 6:00 P.M.

The National Gallery's huge **Museum of Modern and Contemporary Czech Art**, with several thousand paintings and sculptures, should be moving into its new permanent home in the Veletržní Palace on Dukelských hrdinů Street in Prague 7 (Holešovice) sometime in 1994. The seven-story Functionalist former trade fair building (1928), a modernist architectural landmark, was designated almost twenty years ago for this collection, and a multimillion-crown renovation has been under way ever since. When completed, it will be one of Europe's largest modern art museums, with four floors of striking exhibition space surrounding a bright and airy atrium.

See listings at the back of this book for addresses and hours of other museums.

SHOPPING

Prague is not yet a shopping city on the order of London, Paris, or New York, so if you're here to shop you will be disappointed. But you're probably not. Yet there are sur-prises for enterprising, searching souls in the know. Dur-ing the Communist period, if you were paying in foreign currency, everything was cheap but there was little to buy. Prices have gone up considerably, but there is a great deal more of everything—so stock up before prices increase further. You can now choose from quite a lot of what is available in any major European capital.

As for locally made goods, gloves are an unexpected find. Well-made, wool-lined, soft leather gloves are cheap here: about fifteen dollars will buy what costs seventy-five dollars in the United States. Other good buys here are the high-quality Supraphon label records, CDs, and published music encompassing the Czech and world repertoire.

Czech artists have long been known for their strong, imaginative, whimsical graphic design: look for posters, T-shirts, and a world of merchandise—postcards, mugs, books, calendars, and assorted para-phernalia—imprinted with colorful designs.

Glass, particularly hand-cut crystal, is a popular target of many shoppers. There are several outlets for it all over town, but the best and most famous is probably Bohemia Moser, Na příkopě 12. Of course, it's always a good idea to do some comparison shopping.

Czech glass art, or glass sculpture, has an interna-tional reputation. It is part of a tradition of glasswork that began in the Middle Ages and in the nineteenth-century evolved into a singular and unusually demanding three-stage art-educational program of ten years' duration. Prices start at around 2,500 Kč for smaller pieces and rise into the hundreds of thousands of crowns. Galerie Bohm, at Anglická 1 in Vinohrady, is the most important gallery for this art; others are listed in the back of this book.

Porcelain, especially the ubiquitous, traditional, ever-loved blue-onion pattern (trade name Rokoko), is of good quality here, easy enough to find in the center of the city. The store Český porcelán on Perlová 1, for example, sells originals from the Dubí factory, identifiable by their slightly bleeding blue dye. (Dubí is the Czech version of Meissen, the famous German china.) A coffee cup costs about 125 Kč.

Hand-embroidered linens are also a recommended purchase; as you might expect, prices are generally a lot more reasonable when you buy on the street directly from the woman who made them. But if you prefer top-grade hand-woven linen edged with handmade lace, you'll pay from 6,800 Kč up at handicrafts shops, such as the one at Jilská 22 in the Old Town.

Antiques (look for signs saying *starožitnosti, antikva, vetešnictví, hodinářství*) and collectibles, including second-hand books in several languages, are available, though quality items are scarce. The largest concentration is in Josefov, the Jewish Quarter (see Walk 2). Prices are high, but discriminating eyes, as ever, can sometimes spot a bargain, often someone else's mistake. Look also for vintage art of the early twentieth century, particularly art nouveau, in ceramics, jewelry, and sculpture. Keep an eye out for Czech cubist work too, though you'll find few bargains, as this period is in great demand by collectors. If you get lucky, note that if the item was made before 1920 you will have to pay duty on it and restrictions may apply. Before you buy, be sure to ask the age of the item and whether you will have to pay duty. In the case of valuable pieces, it may be best to hire a private agency to expedite passage through customs, so inquire at the store. Semiprecious stones, specifically local garnets, are available in quantity in jewelry stores. And don't forget to look at costume jewelry, another worldwide Czech export of considerable repute.

LANGUAGE

Czech belongs to the same family of Slavic tongues that includes Russian, Belorussian, Polish, Bulgarian, Serbo-

Croatian, Slovenian, and Ukrainian. Slovak is derived from Czech and consequently is extremely similar to Czech. The Czech alphabet is Roman, not Cyrillic as is the Russian. Its origins as a literary language lie in the thirteenth century. Czech is not easy to pronounce for foreigners and the grammar is as complex as the history. If you studied Latin, or any language with complicated declensions (in which the endings of nouns and adjectives change constantly depending on how they're used), you will have fewer problems. But you can become proficient. As with any language, phonetics are key, so listen carefully for the sounds, the rhythms, and the intonation. It is beyond the scope of this book to give more than a few *very* general hints: The trilled ř (the little *v* on top is called a *háček*) is the toughest sound to master: it's roughly produced by pronouncing *r* and *z* simultaneously—tongue action is everything. The *j* is usually pronounced like the *y* in "yet," and the *č* (with a *háček*) is soft, as in "chew." *Ch* is pronounced "kh," and *š* (with a *háček*) is "sh." The most common error is to pronounce Czech words like Russian words: the accent in Czech is generally on the first syllable, not on the last or second to last, so think up front. For example, the name Procházková is pronounced "PRO-khaz-ko-va," *not* "pro-khaz-KO-va." Another example: *národní* (meaning "national") is pronounced "NAH-rod-ni," not "na-ROD-ni." The accents mean business in Czech: both *a*'s in Procházková are dragged out to "ah" sounds.

But not to worry. Czechs are studying English like mad, and you won't have any problem making yourself understood in rudimentary matters. Most of them will be pleased and amazed by your efforts to speak Czech but probably won't let you get too far because they will insist on practicing their English.

Glossary of Useful Phrases

Hi	*Ahoj*
Good morning	*Dobrý den*
Good evening	*Dobrý večer*
Good night	*Dobrou noc*
Good-bye	*Na shledanou*
How are you?	*Jak se máte?*
Thank you	*Děkuji*
Please	*Prosím*
Not at all	*Není zač*
Yes	*Ano*
No	*Ne*
Today	*Dnes*
Tomorrow	*Zítra*
Yesterday	*Včera*
Sorry, I don't understand	*Promiňte, nerozumím*
Border crossing	*Hranice*
Customs	*Celnice*
Passport	*Pas*
How many days have you come for?	*Na jak dlouho jste přijeli?*
For several days	*Na několik dnů*
A week	*Na týden*
Two weeks	*Dva týdny*
A month	*Na měsíc*
Nothing	*Nic*
Have a good trip	*Šťastnou cestu*
Pleasant stay	*Příjemný pobyt*
Is this space free?	*Je tu volno?*
Entrance	*Vchod*
Exit	*Východ or výstup*
Transfer	*Přestup*
Help!	*Pomoc!*
Hospital	*Nemocnice*

LENGTH OF WALKS

It is difficult to do more than roughly guesstimate the length of these walks, especially if you stop for lunch, shopping, museum exploring, resting, and so on. I have found that photography is a great time robber: you can easily extend a walk by more than an hour if you are taking photographs and are careful about framing each shot. So if your time is limited, I suggest either snapping fast with lightweight, fully automatic equipment or, if possible, taking your pictures at another time. (Some people think that the best time to see Prague is before 6:00 A.M. Certainly for photographers it is worth knowing that Charles Bridge is at its most extraordinary at sunset and in the early-morning hours.) Unless you're a weightlifter, being free of photography gear and baggage of any kind makes for more enjoyable, less tiring walks. And I warn you, Prague's hills and cobblestones—even the sidewalks are cobbled—will seriously tax any but the most comfortable, sensible shoes.

A NOTE ABOUT HOUSE NUMBERS

Just as simplification is anathema to the local bureaucracy, every building in Prague has two house numbers, both of which are usually, but not always, visible. The small white-on-red plaque is the permanent number preceded by *čp*, which stands for *popisný číslo*—"registry number." The white-on-blue plaque is the "new" (since 1868) number, which identifies the buildings of one particular street and can be changed in case of new construction. This book uses one or the other number.

CHRONOLOGY

The history of the Czech Republic (Czechoslovakia from 1918 to 1992) is somewhat complex; as the sole democracy east of the Rhine before World War II, it is the only country to have reverted to democracy from Communism. Before that, and in between, it was a fascist "protectorate," a feudal monarchy, and province of a benign despotism (the Austro-Hungarian Empire.) You will be hearing a great deal about the history of the country throughout the five walks that follow, but here is a general time line of events:

5th cent. B.C.?	Celtic tribes Boii (Bohemia) settle area
c. A.D. 100	Germanic tribes move into area
c. 500–600	Slavonic tribes move into area
c. 830	founding of Moravian Empire
863	Christian missionaries Cyril and Methodius arrive from Constantinople
921	birth of "Good King" Wenceslas I (Saint Václav), early Přemyslid, Bohemia's founding dynasty
1061–92	reign of Vratislav II
c. 1119–25	Kosmas Chronicle, the first written record
1158–1174	reign of Vladislav II
1198	ascension of Otakar I; Bohemia becomes a kingdom
1253–78	Přemyslid Otakar II expands domain into Austria
1254	privileges (royal charter) granted to Jews
1300	Wenceslas II gains Poland and Hungary
1306	Přemysl family rule ends; John of Luxemburg becomes king
1346	Charles IV becomes king and Holy Roman Emperor
1348	Charles University founded
1415	Jan Hus martyred at Constance
1419–34	Hussite Revolution

1458	ascension of King George of Poděbrady
1471	ascension of Vladislav, beginning of Jagellonian dynasty
1526	ascension of Ferdinand I, beginning of Hapsburg dynasty
1564	Maximilian II becomes king
1576	Rudolf II becomes king
1609	Letter of Majesty guaranteeing religious freedom
1618	Defenestration of Prague; start of Thirty Years' War
1620	Czechs defeated by Swedes at Battle of White Mountain
1648	Peace of Westphalia; end of Thirty Years' War
1740	Maria Theresia becomes queen
1780	Joseph II becomes king
1781	nonteaching religious orders abolished
1784	Prague's four towns joined into one municipality
1790	Leopold II becomes king
1792	Francis I becomes king
1834	Jungmann's Czech dictionary published
1848	Slav Congress in Prague; city bombarded; Franz Joseph (last Austrian emperor) becomes king
1850	Tomáš Masaryk born; son of Slovak serfs
1866	Hapsburgs lose war to Prussians; Upper Silesia ceded to Prussia
1867	Austria refuses Bohemia home rule
1882	new academic generation emerges from Charles University; Masaryk a teacher
1914	World War I begins; anti-Austrian Czechoslovak Legion forms: Masaryk escapes to Serbia

1915   Masaryk, in exile, advocates union of Czechs and Slovaks and independence

1918   independent state formed; Masaryk returns to Prague as first president of Czechoslovak Republic

1920   new constitution adopted

1935   Edvard Beneš elected president

1938   Sudetenland ceded to Hitler at Munich

1939   Hitler invades; occupation armies dig in

1942   assassination of Reinhard Heydrich; reprisals follow

1945   World War II ends; Beneš elected president

1948   Communists take power; Klement Gottwald elected president

1952   Slánský show trials purge Communist elite

1955   Czechoslovakia joins Warsaw Pact organization

1968   Alexander Dubček becomes First Secretary; advent of Prague Spring; Warsaw Pact forces invade

1969   Gustáv Husák declared president

1977   Charter 77 human-rights organization founded

1989   Communists overthrown; Václav Havel assumes presidency

1990   general elections

1992   general elections; Havel resigns; Mečiar wins in Slovakia; dissolution negotiations begin

1993   Czechoslovakia splits in two: Slovaks separate; Havel elected first president of Czech Republic

Walk · 1

Baroque Prague

FROM THE KLEMENTINUM
TO MALÁ STRANA

Charles Bridge facing Malá Strana

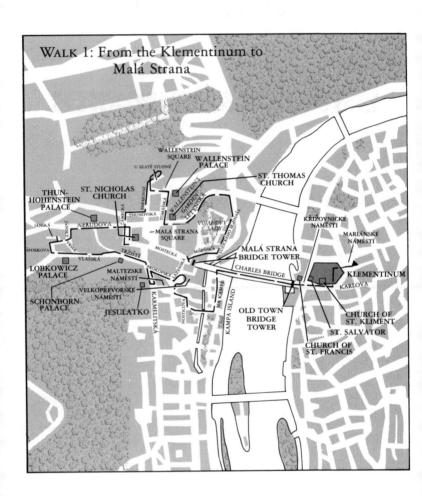

WALK 1: From the Klementinum to
Malá Strana

WALLENSTEIN
SQUARE
WALLENSTEIN
PALACE

U ZLATÉ STUDNĚ

ST. THOMAS
CHURCH

THUN-
HOHENSTEIN
PALACE

ST. NICHOLAS
CHURCH

JÁNSKÁ

ŠPORKOVA

VLAŠSKÁ

LOBKOWICZ
PALACE

SCHONBORN
PALACE

MALTEZSKE
NÁMĚSTÍ

VELKOPŘEVORSKÉ
NÁMĚSTÍ

JESULATKO

KARMELITSKA

NERUDOVA

THUNOVSKA

TOMÁŠSKÁ

MALÁ STRANA
SQUARE

MOSTECKÁ

LÁZEŇSKÁ

PROKOPSKÁ

NA KAMPĚ

MÍŠENSKÁ

WALLENSTEIN'S
GARDEN

LETENSKÁ

VOJANOVY
SADY

U LUŽICKÉHO SEMINÁŘE

MALÁ STRANA
BRIDGE TOWER

CHARLES BRIDGE

KAMPA ISLAND

OLD TOWN
BRIDGE
TOWER

KŘIŽOVNICKÉ
NÁMĚSTÍ

MARIÁNSKÉ
NÁMĚSTÍ

KLEMENTINUM

KARLOVA

CHURCH OF
ST. KLIMENT

ST. SALVATOR

CHURCH OF
ST. FRANCIS

Starting Point: Mariánské Square, Old Town
Metro/Tram Lines: Metro Green Line A, Staroměstská stop; or trams 17 and 18 to Jan Palách Square.
Length of Walk: Three hours at least. Please note that this is one of the longest walks, most crowded with worthy sights, and could take anywhere from three to four hours, depending on your energy level (there is a bit of climbing). There are also a few rest-stop possibilities closer to the end.

Our destination is the left bank of the Vltava River, the still exclusive—at least in spirit—Malá Strana (literally, "small side" or "Little Quarter") district, chockablock with aristocratic baroque architectural treasure. Like clinging courtiers hoping for a royal favor, the palaces, churches, and palatial gardens built by the noble families of the Czech lands cluster obsequiously between the river and the slopes of Hradčany, the Castle Hill part of town. It's long been a fairly quiet residential area, though these days most of the grand palaces have been taken over by embassies, institutions, or the government. You'll soon see why Czech film director Miloš Forman returned to his home stamping ground and filmed parts of *Amadeus* in this neighborhood. There's little commercial hustle here, except on Mostecká (Bridge) Street, the tourist-thronged main shopping thoroughfare, but our walk ends at its mouth.

Though headed for the left bank, our walk starts in the Old Town (Staré Město), which is on the right bank, at the Klementinum, a former Jesuit college that today functions (just barely) as the equivalent of Washington's Library of Congress. Setting out from the right bank of the river will allow us to approach the opposite side via Charles Bridge, a centerpiece of medieval Prague, and also visit Kampa Island on the way. There is some question as to whether you will be able to enter parts of the Klementinum: as of this writing some of the areas I will be describing are closed to the public, pending restoration and better access. The hope is that the library will have resolved its storage, space, and technology problems by the time this book reaches your hands. The Klementinum is undergoing extensive reorganization following nearly a half century of gross and expensive neglect under largely indifferent administrations (Nazi and Communist). In the meantime, just duck and try to look as if you belong here. (Psst, hide your camera.)

Our specific point of departure is **Mariánské náměstí** (*náměstí* means "square"), where the atmosphere is all business. Crisscrossed by locals bent on personal missions, the square is surrounded by three major institutions. On the north side stands the **State Public Library**—the slightly severe looking, travertine-marble–faced building of late-twenties vintage with the six statuesque allegories on the balcony. On the east side is the **Magistrát**, the late-secessionist (1908) *New* Town Hall (as opposed to the Gothic *Old* Town Hall in nearby Old Town Square). The five independent towns each had its own administrative center before they were incorporated into Greater Prague in the 1700s. You will recognize the Magistrát by the several small flags lined up over the entrance. Opposite the New Town Hall is the **Klemen-**

tinum, the massive, yellow-stuccoed baroque structure you will immediately identify as the oldest building opening directly onto the square.

On the far southeast side of the square is the rear garden wall (the garden itself is not visible) of the Clam-Gallas Palace (the entrance is on Husova Street, just off the square). Note the neoclassical female statue set into a wall niche. Sculpted by Václav Prachner in 1812, *Vltava* is a symbol of the wild river that regularly flooded the low-lying shores of the city and turned the streets into swamps before they were raised in the late thirteenth century. In fact, in the Middle Ages Mariánské Square was called In the Puddle, and the Gothic church that once stood here was Mother of God in the Puddle. But to the neighborhood housewives and servants who frequented the fountain as a primary source of water and turned her into a popular distribution center of local gossip and town news, the statue was always Terezka. Even when the water supply eventually moved indoors and Terezka was cut off, an admirer who lived across the street, an elderly bachelor of odd habits and mien, remembered her in his will and left her ten thousand gold pieces. (The will was successfully contested by his heirs.)

Before we enter the Klementinum, take a look at the stone statuary at each corner of the Magistrát building, the work of Ladislav Šaloun, best known for his huge, controversial memorial to Jan Hus in the Old Town Square, which we will see on our second walk. On the left is the Iron Man, a knight who frequented the armorers' guild. Praguers tell a story of his transformation into the ferrous metal when a spell was cast on him for doing away with his girlfriend, and ever since he has shown up centenially, trying to reverse the curse by making out with a virgin. The more remarkable figure, on the right, is the illustrious Jehuda ben Bezalel, better known as Rabbi Lowe, sixteenth-century seer and scholar, and creator of the golem. (We will meet Rabbi Lowe again on Walk 2.) This allegorical work, of an unstructured, sway-

Rabbi Judah Lowe by Ladislav Šaloun at New Town Hall

ing fluidity, is a loose interpretation of one of the multifarious legends associated with the rabbi. When his time came (at age ninety-seven), even death dared not face the formidable rabbi directly, but found a way to surprise him by hiding in a rose whose sweet perfume Lowe inhaled. The rose was proferred by his granddaughter, who is here turned into a naked female clinging wantonly to his flowing robes. Apparently the Nazis didn't approve of the piece and banished it during the occupation.

One of the Prague family jewels, the Klementinum (also called Collegium Clementinum) is second only to Prague Castle in size. It is a massive compound of buildings and courtyards that over the centuries has housed a Jesuit college, an elementary school, three large churches, several chapels, a printing center, a theater, a number of science institutes, an astronomical tower, the archbishopric's seminary, and Prague University lecture halls and libraries—an early mixed-use structure if ever there was one. Today it's devoted exclusively to books. As the chief research library of Charles University and the main branch of the Czech State Library, it holds at least five million books in national, Slavic, French, technical, and economic divisions. The collections include at least twelve hundred papyrus scrolls, six thousand medieval manuscripts, and more than three thousand incunabula (books printed before 1501).

To appreciate the Klementinum's portentous historic significance, however, let's detour to some key events of Czech history and go back to 1556 and the Counter-Reformation. A vanguard of Jesuits arrived in Prague with a mandate from the Catholic emperor to begin the re-Catholicization of Czech heretics, who by now were 90 percent of the population. It was in Prague that opposition, in the person of Jan Hus, rector of Charles University and the most popular preacher in Prague, first seriously threatened the corrupt Roman Church. Hus railed against such widespread practices as selling indulgences (insurance policies "guaranteeing" entrance to heaven). Just as important, he defied the supremacy of the Pope by proclaiming the scriptures as the ultimate authority on the word of God. For his valor and patriotism, in 1415 he was burned at the stake, a not uncommon fate of reformers and truth sayers through the ages. But the Hussite wars that followed were waged equally against Rome and against the German emperor. The Jesuits were expelled from Bohemia at the time of the revolt of the Protestant Bohemian nobility in 1618–20 against the Hapsburgs (Bohemia became one of the dynastic kingdoms of the Hapsburgs in 1526), but two hundred years after the martyrdom of Hus, they returned in full force when the Czechs were trounced at the Battle of White Mountain (1618), fought just outside Prague. This cataclysmic battle, the first of the Thirty Years' War, marks a tragic watershed of Czech history; everything that happened here in this period is qualified as being either pre–White Mountain or post–White Mountain. The Thirty Years' War is often described as a time of crucifixion for the Czechs, and the numbers tell the story: the population dropped from three million in 1618 to 800,000 in 1654. And that's why the Klementinum, as the most sprawling and potent evidence of the power of the Catholic Church and the ruling Hapsburgs—*Cuius regio, euis religio* ("Choice of religion belongs to the ruler") was the law of the day—originally represented such dramatic defeat to Czech patriots who had dared challenge Rome.

With the Klementinum as its arsenal and nucleus of energy, the Society of Jesus gave new meaning to organized, perfervid proselytizing as it sought to "destroy Luther's servants by sword, fire, water, and rope." Their success was on a scale such as the world has rarely seen. Over a period of more than two hundred years (until the order was dissolved by Joseph II in 1777), the Jesuit religious war machine marched in lockstep. As their ardor and efficiency mounted, book bonfires became competitive in the Klementinum courtyards; one member of the order, Konias, boasted that he fed sixty thousand heretical books to the flames all by himself. On the plus side, the Jesuits imposed their rigorous ideas about education and ethics and raised the level of teaching and learning, not only in Bohemia but all over Europe. To accomplish their mission in Prague, the canny Jesuits picked an exceedingly visible and valuable piece of real estate, on the doorstep of the primary communications artery in the city, Charles Bridge, facing the Castle high on a bluff of the opposite bank. Making way for what ultimately became the present Klementinum, which Praguers called the Jesuit City, the order began by displacing a Dominican monastery and ended by razing thirty-two houses, three churches, several gardens and courtyards, and two streets. The complex also featured Prague's first sewage system, flushed by water from the monastery's fountains into the river.

We'll start at the Mariánské Square entrance. The Klementinum's facade is probably the 1726 work of that genius of the Prague baroque, Kilián Ignác (K. I.) Dientzenhofer, a member of a remarkable dynasty of Bavarian architects whose name is connected with several of the city's superior monuments. (Including Christoph, K. I.'s father, there were six busy Dientzenhofer brothers, all of whom apparently began their careers in Prague, though only Christoph, who was illiterate, actually settled here and became a Bohemian architect, as did K. I.) Some of the other celebrated names in Prague architecture of this eighteenth-century period are Lurago, Caratti, Palliardi, Santini Aichel, and Kaňka, the latter one of the few native-born Czechs. The population's drastic decline after the dreadful hardships of the Thirty Years' War decimated the ranks of local artists and craftsmen. For all of them, of course, the Counter-Reformation was a bonanza, evidence of how a political and a religious idea could also incrementally transform the appearance of a city.

It was an equally rare opportunity for a new social class to take root. Pivotal to the Hapsburg strategy of removing the rebellious Protestant nobility was replacing it with a new, smaller aristocracy loyal only to the crown.

The country was stripped of its ancient feudal hierarchy, which went into exile, and in its stead came foreigners from all over Europe: Italian, French, and Austrian German were heard on the streets; the official language became German, not Czech. On the wracked ruins of Charles IV's Gothic stone city appeared a panoply of stuccoed princely palaces, the tightly contrived baroque gardens, the commodious courtyards, the breezy arcades, and the highly elaborated churches so reminiscent of Italian architecture. The churches especially were designed to arouse awe and grandly sacrificed the simple symmetry of the Renaissance for drama, contrast, and emotion. Though not the first of the new rhetorical art to materialize in the city, these creations marked the invasion of the baroque and its distinct style. French artist Paul Claudel said, "The art of the baroque found perhaps its happiest expression in Prague, more than in Vienna, in Bavaria, or in Italy. Here it achieved the difficult moment, the balance between sincerity and lyrical transfiguration." Aesthetic qualities aside, it has not turned out to be maintenance free: unless prescribed materials are used, the fragile lime skin of the stucco facades must be renewed every few years or it peels and swiftly crumbles to dust. Equally noticeable are the effects of lignite, the soft brown coal dust–producing fuel still in common use for heating, which makes for the blackened stucco you see on many buildings.

Culturally speaking, baroque mysticism wove itself into the fabric of nineteenth-century life: the ineluctable memento mori (reminder of death), "the desire to survive the running out of time and the disappearance of space into a world catastrophe," as the radical painter Oscar Kokoschka wrote much later of his baroque-saturated childhood. The style reached its most dramatic, heretofore unimagined, heights of ornamentation and opulence in the achievements of architecture, art, and music: *ad maiorem dei gloriam* ("to the greatest glory of God").

Walking through the entrance of the Klementinum

will take you via a short passage into (unfortunately) asphalted courtyards. Turn left, then try the door of the **Mirrored Chapel** (**Zrcadlová Kaple**), designed 1722–24, probably by K. I. Dientzenhofer, for a brief look around. (It's on the right just before the underpass into the next courtyard.) If you're lucky, it will be open and a rare-book collection will be on exhibit or a concert taking place. The Mirrored Chapel has not been used for worship since 1924 but has splendid acoustics. Inside is a graceful, soft-hued baroque vision of gilded stuccowork, with deep sandy pink walls and coral insets, greenish, coral-veined marble, faux marble trim, pale ivory statuary, and mirror panels, the whole quite warmingly elegant.

Back in the courtyard, proceed through the arches and note the green-domed tower, crowned by a baroque Atlas, behind you. This is the astronomical tower, built in 1721, that served the Klementinum monks as an observatory and still functions as such, two hundred years later, gauging key meteorological indicators for the city. Up until 1918 the tower was a kind of timely symbol of the unity of the Austro-Hungarian Empire. (Franz Kafka mentions it in his novel fragment "Wedding Preparations in the Country.")

In a daily ritual of institutional clock tower timekeeping an official appeared on the balcony with stopwatch in hand. At exactly noon he waved the red and white Hapsburg flag in front of the clock face in the direction of the Castle, a signal from one keeper of royal and imperial time to another, who then gave the signal to fire a cannon, called the Marianschanze gun, from a Letna Park stronghold across the river. Clocks on towers all over town were set to the boom as it sounded, and people synchronized their watches. But this was not just a call to dinner. Rather, it was perceived as a comforting gesture and reminder of the imperial embrace, of the stability and security that the Austro-Hungarian monarchy represented to many people, which had actually started to loosen some time before as timepieces in Bohemia diverged and finally came to a stop after World War I. That's when the ancient Hapsburg Empire, a multicultural state in which regional loyalty largely overrode narrow tribal and religious interests, drew a shuddering breath and died, and the new Czechoslovak state was born. And not all eyes were dry: many of its subjects were actually sorry to see it go. Today, with savage tribal nationalism shattering the region into we know not how many pieces, we can say the sorrow wasn't just nostalgia.

Now turn right and walk to the entrance marked "Národní Knihovna"; this is the main building of the National Library. Walk straight ahead, past the porter's booth, and note the glassed-in, ivy-strewn courtyard on your left with the fountain—this was once the vaulted cloister of the monastery, and it's possible to imagine what the whole place might have looked like before it became a public institution, with scurrying, unhealthy-looking black-robed monks bent to the task over massive pale vellum-bound tomes. Believed to be the oldest in the city (1658), the solar clocks, divided into twenty-four-hour segments and frescoed high up on the courtyard walls, are a persistent theme of the whole compound—religious reformatory zeal extended to the heavens: astrology and astronomy.

Next, turn into the Main Reading Room, opposite the cloister. This vast room dating from the seventeenth century used to be the monks' summer refectory; in 1791 it was reportedly the scene of the first industrial exhibition in Europe. The giant, dark porcelain rococo stove that dominates one wall is decorated with scenes of Jesuit life, and is reportedly the largest in Europe. Behind the stove, over the door on the left, note the painting of an eye in a pyramid, with the inscription *Omnia vide* ("Sees all")—presumably to keep the monks alert and penitent while they ate. Over the door on the other side is an ear, *Omnia audit* ("Hears all"). It is not known if these paranoia-inducing reminders keep book pilferage down.

Back at the cloister, go to the end of the hall, turn left, go up the stairs, and turn right at the top of the first floor (*první patro*), as opposed to the ground floor (*přízemí*). There, in the New College wing, you will find a long hallway with stucco cartouches on the barrel-vaulted ceiling featuring somewhat murky scenes from the life of St. Francis Xavier, whose career ranged far and wide and included highly successful missions to Asia. Apparently the Jesuits thought that his example would prove inspirational to the flocks of acolytes who traveled these corridors. Another such pictorial saga, the exemplary life of the supreme mystic himself, one of the greatest figures in Western Christianity, St. Ignatius of Loyola, founder in 1540 of the order, is in the passage below this one. Unfortunately, the corridor is currently used for offices and book storage of the piled-one-on-top-of-the-other-on-the-floor variety, testimony to the deplorable state of affairs at the library.

There are a number of other rooms in the Klementinum worth a visit. For example, there is the rococo Music Library with its astronomical models, and the New Mathematical Hall, which is today the manuscript department of the library (although it's currently off limits, I mention it in the hope that it will one day be reopened). If the great Baroque Hall has finally been restored and is open, you will find yourself in the most magnificent room in the building, one of the splendiferous ecclesiastical libraries of Europe. (It's on the first floor above the Mirrored Chapel, but place of access is momentarily uncertain.) This two-story stunner was built in 1722 and designed by K. I. Dientzenhofer as the Jesuits' library; the shelves are full of their endeavors. Some of the most valuable incunabula here, on display in glass cases in the window alcove (in facsimile), include the Vyšehrad Codex of 1085, which was used to swear in Czech kings during coronations, and the illustrated Velislav Bible from the fourteenth century. There are also manuscripts of Jan Hus and John Wycliffe, the latter a highly influential British theologian whose works set Hus's thinking on fire. The frescoes on the vaulted ceiling are by Jan Hiebl and symbolize science and learning; in the center is an illusionistic Temple of Wisdom. A graceful baroque steel-and-metal balustrade surrounds the upper gallery, and several valuable eighteenth-century astronomical globes made of painted copper sheeting march down the center of the room; when they populated the Mathematics Hall, they turned on a clockwork mechanism. The portrait dominating one end of the hall is of the Hapsburg emperor Joseph II, who, though he abolished the monasteries and therefore the Jesuits' raison d'être in the Klementinum, enormously enriched the library via extensive collections taken from many of those monasteries. In the antechamber are astronomical table clocks, remnants of a Jesuit mathematical museum founded in 1722, and a portrait of František Josef, Count Kinsky, who initiated transfer of the Jesuit book collections to state ownership in 1777.

Exit the Klementinum library building the way you entered and turn right onto **Karlova Street**. Behind the wall on your right is the **Church of St. Kliment**, and farther along, up the shallow stairs and behind the wrought-iron gates, is the **Vlašská Chapel** (Vlašská means "Italian"); both churches may be entered from this corner portico, designed by František Kaňka. The Vlašská Chapel (1590–97), with its elliptical layout, was built to minister to the spiritual needs of the Italian artisans who settled in the city in great numbers, participating in its construction and decoration. Next door is the portal to St. Kliment Church, originally Jesuit, which has served the Prague Greek Orthodox community since 1930. The current membership fled here in 1976 following a military coup in Greece; note the icons in front of the presbytery. The building was designed in 1711 by Kaňka; inside, the sculptures of church fathers and evangelists are by Matthias Bernard Braun, one of the star local sculptors. Because of its stylistic purity and the unified design of its adornment, this church is rated by some as a prime example of Prague baroque, though its altar, curiously, is trompe l'oeil.

Walking to the end of curving Karlova Street toward the bridge, almost always thronged with crowds surging lemminglike toward the water, their thudding footfalls hitting the cobblestones and glancing off the walls, you will pass the Prague **Unitaria**, a handsome baroque house with stately portal at **no. 8**. In a city so torn by past religious upheavals primed to force feed "the only true faith," it is a curious and ironic juxtaposition that the largest enclave of liberal religion (Unitarianism) in the world should have once thrived a stone's throw from the main Klementinum church. Between the two world wars this congregation drew thousands, led by the charismatic—and radical for their time—freethinkers Norbert F. Čapek and Karel Hašpl. (The group was originally inspired by Charlotte Garrigue Masaryk, a Unitarian from Brooklyn, New York, wife of the remarkable statesman Tomáš Masaryk, first president and founder of the 1918 Czechoslovak Republic.) For his outspoken though necessarily occupation-muted efforts, Čapek died a gruesome death at Dachau, a victim of Nazi medical experiments. The immediate pretext for his arrest was that his radio dial was tuned to Radio Free Europe.

A few doors down at **no. 4**, marked by a plaque, is the Renaissance house, its facade frescoes faded to fragments, where the great astronomer Johannes Kepler, one of the founders of modern science, lived around 1610 and discovered the first two laws that govern the elliptical movements of the earth around the sun. If you can enter the courtyard through the vaulted passageway, you will see bronze and plaster reliefs of Kepler with a flowing beard. A Protestant who appreciated the relative religious tolerance of Prague under Emperor Rudolf II (Kepler had battled to save his mother, Katherina, from witchcraft charges in Germany and succeeded only because of his position as imperial mathematician), he came here in

Klementinum entrance from Křižovnické náměstí

1600 to work with Tycho Brahe, that other astronomical star at Rudolf's experimental science- and magic-obsessed court.

At **Knights of the Cross Square (Křižovnické náměstí)** turn right; on the corner (of Karlova) you will find yourself in front of another part of the Klementinum, the **Church of the Holy Savior**, or **St. Salvator**, first church built by the Jesuits here in 1578, completed in 1714, and designed by Carlo Lurago and Francesco Caratti. It was once the primary Jesuit church in the Czech lands. Right next to the church, on your left, you will see the sixteenth-century main entrance of the Klementinum, in the courtyard of which is a swashbuckling statue of a Prague student. This nineteenth-century work by Josef Maxe is in honor of the young men who, commanded by Jesuit priests, helped defend the Old Town from the marauding Swedish Army in 1648, during the final fight of the Thirty Years' War. Two hundred years later, the Klementinum became a hotbed of revolutionary activity during the nationalist struggles with the Austrian Empire; the students acted on their own initiative this time, manning the barricades they'd built around their college.

Before we leave the Old Town and cross over the bridge into Malá Strana, take a look at the baroque **Church of St. Francis** (1679–89), also known as the **Church of the Crusader Knights**, a soaring creation of the Burgundian architect Jean Baptiste Mathey for the Knights of the Cross, a homegrown Czech religious order dating back to 1234. Establishment of the order was the brainchild of Princess Agnes, daughter of the Přemysl king Otakar I, who twice tried to arrange politically apt marriages for her and failed. So she disappeared from court and public life into a convent, a severe, self-abnegating one at that, based on the ideals of St. Francis of Assisi and bound by vows of profound humility and poverty. Though it took over seven hundred years to canonize Agnes of Bohemia (it finally happened in November 1989), the monastery and church she founded were two of the first Gothic structures in the land, and their remains (from 1270) are evident in the crypt. Inside the rather intimate, oval-shaped sanctuary are a number of paintings (1722–23) by Václav Vavřinec Reiner, the most distinguished Czech painter of the period. Note the dynamic cupola-vault fresco of the Last Judgment and the paintings of the four evangelists and church fathers underneath. The full dome is a landmark, and the layout is striking for its expanded cruciform configuration.

Until the middle of the nineteenth century there was a two-story guardhouse on the square, to the right of the approach ramp to the bridge. Now an 1848 Gothic-style memorial to the emperor Charles IV, urban planner par excellence and author of Prague's golden period, stands in situ nearby. The monumentally Gothic **Old Town Bridge Tower** (fourteenth century) forms the entrance to the bridge; it was part of the fortification walls of the Old Town, and as was the custom with these towers through-out Europe, its cellars served as dungeons, as did the rooms in the tower. Notice the figures of happy-looking couples carved on the corners, which some Prague cynics refer to as a bit of Old Town satire. Since the bridge it-self is not on the program, we will not linger except to point out that it was designed in 1357 by the young German architect Peter Parler, whose other legendary monument in Prague is St. Vitus Cathedral, heart of the Castle complex.

You may already have noticed that this ancient con-necting thoroughfare is not a straight line but a continu-ation of the crooked streets of the medieval town we've just left. That's because it was built on the remains of an older Romanesque bridge, the Judith (1170), destroyed in a flood. The thirty sandstone statues and groupings on each side were a later, seventeenth-century addition, and most are superior examples of baroque sculpture of the period. They formed a highly visible part of the Catholic restoration, the realization of a kind of *via sacrum* to the cathedral. The first one to be erected (1683) was St. John of Nepomuk, cast after a model by Jan Brokoff—you can see it in the center on the north side. One of only two bronze pieces on the bridge (the other is the crucifix near the Old Town side, which has stood there since the four-teenth century, though this is the fourth version), the figure of St. John Nepomuk was imitated on bridges all over Bohemia and Central Europe. The Counter-Reformationists turned the former cleric into a cult figure, a propagandist for Hapsburg power, aimed at diverting heretics from lingering thoughts of the sacrificed Jan Hus. The anti-Hussites spread the story that St. John Nepomuk was confessor to the pro-Catholic queen, whose husband had him tortured and thrown into the river for refusing to divulge her confession, hence his star-studded martyr's halo. The facts are more mundanely political: King Wenceslas IV toppled him into the Vltava for disregarding the king's wishes over a priestly appointment. Since the 1970s five replicas have replaced the original statue groupings on the bridge because of Prague's corrosive pollution. Guess which ones they are. You can't miss the living groupings here, for this has long been a magnet for young and old Praguers with something to sell, if only a song and a few twanging guitar or accordion chords. At this point, we still have most of our walk to do, but what a stunning approach to our destination, Malá Strana!

As you near the other side, watch for the statue just below the bridge on your left. The stalwart-looking figure with the lion at his feet and sword in hand is **Bruncvík**, a knight about whom multifarious legends abound, though he is usually associated with the medieval epic *The Song of Roland*, in which the hero, marred only by pride, crusades valiantly against the infidels. One of the Czech versions recounts that Bruncvík's mighty sword is hidden in the bridge but will be found in case of a threat to the town. Spreading the Pale Knight's fame to unexpected places, the great Russian poet Marina Tsvetayeva wrote a poem about him, recalling a rare happy period of her life, when she lived in Prague in the 1920s: "Pale Knight, you are the guardian/Of the running river . . ."

The true story of Bruncvík, however, has more to do with crass commerce than gallantry. In past centuries the bridge and the towers at each end belonged to the Old Town, which was empowered by royal decree (implemented by the Jagellonian Vladislav II) to control traffic for both security and customs purposes. Malá Strana and the Old Town were then separate municipal entities, ringed by their own armed fortifications. The municipal coat of arms and a statement of rights and privileges were carved into Bruncvík's pedestal, so from the fifteenth cen-

An entertainer on Charles Bridge

tury the knight's job was to serve as a warning to bridge crossers to pay up. The present statue of Bruncvík is an 1884 version of the original Gothic one, which was shot up in a bridge battle of the Thirty Years' War.

Before we turn left at the divided stairway off the bridge and descend to Kampa Island, a few more words about the Malá Strana district, of which Kampa is a part. Over the centuries this tumult of streets and squares grew slowly on the slopes under Hradčany, the Castle quarter, near the axis of a key international trading route. Archaeologists excavating the metro in the 1970s found traces of early settlements from as far back as the seventh century, though most were from the twelfth and thirteenth centuries. Many of the Romanesque and Gothic structures disappeared when two thirds of the town was destroyed in a 1541 fire, which actually proved lucky, in a sense, because it made room for the construction of the baroque showplaces, secular and religious, that are on our route. Though they are the bounty of a building spree by aristocrats and opportunists loyal to the victorious Catholic Hapsburgs after the devastation of the Thirty Years' War, they are remarkable remnants of a vision and craftsmanship that we will never see again and that produced not a few masterpieces. While lamenting the demise of the nobility is not on our agenda, fortunately art outlives us, and Prague has lovingly, miraculously preserved an unusually large amount of it, given the age of the city and the inevitable losses from tyrants, predatory foreign armies, and militant religious orders.

One of the most romantic and peaceful nooks of Malá Strana, **Kampa Island** is a hideaway from the normal bustle of the city. Before the sixteenth century it was simply called Island Under the Bridge. It has often been described as a bit of Venice, washed on one side by the bucking waters of the Vltava and on the other by the rushing Čertovka—a slender but lively arm of the river. Čertovka means "little devil," though no one knows the origins of the name and few think it has anything to do with satanic magic, as do numerous other Prague myths. Supposedly the name comes from a sharp-tongued washerwoman who lived in a nearby house known as the Seven Devils. Before the end of the last century the stream was named after the various owners of the three mill wheels that once turned purposefully on its shores. Of these mills only one is still functional and has been there since the sixteenth century, except when it was recently removed while the Čertovka was temporarily dammed during repair of sodden house foundations along the canals. Another tribute to clothes washing is an early Gothic (originally Romanesque) church here called St. John of the Laundry (once it actually did function as a laundry!). Although it's not on our itinerary, you'll find it at the southernmost end of the island on Říční Street.

In front of you is the villagelike square of Kampa Island. With its acacia trees and quietly evocative sixteenth- and seventeenth-century baroque houses flanking it, this square is like few others in Prague. A twice-yearly potter's market used to be a tradition here, and good-quality ceramics may still be bought in the shops. Considered the most beautiful house, with a rococo facade, is **no. 510, At the White Shoe. No. 498, At the Blue Fox**, has a notable house sign dating from 1664, when it was rebuilt by a hatmaker. The elegantly imposing palace on the riverbank, just below the square, was built at the end of the seventeenth century and once belonged to the superwealthy and powerful Liechtensteins, masters of not a few great estates in Prague and the Czech lands. The family coat of arms above the portal is the only reminder that the classicist structure, restored in 1864, was originally baroque; today, after more recent restoration, it serves federal government purposes. On the right stands a bust of scholar Josef Dobrovský, best remembered as one of the early fathers of the nineteenth-century Czech national revival, the self-determination movement that helped the country find its identity after being submerged in a German-dominated state for three hundred

Arcade sidewalk near Maltese Square

years and that led to independence in 1918. Dobrovský's research and writings accelerated the process, heralding a new age. He lived here for a time in the small vine-overgrown cottage in the Nostic garden behind the statue. The bust on the wall is of historian Zdeněk Wirth, who also lived here, as did the popular stage and screen performer Jan Werich—half of the much-loved thirties' comedy team of Voskovec and Werich—from the end of World War II until his death. So you know this captivating spot is an exclusive address.

Just past the statue, turn right, cross the bridge, and walk through the park, following the path on the right to **Nosticova Street**. Proceed to **Maltese Square**, past the sprawling early baroque Nostic Palace on your left; today it's the embassy of the Netherlands and a venue for concerts in the Prague salon. It also houses the fifteen-thousand-volume library of Josef Dobrovský (the scholar was a tutor to the Nostic children), a private Nostic family collection open to the public by special request. From the square turn right on **Lázeňská Street**. The early baroque building on the corner is the restaurant **U Malířů** (**At the Painter's**), here since 1543—its nucleus is Gothic—when an artist owned it. Before the upending events of the Velvet Revolution of 1989, it was a popular haunt of intellectuals and artists, as well as of regular citizens. Today it's still a cozy, but extraordinarily pricy, French eatery (mercifully not much spiffed up), though in summer you can snack slightly more reasonably on a makeshift terrace in front. Next door is **U Vladaře**, an informal, popularly priced eatery in the *vinarna* ("wine cellar"), with a restaurant and nightclub next door.

A few words about the Gothic-appearing **Church of Our Lady Under the Chain** (**Kostel Panny Marie pod řetězem**), whose twin towers now loom massively in front of you. This former religious citadel is the oldest church in the district, built around 1250 by the Knights of Malta. It is a remodeled eleventh-century Romanesque basilica; some of the original remains can be seen embedded in the right wall of the front courtyard. Of a fourteenth-century Gothic reconstruction only the stern towers and an anteroom were completed. The story of the church's name derives from the time the Virgin Mary supposedly helped the knights guard the river's first bridge, the Judith, predecessor of the Charles. To cover all approaches to the Castle, King Vladislav ordered the knights to build a kind of fortified monastery with a gate that closed with a chain on the riverbank near the bridge. If you can get into the baroque interior of the church during masses or attend the services held here in French on Sundays, you will see the chains still hanging over the main altar painting by Karel Škréta, one of the period's outstanding Czech artists.

As you face the church, the baroque building on your left, on the tiny square, is a former hotel, **U Zlatého Jednorožce, čp. 285**, marked by a prominent plaque, indicating that Beethoven stayed here in 1796 (and supposedly while here composed some mandolin pieces). Mozart also stopped here in 1789 en route to Berlin.

Now follow Lázeňská Street, but before you turn the corner, note the superb baroque Grand Prior's Palace on your left, built by the Knights of Malta (originally the Order of St. John of Jerusalem), who adopted the Malta appellation in the sixteenth century. Though the order goes back as far as 1099, the Prague branch dates to 1169. Its purpose was to care for the sick and indigent, and conduct crusades against heretics. Membership in this ancient aristocratic religious group was highly restricted: applicants had to prove they were descended from at least sixteen noble ancestors. Many sons of the great landed families of Czechoslovakia and Austria were members. Today the order still has extensive property holdings throughout Europe and continues its work. You can see the eight-pointed Maltese cross on the facade of the palace, recently renovated, as the Grand Prior is back in residence. (A museum of old musical instruments that used to reside here has been cleared out.)

Around the corner is a delightful surprise—secluded, tree-shaded **Grand Prior's Square** (**Velkopřevorské náměstí**), a Malá Strana treat, and if you didn't know exactly where it was, you would most likely miss it. On your right is the pastel baroque **Buquoy Palace, no. 486**, another of the landed gentry's opulent pieds-à-terre, today the French Embassy. The palace belonged to the Buquoys, an old French family related to the counts of Artois and ennobled by Phillip II of Spain—Thirty Years' War arrivistes who stayed until the end of World War II.

Opposite, you can't miss the **John Lennon Wall**, densely layered with late-twentieth-century grafitti and portraits of the singer, a hero to the pacifist youth subculture of Central and Eastern Europe during the Com-

munist period. The young idealists made what they could
of a forbidden public opportunity to synchronize the
singer's lyrics and rhythms with their own personal dis-
closures, and spilled their feelings and dreams onto its
masonry. Sample flower-child writing: "People don't die,
they're changed into flowers." For a time a constant battle
was waged with the police, who would come and wash
away the "subversion." Now, no one knows what will
happen to the wall, because the garden to which it belongs is back in the hands of the Knights of Malta. But
Lennon fans still tend the flame and regularly place flowers and candles under his portrait.

At this point retrace your steps back to Maltese
Square, and walk past the monument in the center, a
memorial to St. John Kritel, patron saint of the Knights
of Malta, by Ferdinand M. Brokoff, a celebrated Prague
sculptor of the baroque period. The classicist building
behind it, **no. 480**, was the main Prague post office from
1622 to 1723. Then continue up Prokopská Street to
Karmelitská, turn left, cross the street, and go up the
stairs to the **Church of Our Lady Victorious (Panny
Marie Vítězné)**, open from 8:30 A.M. to 4:00 P.M. The
well-lit, heavily encrusted, and richly carved silver altar
on the right contains an elaborately gowned sixteenth-
century wax figure of the infant Jesus, Jezulátko, with a
very large and sumptuous wardrobe, changed often. It
was brought here from Spain in 1628 by one Polyxena
of Lobkowicz, an extremely devout Spaniard who married into local Catholic society. An object of veneration
and source of miraculous healing powers, the effigy, also
known as the *Bambino di Praga*, is visited by a constant
stream of prayerful, tearful pilgrims from around the
world and particularly from Latin America. The Jezulátko
has turned the church into a kind of Lourdes shrine, a
repository of hope for the hopeless, perfectly in tune with
Prague's age-old reputation as a citadel of lost causes and
mystical font of the supernatural, every legend stocking a
virtual library of weird variations.

Exiting the church, turn left and follow **Karmelitská Tržiště**, a street named after the outdoor markets that used to be here in the seventeenth century—*trh* means "market" and *tržiště* means "marketplace." Before you reach the corner, note the plain-faced late-Renaissance **Vrtba Palace (čp. 373/25)**, behind which—you couldn't guess from the facade or from the almost gloomy entranceway to the small courtyard—is one of the glorious, deeply terraced baroque gardens of Malá Strana. If its restoration is complete and it is open, the Vrtba garden is worth a visit for its superb design, by Czech architect Kaňka, on a small plot of land, and also for the work of monumental sculptor Matthias Bernard Braun, who did the vases. Note the memorial plaque to Czech artist Mikoláš Aleš, of almost equally gilded reputation, indicating that he maintained his studio in a small house below the slope; he cherished the privacy afforded by the tucked-away garden.

Walk up Tržiště to the **Schonborn Palace**, now the American Embassy, on your left. The exquisitely carved gates of its portal date from the construction of the building, 1643–57; the lower section is from 1715. Writer Franz Kafka lived here for a few months in 1917, when it was an apartment house. Despite the unsurprising palace drafts and dampness, he was more than pleased with his two spacious rooms in a quiet first-floor wing; they had electricity and a view of the garden but were sans bath, which didn't seem to bother Kafka.

In the extensive gardens behind the embassy, and most visible from the entrance courtyard in winter, is a pale yellow stuccoed gloriette of particular charm, a kind of small summer pavilion called a *letohrádek*. The American flag, a triumphant but frustrating symbol of unattainable freedom during the Communist occupation, flies from its roof and can probably best be seen from Prague Castle. Stepping into the forecourt entrance of the embassy, you can glimpse a pair of Herculean figures, from sculptor Matthias Braun's studio, guarding the inner

Hercules at Schonborn Palace

sanctum of the compound. Beyond them the grand stone double staircase rises up to the terraced gardens on Petřín Hill.

Continue up the left side of the street, which becomes **Vlašská**. Here the Italian colony of artisans whose chapel we looked at earlier in the Old Town settled in the sixteenth century, though some had arrived during the early Middle Ages. The police station just past the Schonborn has a considerably shorter history, having been installed by the Communists to keep an eye on the Americans. Still farther up on your left, at the sign of the Three Roses, was the former entrance to the American Library (since moved to Hybernská Street), part of the embassy, in the dark days of Communism visited only by fearless Praguers who were willing to take the risk of having their presence reported to the STB (Státní Bezpečnost, or Secret Police). The daring younger Czechs who came here report that they were often treated less than graciously by the Czechs who worked at the embassy, some of whom, having also received clearance by the STB to work there, were doing double duty for the police.

Farther up the street on the right, the **Italian Cultural Center** is the last remaining institution of the ancient Italian expatriate community in Prague. The plaque states that the community founded a hospital here in 1602 and an orphanage in 1804. These days it's a venue for cultural events sponsored by the Italian government. Opposite stands the immense **Lobkovic Palace** (1703–07), which houses the German Embassy. The palace was originally designed by Giovanni Battista Alliprandi and later augmented by Ignác Jan Palliardi, both busy Italian architects of the Czech baroque who worked in Prague. The remarkable baroque architecture—a rotunda between symmetrical wings—includes two loggias, which, along with the beautiful gardens, are best seen from the rear. The palace and its grounds earned a place in recent history when the area was overrun in 1989 by thousands of East Germans fleeing into West Germany via Prague. In the trampling rush and confusion many abandoned their pressed-cardboard Trabant cars on the surrounding streets of Malá Strana. The event is commemorated by a witty footed Trabant sculpture in the garden. The garden is closed to the public, but to see the sculpture walk farther up the road about two hundred meters and turn left. Follow the path to the woods, turn left again along the road, and peer through the iron-fence railing into the compound. You will see the Trabant on the left, an actual car covered with wire mesh and painted bronze, entitled *Quo Vadis* ("Where are you going?"). First on view in the Old Town Square, it was acquired by the German government from David Černý, a young Czech design student in Prague, who was also responsible for painting a Soviet tank bright pink in another memorable post–Communist-era incident.

From here we'll go back down Vlašská Street and turn left at **Šporkova**—there's a tiny "Greek" restaurant here called **Faros**, which offers decent food and quick service. Šporkova is a cozy lane that turns in its upper part into **Jánský Vršek** and winds romantically up to a tiny dead-end lane called Jánská. Note **no. 320** hidden away in the corner on Šporkova near an ivy-shrouded stone statue of St. John Nepomuk. This finely decorated baroque building seems to have earned its name **At the Stonemason's**, for it was home to generations of them. It was remodeled in 1729 by a devout owner who carved emblems of his faith into the facade; the last of the dynasty was Josef Kranner, master builder of St. Vitus Cathedral. The Latin inscription says, "In the merciful hands of God's providence you will be a stonemason."

Now wind your way to Jánský Vršek Street and take the steps up to **Nerudova**. You are now on the main drag on Malá Strana. On the corner stands the rococo **Bretfeld Palace**, built by an aristocratic art and book collector. His extensive holdings were thought to have come from the spoils of defunct monasteries, but he also achieved renown as an exemplary host specializing in grand balls and entertainments. Among his guests were Mozart in 1787 and, earlier, that prolific rake Casanova. For several centuries Nerudova was the next-to-last stretch of the Royal Road (Královská Cesta), the principal approach to Prague Castle and route of the traditional coronation processions of Czech kings (kings of Bohemia). The ceremonial corteges started at the Powder Tower (Prašná Brána, on Republic Square) in the Old Town, wound their way across Charles Bridge, up Nerudova—whose narrow and steep incline must have been a scramble for the horses and carriages—to the Castle, and ended at the Cathedral, where the monarch was consecrated. The first coronation, in 1086, was that of Vratislav II of the Přemyslid dynasty; the last was in 1836, when the Hapsburg Ferdinand V was crowned. His successor, Franz Josef, whose long reign marked the end of the three-hundred-year Hapsburg era, refused to be crowned in Prague.

Now we'll walk down Nerudova. The thoroughfare was

named after a major figure of Czech literature, poet and journalist Jan Neruda, who lived a bit farther up the street. (If you feel like taking a slight detour, turn left instead of right at the top of the stairs and walk to his house on the left, **no. 233**; a huge sculptured plaque marks the spot known as **At the Two Suns**.) In addition to being home to many of Prague's literati and illustrious artists, the climbing, curving, hopelessly charming street is famous for its profusion of house signs—a forest of them formerly bristled on wooden dowels over the street. They served as address identifiers in the fourteenth century, before anyone thought up a numbering system, and often indicated some distinct feature of the house or the profession of the owner. For example, **no. 220, At the Golden Horseshoe**, boasts over the doorway a painting of St. Wenceslas's horse being shod that incorporates an actual horseshoe. This Renaissance house was also the site of the area's first pharmacy.

In the Middle Ages this upper section of the street belonged to the Castle district (Hradčany) and was divided from Malá Strana by a fortified wall complete with tower, drawbridge, and moat. Nearby on the left is **no. 210, At the Three Violins**, home to three families of violin makers, who lived there from 1667 to 1748. They were preceded by a court chamber painter to Rudolf II, Bartoloměj Spranger; today it's a tiny family-owned restaurant. Note **no. 212, At the Golden Goblet**, where a goldsmith once resided. The baroque facade of **no. 213** has been neatly and purposely scraped away in a couple of spots to reveal the original Renaissance black-and-white geometrical sgrafitto work underneath (sgrafitto is a process by which an outer layer of stucco is scratched through to show a different-colored ground). The **Thun-Hohenstein Palace** (1710–20), at **no. 214** on your left, now the Italian Embassy, was designed by the great Jan Santini Aichel. The handsome but low-key baroque structure stands in contrast to the extravagant plumage of the eagles, sculpted by Matthias Bernard Braun, flanking the portal, above which perch figures of Jupiter and Juno. The eagles are a heraldic symbol of the Kolovrat clan, for whom the palace was built; the Kolovrats claimed a number of distinguished diplomats and officials of the Austrian Empire. The palace was inherited by the Thuns in 1768, one of whose members made it into a lively literary salon for prominent locals. The Thuns date back to the eleventh century and are also closely tied to the highest echelons of imperial service; five Prague palaces bear their name. Also note the impressive baroque **Morzin Palace**, another Santini Aichel project, now the Romanian Embassy, across the street. Two Moors, sculpted by the eminent Ferdinand M. Brokoff, hold up the balcony; the busts represent Day and Night, and allegorical representations of the four continents then known (Europe, Asia, Africa, and the Americas) preside on top. The oldest pharmacy in Malá Strana, called Fragnerova and known as the royal pharmacy because it was also frequented by the court, once stood at the bottom left of Nerudova. It's marked by an oval plaque up on the wall; today a pub called **At the Tomcat's** occupies the premises.

Opposite is the upper part of Malá Strana Square. As long as we're here, we can hardly avoid taking a look at **St. Nicholas Church**, the chief Jesuit stronghold in Malá Strana and Prague's most extraordinary baroque church, a fixed supernova in the architectural galaxy of European high baroque. Its powerful verdigris-tinted copper dome and bell tower reign over the rooftops of the city like a tall clarion queen standing by her rotund king. The couple form an ineluctable part of the Prague panorama, appearing in changing juxtaposition as the viewer moves around town. The design and construction of this monument was a joint effort of father-and son architects Christoph and Kilián Ignác (K. I.) Dientzenhofer: K. I. took over after his father died, and the tower was executed by K. I.'s son-in-law, Anselmo Lurago. Though the foundation stone was laid in 1673, the building was not finished until nearly a hundred years later, in 1759, and is considered the last major achievement of the Bohemian baroque.

Christoph built a nave of such extreme undulating fluidity that its effect is to momentarily shock and perplex. The Dientzenhofers were said to be inspired by the Italian master Guarino Guarini's unconventional ideas about roof vaulting, and the wavy construction may have scandalized the Jesuits, who later ordered it obliterated by a vast illusionistic fresco by Jan Lukas Kracker in 1760. The dome, designed by Kilián at the end of his career, is considered a stroke of genius for its massive sobriety, balancing the nave's swirling underwater effects; the unexpected contrast of dome and tower sets concavity against convexity. Commanding the interior pillars under the cupola are four oversized, crook-armed, mitred bishops by Ignác Platzer. They play their heretic-winnowing and soul-saving roles perfectly—you could almost be seduced. You certainly can't ignore them. A gilded statue of St. Nicholas himself sits on the main altar, guarded by the two Jesuit heroes St. Ignatius and St. Francis Xavier, on either side. Note the large windows intended to enlighten worshipers who had lost their way, with divine rays, no doubt also overwhelming them with the beauty of their new church. Mozart played the organ here on one of his visits to Prague. When he died in 1791, a requiem mass attended by four thousand people was performed in his memory. During the Communist period worship was discouraged and services were held here only in conjunction with concerts.

Next go back to Nerudova and turn left on **Zámecká Street**, climb the small hill to **Thunovska**, and turn right. You can't miss the large bust of Winston Churchill at eye level on your left, beyond which is the **British Embassy** at **no. 14**. Mozart was a guest here when the palace used to belong to his friend and patron, Count Thun.

Now walk down to **Snemovní Street** (*snem* means "assembly"). Since 1870 the neobaroque palace on your right, **no. 176** (another former Thun abode), has served as an assembly hall for federal congresses, notably during the establishment of the First Republic. It was then seat of the Czech National Assembly; today it is where the Czech National Council meets. The huge granite plaque on the facade recounts the highlights of the hall's historic role. This quiet street, like so many in Malá Strana with its baroque gems, reminds me of the characterization that the sleepy quarter was given by a turn-of-the-century observer, Emil Utitz, a school friend of Franz Kafka: "Grass still grows there between the cobblestones, and the people sit in front of their doors as though they are living in the country . . . and the old people . . . give this quarter of the city a refined stillness." Well, you won't find much grass between the cobblestones now, but sometimes there's an unmistakable air of serenity, warily preserved and preferring to stay that way.

Follow the street past the small square up to what looks like its end but in fact is a right turn. Here the street changes its name to **U zlaté studně** (**At the Golden Well**). At its very narrow end is a house of the same name, **no. 166**, said to be nearly six hundred years old, which used to lead to a terraced restaurant with a superb view of Prague. Though closed at this writing, it is such an extraordinary site that someone is sure to restore it. The cast-iron plaque overhead is of Christ and the Samaritan woman at the well. Next door is the freshly repainted **U Malířů** (**At the Painter's**), once owned by a noted Czech artist (no relation to the one on Maltese Square).

Walk back down the lane to the diminutive **Square of the Five Churches** (Funfkirchen in German, **Petikostelní** in Czech, but not, it seems, on any map in any language), surrounded by wonderful sixteenth- and seventeenth-century houses with courtyards. Note especially **At the Golden Swan** on the corner, a small though remarkably genial Renaissance building from 1589. Though heavily restored, the courtyard gate, gallery, and gabled facade with sgrafitto are quite authentic-looking.

Nearby, **no. 163**, **At the Three Roses**—look under the ivy—supposedly once belonged to one Jeronymus Makovský. This character was personal footman to the Emperor Rudolf II, who treated him well and even ennobled him. He became enormously wealthy by taking hefty bribes to arrange audiences with the mistrustful, mentally wavering emperor. Rudolf paid little attention to matters of state but quite a lot to culture and science, or what science encompassed in those days—astronomy and astrology, alchemy and necromancy. And because he pulled together the most spectacular art collection the world had ever seen, he will live forever as acquisitor *non plus ultra*. After the Thirty Years' War the trove was scattered around Europe; you can see bits and pieces of it in many major museums. As for Makovský, he became one of the most successful parasitical parvenus at the court, rarely allowing anyone to see Rudolf because Rudolf didn't want to see anyone. The valet began making political decisions and delivering imperial pronouncements himself; in time, his conduct became so outrageous he ended his days in the dungeons of Křivoklát, a fortress reserved for dangerous criminals and enemies of the state.

At the bottom of the street you will find yourself in **Wallenstein Square** (**Valdštejnské náměstí**). The slightly austere though sumptuous baroque palace facing you was built for one of the most notorious and, naturally, most interesting figures of the convulsive Thirty Years' War, Albrecht von Wallenstein (1583–1634). Some Czech historians point out that just as the Klementinum is an emblem of the looting of Prague by the Jesuits in the post–White Mountain period, so Wallenstein's palace represents the bounty of a ruthless adventurer. In the annals of capable careerists hungry for power and fortune, few have come so far so fast as this orphaned son of a small Protestant landowner, an ex-Lutheran turned Catholic who, as the military governor of Prague and the emperor Ferdinand's chief *condottiere*, became one of the most feared army commanders on the battlefields of Europe.

He was in a position to profit and did so, royally: ultimately he may have had his sights set on the Castle itself. Guided by astrology, he ordered his horoscope cast by Johannes Kepler and retained him on his payroll. When Kepler died, the astrologer Seni took over—some said he was also being paid by the Viennese court to spy on his employer. Wallenstein's Prague palace was but a fragment of the property he accumulated: sixty-six estates in all, including the province of Friedland and the town of Jičín. Soon he controlled nearly a quarter of Bohemia and had raised a personal army. No wonder the emperor became nervous.

When word reached Ferdinand that Wallenstein had started keeping company with suspiciously subversive elements, the monarch ordered the general's death. Among the assassins were his own men, members of a British soldiers-of-fortune contingent. Wallenstein's death and life have been commemorated in song, art, and drama: among the literary efforts was the great German poet Schiller's play about the general as hero. Written in 1796, it's known as his best historical and classical dramatic work. More than a hundred years later the German novelist Alfred Doblin portrayed Wallenstein as a business tycoon, profiting from inflation and currency devaluation, a kind of seventeenth-century Wall Street raider of the smash-and-grab school of finance.

To make way for this vast private residence, twenty-seven houses, a brick yard, and four gardens were razed. Built in less than three years (1622–24) by architect Andrea Spezza along the lines of the Palazzo Farnese in Rome, it was the first such baroque edifice in Prague, with several wings encompassing five courtyards, an indoor riding arena, stables for three hundred horses, a chapel, and extensive formal gardens. Nor did Wallenstein cut corners on the interior furnishings, said to have been predominantly in blue: at least 182 Belgian tapestries and 62 carpets were included in the inventory register confiscated following his death. In the front wing facing the square, through the central portal, is the baronial marble Knight's Hall, one of the great public rooms. It is open only for concerts. (The rest of the palace is mostly used by the federal Ministry of Culture.) The ceiling, decorated with rich stucco detailing, includes a huge central portrait of Wallenstein himself in a chariot and raiments of the god Mars on triumphal parade. The fireplaces are also original, though the walls were inset with marble from the Černín Palace in Hradčany in 1853. After Wallenstein's demise the palace was said to have been returned to his nephew Maximilian, whose descendants lived here until 1945. Another version of the palace's fate is that it was acquired by Count Matyas Gallas, an Italian mercenary and founding member of the powerful Clam-Gallas family, in a package steal that included two other Wallenstein properties in Bohemia.

It's also worth noting the **Jan Amos Komenský (Comenius) Museum** located in the palace indoor riding arena, whose entrance is through the passageway on the left. Komenský is known as the founder of modern pedagogy—the French historian Jules Michelet called him the Galileo of education. He was a bishop of the Bohemian Brethren, a Protestant sect, and a post–White Mountain exile said by Cotton Mather to have been invited to America by Massachusetts Governor John Winthrop to become the first president of Harvard College. Time spent at the museum is not calculated into the timing of this walk; you may want to make another trip.

The same is true of the famous baroque/rococo **Terraced Gardens** behind the palaces on your left as you face Wallenstein's *residenz*. They are not specifically on our route, but it is difficult to pass this area of Malá Strana without saying a few words about them. As of this writing the gardens are closed and in a sad state of disrepair, with no word about completion of their restoration. If they have since been reopened, you owe it to yourself to check them out, because they are unquestionably among the glories of Prague. They feature elegant pavilions, loggias, terraces, tritons, fountains, great sculptured vases, and statuary; and it is the intimacy of even the more spacious ones that distinguishes them. Behind the eponymous palaces are the Ledebour garden at no. 162, the Palffy garden at no. 158, and the Kolovrat garden, no. 154. The Furstenberg garden at no. 153 belongs to the Polish Embassy, so you won't likely get into that one without an invitation.

By now you might be hungry; try the **Valdštejnská Hospoda** on the corner of **Tomášská Street**. The 1820 classicist building is called **At the Three Storks (U Tří Čápů)**; it used to house the brewery belonging to the nearby monastery of St. Thomas Church. The establishment has recently been privatized, but even during the Communist years it was a few cuts above average, and you'll likely enjoy the innlike atmosphere—dark wood beams on whitewashed, rough-stuccoed walls and stone fireplaces.

Now turn down Tomášská Street and note one of the most remarkable house signs in the city, the fine Brokoff **sculpture of St. Hubert**, patron saint of hunters, and the stag on the left over the door at **no. 26, At the Golden Stag**. The building is a mansard-roofed 1725 baroque design of K. I. Dientzenhofer.

Continuing down Tomášská Street, turn left at the corner and walk to the stubby dead end in the middle of the block on your left, where you'll find the entrance to the Augustinian **St. Thomas Church**, whose history is typically multilayered: Romanesque, Gothic, Renaissance, and baroque. In its early Gothic three-nave basilica incarnation (1285–1316), it was one of the largest and most expensively outfitted churches in Prague before being nearly destroyed in two fires (1491 and 1541). Its present late-baroque design (1723–31) anticipates the advanced projects of the enormously prolific K. I. Dientzenhofer.

Inside, look closely at the powerful yet gracefully drawn and clear-hued frescoes of Václav Vavřinec Reiner

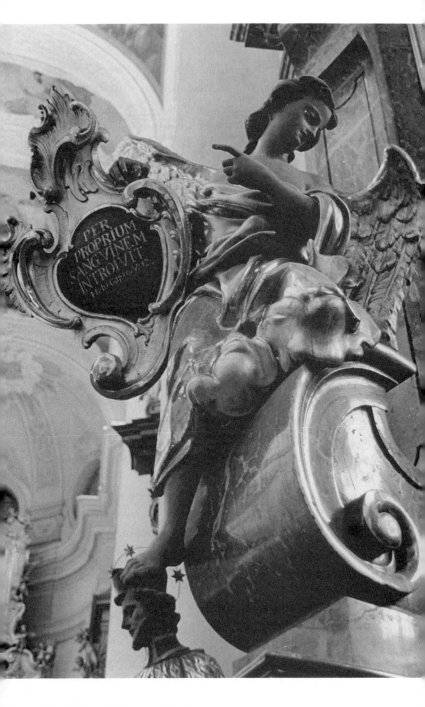

PER
PROPRIUM
SANGVINEM
INTROIVIT
Heb. Capit 9. v. 12.

Detail from St. Thomas Church

on the vaulted ceiling: above the main nave are scenes from the life of St. Augustine, over the cupola and the presbytery are depictions of legends of St. Thomas, and under the cupola, at the base of the dome, are exuberantly detailed allegories of the four corners of the world. In the center of the nave, notice the burning heart in one of the two gilded, cherub-encrusted glass boxes. This oft-repeated motif of the Augustinians, which you'll find throughout the church, stands for spiritual ardor. The relic boxes contain remains of St. Just and St. Boniface. The paintings on the double-tiered high altar are copies of valuable works by Peter Paul Rubens: one shows the horrific death of St. Thomas, a typical baroque Catholic exercise in dramatic cruelty, and the other is of St. Augustine. The originals have been carted off to the National Gallery in Šternberk Palace on Hradčany. There you will see much more Catholic art (and secular art spanning several centuries), a collection one might call variations on torture, some quite imaginative. Historic churches, especially baroque ones, often offer the unsettling experience of being overwhelmed by the beauty of the architecture while simultaneously sickened by the sadistic art.

If the church is not open, try the **cloister**, dated 1338, partly rebuilt in 1592 and again in the seventeenth century, today a home for retired persons. It may be entered by the door on the left of the main portal into the church, or from the church itself on the left. (Don't give up on the church, however; if no service is in progress, try the sacristan, if you can find him—he might let you in.) In the cloister, the Chapel of St. Barbora is through two Renaissance portals inscribed with the date 1596. Note also the burial tombs embedded in the walls around the loggia. One is that of a poet, Elizabeth Jane Weston, an Englishwoman who lived in Rudolfine Prague. Rudolf attracted a diverse and sometimes dubious international crew of artists, scholars, experimenters, and hangers-on to his court, and Weston, who died in 1612, was one of the English group, acclaimed for her Latin verse. Her stone can be found on the far side of the first loggia.

Now turn left into **Letenská**. At **no. 12** stands what is probably the oldest pub (1352) in Prague, **U Svatého Tomáše**, originally part of the brewery of St. Thomas's monastery. Like the church and cloister, this too was originally a Gothic structure, later remodeled as baroque. The brewery operated until 1953. Near the end of the nineteenth century a group of artists and literary types used to meet here. They called their circle Mahabharata, after the Hindu epic, and referred to themselves as Brahmas. The nucleus for this society was one Jakub Arbes, editor of a nationalist newspaper who got into trouble with the Austrian political police and lost his job. Under surveillance, he began spending his days in pubs so that his family would think he was going to work. Soon this one became his office. Today the pub mostly draws tourists, who congregate in its large low-vaulted rooms. Though the beer garden is no more, black Branik beer is a fair substitute for the monks' black-style brew.

Continuing on Letenská, walk down the street to the entrance of **Wallenstein's Garden (Valdštejnská Zahrada)** in the wall on the left. It is open daily from 10:00 A.M. to 7:00 P.M. from April 25 to September 30. Enclosed by high walls, this is probably the largest formal garden in Prague. Concerts are held inside the monumental triple-arched loggia built into the back of the palace. Despite its position at the far end, the loggia dominates the entire garden. Designed by Giovanni Pieronni, it is decorated with fine ceiling stuccowork and paintings of the Trojan War. Schiller's play *Wallenstein* was performed here in 1859. Next to it is an aviary where (after Wallenstein's day) rare birds were kept, along with a grotto from the 1630s entirely covered with artificial stalactites. The *giardinetto* in front of the loggia features a bronze fountain with a statue of Venus and Cupid, a cast of the original from 1599; the actual work was stolen by invading Swedes at the end of the Thirty Years' War and taken as

Wallenstein's Garden

booty to Sweden, whence it was returned in 1890. Today it's on display in the picture gallery of Prague Castle. A similar fate befell the fine sculptured bronzes of horses and mythological figures standing on either side of the avenue leading to the loggia. They are copies (1914–15) of works by Adriaen de Vries, court sculptor to Rudolf II. The originals were seized as plunder and removed to Drottingholm Castle near Stockholm, where they remain. The garden itself was laid out in the Italian style; the network of clipped hornbeam hedges and shade-bearing horse chestnut trees was restored most recently in 1955. At the opposite (southern) end of the garden is a large artificial pond with an island. The sculpture here is Hercules and a naiad, also a copy of de Vries pieces, and the fountain is a reconstruction of the original marble. A profusion of roses, large deciduous magnolias, figs, and perennials grows here. And behind the pond is the baroque facade of Wallenstein's riding school, which today functions as an exhibition hall of the National Gallery.

Exiting the garden, follow the street, staying on your right, to **U lužického semináře**, among the oldest streets of Malá Strana, where the houses still have names and where another oasis, a garden called **Vojanovy sady**, awaits your possibly weary feet. Formerly the garden of a Carmelite monastery, it's a quiet spot to rest in; at the opposite end, up a broad, stone-balustraded staircase, jazz concerts are held in the summer. The niched statue by Ignác Platzer on the left as you enter is of the ubiquitous St. John Nepomuk. One of the two tiny chapels in the garden is hung with stalactites to resemble a grotto but is in such a dank, abominable state of neglect that it's impossible to make out whatever frescoes or charm it might once have had. The other, larger chapel of St. Theresa is a purely baroque structure, apparently recently restored, with frescoes of its namesake on the ceiling.

In the homestretch now, you'll see a few restaurants along the street, of which I can recommend **At the Two Hearts** for informality and decent, moderately priced

Míšeňská Street

Czech food. Turn right onto the gentle curve of **Míšeňská Street** and make your way through a small square called Dražické up to the Gothic **Malá Strana Bridge Tower**. Next to it is a smaller tower and what's left of the twelfth-century Judith Bridge, Charles Bridge's predecessor. Romanesque at its core, the Judith Tower's Renaissance gables are sixteenth century. Together, the two towers form a matchless and inseparable introduction to Malá Strana. Another curiosity: the small two-story building set against the Judith Tower used to be the customs house when tolls were paid on the bridge. Inside is a late

Romanesque relief fragment more than seven hundred years old. Originally set into the east side of the tower, it was visible from the bridge until the sixteenth century. What the relief represents is uncertain; most bets hold that the kneeling figure is the contractor charged with building the town, and the seated figure is the Přemysl King Otakar II, from whom he took his orders. The fragment is on display in the tiny first-floor corridor leading to the main office of the Club of Old Prague (Klub za starou Prahu), a venerable amateur historical-preservation group.

If you're not ready to quit, I can promise you that the climb up to the viewing crown of the higher bridge tower is well worth it for an enchanting spectacle of the city, the river, red rooftops, domes, towers, and hundreds of spires, with photo ops to match. As towers go, this one is in the moderately-easy-to-climb category—up wooden steps, with two spacious resting possibilities. The tower is an early-fifteenth-century Gothic construction, designed to complement the one on the Old Town side, though with less embellishment all around; the coat of arms of the Old Town decorates the facade because the tower once belonged to it. Also on the bridge side are the coats of arms of Bohemia, the Luxembourg dynasty, and Moravia. Nothing like ending up on top!

Walk·2

Franz Kafka's Prague

THE OLD TOWN

Our Lady of Týn Cathedral, Old Town Square

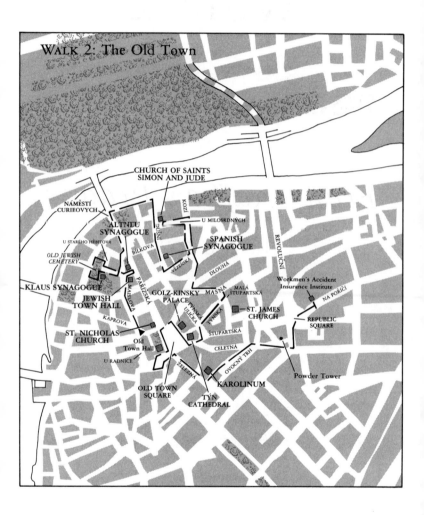

WALK 2: The Old Town

CHURCH OF SAINTS
SIMON AND JUDE

NÁMĚSTÍ
CURIEOVYCH

KOZÍ

U MILOSRDNÝCH

ALTNEU
SYNAGOGUE

U STARÉHO HŘBITOVA

DUŠNÍ

SPANISH
SYNAGOGUE

REVOLUČNÍ

BÍLKOVA

OLD JEWISH
CEMETERY

MEZENSKÁ

DLOUHÁ

KLAUS SYNAGOGUE

PAŘÍZSKÁ

MASNÁ

Workmen's Accident
Insurance Institute

NA POŘÍČÍ

GOLZ-KINSKY
PALACE

MALÁ
STUPARTSKÁ

JEWISH
TOWN HALL

MASLOVA

KAPROVA

TÝNSKÁ
ULIČKA

TÝNSKÁ

ST. JAMES
CHURCH

REPUBLIC
SQUARE

ST. NICHOLAS
CHURCH

STUPARTSKÁ

Old
Town Hall

CELETNÁ

U RADNICE

ŽELEZNÁ

OVOCNÝ TRH

Powder Tower

OLD TOWN
SQUARE

TÝN
CATHEDRAL

KAROLINUM

Starting Point: Just off Old Town Square at intersection of Maislova, Kaprova, and U Radnice streets. Do not attempt this walk on Saturdays or any Jewish holiday; weekdays are best to avoid Sunday crowds.

Metro/Tram Lines: Metro Green Line A, Staroměstská stop; or trams 17 or 18 to Jan Palách Square.

Length of Walk: About three hours.

Franz Kafka, a German-speaking Jew from Prague, is one of the rare twentieth-century literary figures whose name has taken up permanent residence in the language. *Kafkaesque* is an adjective with universal currency that defines the demonic forces of our modern age. We use it when we feel that the whole world is putting us on trial and no one will tell us the charge, when a suffocating bureaucracy makes us swoon. Or, as one Kafka biographer, Frederick Karl, told this writer, "When you enter a surreal world in which all your control patterns, all your plans . . . begin to fall to pieces . . . You don't give up. What you do is struggle with all your equipment, with whatever you have. But of course, you don't stand a chance . . ."

To understand how Kafkaesque came so perfectly and

devilishly to fit the zeitgeist, it helps, even if you've only read, say, *The Metamorphosis* or *The Trial*, to retrace Kafka's footsteps in his hometown and try to penetrate beyond the surface stone and stucco. But you don't have to look too far, because it all appears very much the same as it did in Kafka's day. Our walk will encompass many of the buildings, streets, and squares that made up the historical and cultural world of Franz Kafka. It should take a little over three hours, depending on how long you choose to linger at the various exhibitions along the way. Avoid this walk on Saturdays, when the Jewish quarter's treasures are closed for the Sabbath, or on any Jewish holidays. Weekdays are best because Sunday is overcrowded, especially during high tourist season. And remember to buy your single ticket for admission to all the sites covered here before you begin: do this at the High Synagogue and backtrack to the Maisel Synagogue. If you don't want to go back, simply pay the modest entrance charge at the Maisel when you come to it. (Museums are run by the state at this writing and are cheap.) Perhaps in time this system will change, and all-inclusive tickets will be sold at the Maisel. Last tickets are sold a half hour before closing time, 5:00 P.M. April to November, 4:30 P.M. the rest of the year.

Franz Kafka was born a citizen of the Austro-Hungarian Empire and died a citizen of the sovereign state of Czechoslovakia. So this walk is also a journey back to turn-of-the-century Prague, when momentous social movements were preparing the heaving ground for the new nation in the aftermath of World War I. Then came the exhilarating years of the First Republic between the two world wars, when the country became an industrial powerhouse ranked tenth in the world. The walk will also briefly take us much further back, to the eleventh century, when the earliest commercial center appeared around the Old Town Square.

While most of this walk is smack dab on the beaten tourist track—the Old Jewish cemetery is the most consistently mobbed historical attraction in Prague—our eyes will focus on Kafka's surroundings as he moved from one address to another in the Old Town and beyond. Imagining the area in the context of some of the seminal events of the author's life should not present any problems for anyone with a sense of history, a sense of literature, and a sense of what Kafka and Prague between them have given the world. This walk is also for those non-Jews to whom it might not occur to visit what's left of Josefov, the former Jewish ghetto, one of the most fascinating parts of *fantastická Praha.*

Before we set out, however, some background on the author and his milieu. Recognition of Kafka as a Czech writer, rather than the narrow view of him as a German writer—though he was educated and wrote in German—is a relatively recent phenomenon. It is more recent than the apotheosis of Kafka, which is a post–World War II reality. During his lifetime Kafka was scarcely known outside his small Prague circle of predominantly German Jewish comrades and colleagues. He is, in fact, the country's most famous writer, posthumously one of the most illustrious of all Prague's prodigious literary figures; the poet Rainer Maria Rilke is the other. But Rilke, the "tragic outsider," moved away in his teens, though he once used the words of the Czech national anthem in one of his poems and reworked Czech historical themes and legends in his poetry.

"It bubbles like a witches' broth, a devil's mix of Brod, Werfel, Kafka, and Kisch," wrote Anton Kuh of key members of the Prague literary group in this period. Kafka's other Prague contemporaries were Jaroslav Hašek, Karel Čapek, the painters Kupka and Kubín, and the composers Dvořák, Smetana, Janáček, and Suk. Born, bred, and buried in Prague, Kafka lived here nearly his whole life long. And unlike most of his German-community friends, he spoke and wrote Czech fluently.

It is here in Prague that Kafka has been discovered most recently of all, since the glacier of Communism melted away, revealing what had long been suppressed, what the descendents of those among whom he lived intuited but were the last to know. Such was the power of the word under Communism that, except for a short-lived rehabilitation during the sixties—the time of the aborted Prague Spring of 1968, when the frozen creative world began to thaw and thrive—Franz Kafka was viewed as a dangerous subversive, and his all too lucid, yet opaque, vision was officially blacklisted. He was read only in samizdat (clandestinely published editions) or was smuggled in from the West—omnipresent but never mentioned. Until 1989, that is, when everything changed for everybody—even for a dead writer. Today a Kafka industry markets its product as mercilessly as billboard Marlboro Men squint behind wreaths of cigarette smoke on Prague buildings. The writer's huge, terrifying, liquid black eyes emblazon T-shirts, postcards, brochures—every imaginable tourist artifact. He is the subject of continuously running theater performances, and a recently formed Franz Kafka Society sells books and promotes contemporary literary ventures in his name.

Though Kafka ranged over much of the city, especially the gardens of Chotkovy Sady below the Castle, most of his days and nights were spent near the Old Town Square, in and around the crowded Jewish ghetto. There the houses once had strange, otherworldly names like The Mouse Hole, The Left Glove, Death, Gingersnap, and No Time. Within a radius of a few blocks, roughly a square mile, as Kafka himself once described it to his Hebrew teacher by drawing small circles with his finger as they looked out onto the Old Town Square, he grew up, went to the gymnasium (grammar school), took a law degree, earned a living . . . and inevitably learned what it meant to be Jewish in the ancient capital of Bohemia.

Prague once had the largest and oldest Jewish settlement in Europe. Historians guess that it dates back to the tenth century. Jewish legends claim it may have been as early as four hundred years before the Czechs themselves arrived. The major branches of European Jewry, the Yiddish-speaking Ashkenazim and the Iberian Sephardim, crossed paths here: they came from the Balkans, from Russian-Polish regions, and later, from Spain, Portugal, and Italy. But in Kafka's time Prague was more a provincial town than the metropolis it is today. As the largest city of the Austro-Hungarian Empire after the Dual Monarchy capitals of Budapest and Vienna, Greater Prague had a population of 450,000 distributed over five districts. About 35,000 were German speakers, of whom the great majority, possibly as much as 85 percent, were Jews, a tiny island in a sea of Czechs. The most clearly demarcated district was Josefov, where Jews lived enclosed by walls with gates that locked at night. The region was no melting pot. Prague was a segregated city with fermenting nationalities and minorities boycotting each other at all stages.

But then this city had always been a complex place, historically, politically, religiously, artistically, even journalistically. More than twenty daily newspapers were sold on the streets; the small German-Jewish community had two dailies. Out of all proportion to its size, it had an intense social and cultural life, supporting two theaters, a huge concert hall, a major university, an institute of technology, five high schools, four vocational schools, and the German casino on Na příkopě street, which the Germans called the Graben, echoing the gilded Graben in the heart of Vienna. The Germans also had their own banks and industries. What the community lacked, despite these institutional, cultural, and civic manifestations, was a clear identity in the midst of a burgeoning Czech nationalism and a decaying Hapsburg Empire that had lost its compass. Kafka eventually described himself as a Bohemian (Gustav Mahler, also a German-speaking native, did the same on a visit to New York once, to the disappointment of the German journalists who were interviewing him) and thereby solved the vexing problem, for himself at least, of his unclassifiability.

Let's begin our Walk at **Saint Nicholas Church**, the

Portal of Franz Kafka's birthplace

big white baroque church on the Old Town Square whose
entrance is just off it on its northwest side. This places
us near the intersection of **Maislova**, **Kaprova**, and **U
Radnice** (At the Town Hall) streets, just outside the
boundaries of the old Jewish ghetto. Kafka was born at
no. 5 Maislova (or no. 1/21) on July 3, 1883; the building was demolished fifteen years later and in 1902 was
replaced by the one that abuts the church. The original
structure was once part of a Slavic Benedictine monastery
prelature attached to St. Nicholas and called Tower House.
The baroque portal is all that remains.

When the Kafka family lived here, a seedy, reeking bar occupied a nearby partially hidden basement, and St. Nicholas was known as the Russian church, for the Russian Orthodox order that used it. (Since 1920 it's been run by the Czechoslovak Hussite order.) On the ground floor of no. 5 is an exhibition of Kafka's life and work, opened in 1991, which may or may not be permanent. Mounted high on the corner wall is the memorial marker, a life-size head of Kafka sculpted in black bronze. One of Kafka's biographers, Ernst Pawel, describes it as a "modest memorial, conceived in ambivalence and therefore singularly fitting in its way." It is the 1965 work of artist Karel Hadlik, commissioned by the Communists to signal the first phase of the author's proposed rehabilitation. Though rejecting and defaming Jewish intellectuals as alien and rootless, they had planned to convert Kafka from a "subjective and pessimistic" writer into a satirist of capitalism's wicked ways. This process was halted in its tracks by the invasion of Warsaw Pact troops, extinguishing for another twenty years any thoughts Czechs may have entertained of extended breathing space from police-state persecution.

Before proceeding down Maislova, note the *vinárna* (wine cellar, though not necessarily subterranean) **At the Green Frog**, čp. 13, on the left opposite the Kafka house. In unstanchable operation since the 1600s, its claim to fame is as a watering hole of one Mydlář the Executioner, who did some of his bloodiest work in 1621 in the Old Town Square around the corner. His job then was to decapitate the cream of the old Bohemian aristocracy that had plotted rebellion against the Hapsburgs. The back room of the fourteenth-century building has an early-Gothic vaulted-and-ribbed ceiling and sits on Romanesque foundations at the edge of the "fifth district," as this area was known then. For the specific purpose of making Jews "useful to the State," restrictions on the fifth district were gradually lifted, a process that started in 1784 and continued until 1867, when full political emancipation was granted. Officially the ghetto, once ringed by steel wire, had been abolished and its iron gates flung open for good in 1852 by that great reformer, Emperor Josef II. (In gratitude the Jews named the quarter Josefov.) German-language instruction was mandated and Jews were allowed to engage openly in commercial trades, become artisans and farmers, and attend Christian schools. Prosperous Jews, no longer confined to the ghetto, moved out. Non-Jews moved in, and the area quickly deteriorated into a packed, decaying breeding ground for disease and undesirable elements. At least that was the excuse for what remains an insensitive and controversial forced displacement. At the Green Frog is a survivor of the drastic slum demolition that began in 1893 and effectively destroyed the infested ghetto's thirty-odd streets and some three hundred houses, many of them subdivided into "incredible fractions," as one observer put it. A victim of civic "sanitizing," the ancient Jewish community, which had survived plagues, fires, pogroms, and banishments, was to endure even worse in the twentieth century.

Kafka never forgot the atmosphere of the old ghetto: "In us all it still lives—the dark corners, the secret alleys, the shuttered windows, the squalid court-yards, the rowdy pubs, the sinister inns. We walk through the broad streets of the newly built city. But inside we still tremble in the centuries old streets of our misery. Our hearts know nothing of the slum clearance around us."

Maislova Street and its neighboring thoroughfares are no longer the cobbled crevices of Kafka's youth, and precious little remains of the old Josefov, but we'll see what's left. Walk down to the Neo-Gothic **Maisel Synagogue** on the right. Street and synagogue are named after Markus Mordecai Maisel, distinguished sixteenth-century mayor and public-works developer of the quarter, said to be the wealthiest individual in Rudolfine (Emperor Rudolf II) Prague, some say perhaps in all of Europe. Maisel was also a merchant and banker with close business ties to the emperor, a connection that helped him win concessions for his community. While the street dates to 1592, with few exceptions its architecture reflects the new, grandiloquently conceived Neo-Gothic, Neo-Renaissance, and art nouveau apartment buildings of the Vienna school, that replaced the medieval two- and three-story houses of the old quarter.

The end of the nineteenth century was also a time of intense urban renewal in other districts of Prague; streets were widened and raised and new infrastructure was installed. Sadly and irrevocably, the city authorities did not stop at leveling the ghetto; they went on an "improvement" rampage and flattened numerous valuable landmarks, including some of the oldest Romanesque structures. The Maisel synagogue's present appearance is an 1893–1905 phenomenon; the original, larger, structure was sixteenth century, built to Maisel's specifications as his private house of worship. Today it is used by the State Jewish Museum for exhibiting the more than 30,000 religious and artistic objects—ceremonial art and liturgical implements, particularly silver and metalware—brought to Prague from the ransacked synagogues of Bohemia and Moravia by the Nazis, who intended to stock an "Exotic Museum of an Extinct Race."

Farther down Maislova Street on the right corner, you will see the pink-and-white-painted late baroque **Jewish Town Hall**, also a beneficiary of Maisel's philanthropy. It is often proudly described as a symbol of the Jewish community's autonomy and self-sufficiency during the sixteenth-century period of relative peace and prosperity. Rudolf II's rule of benevolent anarchy helped the Jews flourish, and a kind of "golden age" or renaissance produced contributions in literary and scientific fields such as astronomy, mathematics, historiography, and religious thought, the last of which was generally dominated by the scholar David Gans and especially Rabbi Judah Lowe ben Bezalel, who became a legendary international figure (we'll talk more about him later).

The Town Hall's facade dates to a 1763 restoration that followed two fires—in 1689 and in 1754. The bell tower was added by special permission of Ferdinand III in appreciation of the Jews' efforts at fighting off the Swedes in 1648. (A kosher restaurant on the ground floor might interest you if you want to stop for a moderately expensive meal.) This building is also administrative headquarters of the surviving Jewish community. Turn the corner and note the clock on the roof (below the clock tower) with Hebrew characters; it runs backward, so "clockwise" in Hebrew is the equivalent of counter-clockwise in English. Attached to the building in the di-rection of Pařížska Street is the **High Synagogue** or **Town Hall Synagogue** (**Vysoká**), built by Maisel in 1568. It was originally connected with the Town Hall, accessible only through the first-floor entrance of that building. It served as a center of community social functions and for rabbinical court sessions. Today it is a repository of sa-cred textiles and artifacts, a rich bounty on permanent exhibition. Most of the remaining synagogues and their collections are similarly employed—forlornly, some might say. There are simply not enough Jews left in Prague to use them as they were meant to be used. (At the begin-ning of the eighteenth century, Prague's was the largest Jewish community in the world; today it has shrunk to a couple of thousand.) Still, all the exhibits of the Jewish Museum are eminently worth seeing.

Directly opposite the High Synagogue is the oldest extant house of Jewish worship in Prague, the legendary **Altneuschul** (**Staronová synagoga**). It is also the oldest synagogue still in continuous use anywhere in the world, at the heart of life in the Jewish community for at least seven hundred years. This has made it into a kind of representative synagogue, a symbol of all those that are known only from archaeological and documentary evi-dence and from the pages of medieval illuminated manu-scripts. The German *altneu* means "old-new" and is thought to be a seventeenth-century appellation used to differentiate it from the earlier Altschul or Old Synagogue (1142), a synagogue that stood in a nearby street. Historians estimate that the Altneu's early Gothic architecture is of late-thirteenth-century vintage, though the crenellated brick gable was added about one hundred years later. The low extensions on three sides are also later additions. The northern one, from the eighteenth century, is a women's gallery, since women are not permitted to participate in sanctuary rites.

Inside the Altneu, daylight sends eastern sunbeams slanting hazily from two high-up, smallish round windows into the hushed dimness, and you are instantly enveloped in chiaroscuro mysticism, an atmosphere of great age and mystery. You might feel like sitting down on one of the dark wood Renaissance armchairs ranged around the walls, and looking around.

The smallish, double-naved central chamber with two octagonal pillars is an architectural feature typical of medieval synagogues. Against the eastern wall stands the high-backed chair of Rabbi Judah Lowe ben Bezalel, a mystic who was even more of a legend in Prague—and elsewhere—than was the venerable Altneuschul. Also on that wall, under the tympanum, is perhaps the most sacred spot in the sanctuary: flanked by two Renaissance columns, behind the embroidered curtain, is the Torah, parchment scrolls containing the five books of Moses. The scroll form of the Torah is a reminder of its ancient origins before Gutenberg's press; it is never read with the fingers, only with pointers carved like tiny hands, many examples of which are on display in the museum's collections. The sculptural decorations encrusting the columns are all of horticultural or vegetable motifs because of Jewish reticence over three-dimensional figures (considered idolatrous); notice, for example, the finely carved leaves and branches in the Gothic tympanum above the interior portal. The triangle also represents the tree of life and the three continents then known to Europeans.

The rib-vaulted ceiling gives the impression of soaring space despite the small size of the sanctuary, a mere fifteen by nine meters. Some observers think that the architect achieved this loftiness by lowering the floor's level below that of the adjacent streets, to circumvent restrictions placed on the height of synagogues during the Middle Ages. (The laws were intended to ensure that churches always towered over synagogues.) But it's more likely that the sanctuary's floor was flush with the street level until the Old Town pavements were raised to prevent the periodic river flooding that plagued the area. Note also that the vaults have five ribs instead of the usual four, to avoid the cruciform intersections of Christianity that would be inappropriate to Judaism.

Above the fifteenth-century wrought-iron grille that surrounds the center pulpit, called a *bimah*, a lectern for reading from the Torah, hangs the historic banner of the Prague Jewish community. It too was a gift of Emperor Ferdinand III in 1648, the final year of the Thirty Years' War, in gratitude for Jewish participation in defending the Old Town from the Swedish Army. Originally, Emperor Charles IV had recognized the community with a banner in 1357, a proud possession whose meaning of political autonomy and privileges granted and renewed was of utmost significance for the Jews. Kafka once accompanied his father here and noted a Yom Kippur service in his diary: "Suppressed murmur of the stock market. In the entry, boxes with the inscription: 'Merciful gifts secretly left assuage the wrath of the bereft.' Churchly inside. The pious, apparently eastern Jews. In socks. Bowed over their prayer books, their prayer shawls drawn over their heads, become as small as they possibly can."

The atmosphere of the Altneu is palpably ancient and has riveted scores of artists, writers, and photographers. But equally prehistoric-looking in this neighborhood of large, ostentatious apartment buildings designed to intimidate, is the synagogue's humble and somber exterior, like the carcass of a great, dark, tough-skinned sea creature, beached on its island sward of green. Historians theorize that the synagogue, once surrounded by a marketplace, was preserved by its lucky, freestanding placement. It was protected from fires and other calamities that destroyed many structures huddled together in the congested quarter. (Jewish mythology says that it's the oldest synagogue in the world, having been erected, or brought, by angels immediately after the destruction of the Temple in Jerusalem.)

Stories about the Altneuschul abound. One particularly poignant one concerns the looting and burning of the ghetto in 1389, when mobs chased Jews into the synagogue and massacred them. They were among three thousand who died in the most brutal pogrom Prague had ever experienced. The victims' bloodstains were preserved on the eastern interior wall for five hundred years, until an incompetent restorer plastered them over. Rabbi Avigdor Kara, a noted scholar and poet, witnessed the murders and wrote an elegy, "All of the Hardships That Befell Us," which is recited annually by the Jews of Prague on Yom Kippur, the Day of Atonement.

> The worst of our foes' crimes occurred in the year 5149 [1389], when heavy fell our Lord's scorn on Golden Prague, the city of beauty we mourn . . .
> Without any reason they drew their knives and slaughtered our men, children, and wives . . .

Outside, walk to the northern side of the synagogue to the green, and notice the handsome bronze **sculpture of Moses** (1905) by Czech artist František Bílek, about whom more in Walk 3. It's an oddly agonized view of a dying Moses, not the usual proud profile of the prophet who liberated the Israelites; nor is it a typical example of Bílek's work, which is rarely so baroque.

Now make your way down **U starého hřbitova (At the Old Cemetery) Street**, off Maislova, for the other most remarkable sight in this quarter, the Old Jewish Cemetery. But first notice the **Klaus Synagogue** on your left before the entrance to the cemetery. This particular structure was built in 1694 on the site of a complex containing a small synagogue, a hospital, and a ritual bath (additional contributions of Mordecai Maisel). The Klaus became prestigious for its Talmudic or rabbinical school, which attracted prominent rabbis and scholars to Prague. Among them were David Gans, astronomer, mathematician, and historian, and his mentor, Rabbi Lowe. The synagogue also served as a prayer hall and meeting center for the local burial society. Today it's been turned into an all-important exhibition hall of old manuscripts and literature printed since 1512, when the first Hebrew press north of the Alps was established in Prague. It's a must-see stop for the story of the Jewish community, but the exhibitions do change. Of the interior architectural details, note particularly the richly stuccoed barrel vaulting and the elaborate three-tiered Torah ark from 1696 (restored 1983).

From the Klaus, let's move on through the gates of the **Old Jewish Cemetery** next door. Perhaps you'll be lucky and there won't be too many visitors; if there are, it's best to move away from the bottleneck entrance area. Of course, the crowding here is nothing compared to the terrific crowding under your feet. Gingerly stepping around the remains of the permanent residents is to remember that they are almost as crammed in death as they were in the dense warrens of the ghetto. Few people forget the sight of this place that the Jews call the garden of the dead, the oldest graveyard in Europe. Nothing in the neighborhood, among the houses of worship and study or in the teeming streets, prepares you for it. Though the last burial was in 1787 (the first in 1439), the packed-together, drunkenly tilting-every-which-way gravestones, many half sunken, many submerged entirely, seem to jostle each other under the bumpy earth. And when the sun filters through the leaves of the elder trees, throwing shadows up and down the madly heaving ground, the effect can be hypnotic. How many? Twelve thousand tombstones, 100,000 graves layered twelve deep. Since Jewish religious law forbids the removal of old

Gravestone, Old Jewish Cemetery

graves, when space was exhausted, the ground was covered over with fresh earth to make way for new plots; thus the tablets accumulated. They are monuments to diverse eras in Prague's history and culture, and the Hebraic inscriptions are critical sources for the story of the community's development and of its key personalities.

You will notice that small stones and pebbles have been placed on many of the tombs. It is said that this old Jewish custom dates to the days when Jews wandered in the flowerless desert following the exodus from Egypt. Often you will see notes folded under the stones or tucked into the crevices—secret thoughts or prayers for the dead from well-wishers. (Franz Kafka gets a lot of notes, but you won't find his stone here; he is buried in the New Jewish Cemetery in Olšany: metro line A to Želivského).

For a tour of the graves of some of the most signifi-cant figures in the community, turn left from the en-trance. Note, in the front row, the tombstone of a physician, Beer Teller; the stone is carved with a bear holding medical tweezers. Walk toward the northeast corner of the Klaus Synagogue: embedded there are frag-ments of fourteenth-century gothic tombstones from the original Jewish cemetery in the New Town, site of an earlier, now extinct, settlement. Also in this area, called Hill Nefele, is a child's memorial tombstone from 1903. Now walk down to the east wall, past the Jewish hospital, to the oldest grave in the cemetery, that of poet Rabbi Avigdor Kara, who was buried here in 1559. His marker is one of the earliest type, a large black freestanding rect-angular sandstone block, the surviving inscriptions in high relief. Next we'll detour to the Pinkas Synagogue on the north side of the cemetery, but first note two markers, the tomb of David Gans, the ghetto's first historiographer (died in 1613), into whose stone is carved a Star of David surmounted by a goose (*gans*). Nearby is that of Mordecai Cohen, printer, son of Gershom Cohen, founder of the Prague Hebrew press (1592). Notice the blessing hands and ewers signifying descendants of the biblical priestly clans on the gravestones of members of the Cohen and Levi families.

The **Pinkas Synagogue** was regularly attended by Kafka's father Herrmann during his first years in Prague (he came from a poor village in southern Bohemia); young Franz recalled being more impressed by Judaic tradition and its orthodox rituals here than anywhere else. The second-oldest existing synagogue in the city, it is exemplary for architectural detailing and was originally built in late-Gothic style—note the reticulated vaulting—for the private use of the prominent Horowitz family in 1535. But there was an even earlier Romanesque house of prayer here dating to at least 1479. The remains of a ritual bath, called a *mikvah*, were discovered in the ancient foundations. In 1625 the building was redesigned again in late-Renaissance style and widened, and a women's gallery added. Its sunken position is a result of the surrounding streets' having been raised in the thirteenth century. Unfortunately, and in stark contrast to the Altneuschul, an insensitive overrestoration that dragged on for twenty years obliterated virtually all traces of atmosphere the sanctuary once had and of what it might have looked like inside; you will have to view old photographs to appreciate its pre-Communist condition. Worse, the "restoration" wiped out the memorial to the 77,297 Jews from Bohemia and Moravia who perished in the Holocaust. In a five-year project starting in 1950 their names had been carefully inscribed on the walls, according to region of origin, family surname, date of birth, and deportation date. It was the only memorial to these victims in the country and is currently being inscribed all over again.

Now we'll retrace our steps to the cemetery and continue our tour. Proceeding in a southwesterly direction, notice the large tombstone marking the grave of Rabbi David Oppenheim, a distinguished chief rabbi of Prague and Talmudic scholar. His is one of the more elaborate, three-dimensional monuments of pink-and-white marble, of which there are about twenty, which began appearing in the early seventeenth century. These tombs were constructed like tents from two decorated stone slabs joined as a roof, an effect meant to symbolize the houses of ancient Israel. The rabbi was a bibliophile who is remembered for his huge collection of old Hebrew manuscripts and prints, presently kept at the Bodleian Library at Oxford.

Following the path and turning right will take us to Mordecai Maisel's grave (1601). Rabbi Loew is buried with his wife back near the western wall, so you will have to retrace your steps a bit if you want to pay your respects to the most celebrated figure of the Czech Jewish community of the late sixteenth century, remembered ever after in both Jewish and Czech folklore.

While we're here at his final resting place, let's talk a bit about the life and career of the esteemed rabbi. Shortly after most of Josefov was razed, the city commissioned sculptor Ladislav Šaloun to create statues for the New Town Hall (in the Old Town—see Walk 1). He chose two themes to represent the spirit of Old Prague. One was the Iron Knight of the medieval city; the other was Rabbi Lowe, the personification of Josefov, familiar to every resident. Though born in Poland, Rabbi Lowe was revered as a great scholar and teacher and worked in Prague for thirty-six years. Outside the ghetto, his fame derives from his literary creation, the golem—an artificial being, often ghostly or made of clay, conjured (by using the holy name *golem*), to protect the Jews of Prague, but also a monster that is an affront to God. Originating in the Bible, over the centuries Lowe's tales spun around Europe and beyond, and the golem developed into a kind of robotic Frankenstein figure, eventually losing its Jewish identity except in Bohemia. Variations on the story and the monster were endemic; at the turn of the century one Gustav Meyrink wrote a best-selling novel about Jewish Prague and a golem. The theme is thought to have influenced Kafka's idea of Gregor Samsa in the novella as a creature who could be manipulated and metamorphosed into a giant beetle. Like everyone else, Kafka was undoubtedly steeped in the tradition and knew Meyrink, as did Franz Werfel and other Prague literary figures of the day.

Next stop is the beautiful pink marble tomb of Hendl Bashewi, wife of Jacob, who was a banker and an associate of the mighty mercenary capo Albrecht Wallenstein. It is located in the tightest spot of the graveyard, near the west wall. Jacob Bashewi, who is buried elsewhere, was the first Jew to be ennobled for his services to the emperor. The buzz was that although these tombs that looked like little houses were reserved for distinguished personages, the superrich could buy their way into a final resting place more deluxe than even Mordechai Maisel's. Our last stop, closer to the south wall, is at the grave of another important seventeenth-century scholar, Rabbi Joseph Shlomo Delmedigo of Candia, peripatetic Italian philosopher-scientist and student of Galileo at Padua.

Find your way back to the cemetery entrance and, as you exit, notice the pseudo-Romanesque **Ceremonial Hall** on your left. Designed to resemble a small castle, the building is a 1906-vintage structure that houses a painfully moving exhibition of children's art and poetry from the Terezín (Theresienstadt) concentration camp (located thirty miles from Prague) whence 140,000 people were transported to death camps.

From this exhibit, retrace your steps past Maislova to **Pařížská Street** (called Niklas Street in Kafka's time), where the buildings reach new heights of grandiosity, and walk down to the Vltava (known in the symphonic repertoire by its German name, the Moldau) embankment, to a position just left of the remarkable art nouveau bridge called **Svatopluk Čech Bridge (Čechův most)**. It is named after the nineteenth-century Romantic Czech poet Svatopluk Čech and was built in 1906; winged victory figures crown the pillars on either side. The law faculty building of Charles University stands on the corner. From here you can see across the river to the **Civic Swimming Pool (Občanská plovárna)** on the other side, dating to 1840, a favorite recreational spot of the Kafkas; young Franz first came here with his father. Once also a boating establishment where Kafka kept a rowboat, now it's a wreck; perhaps that will also change. In far better shape is the tiny early baroque rotunda of **St. Mary Magdalene** (1635), used as a chapel by the Catholic Church. But Kafka would have experienced some skewed déjà vu if he saw the rotunda

Ceremonial Hall, Josefov

today: it used to stand lower down on the embankment and was moved to its present spot when the bridge was under repair in 1955, the first such whole-building relocation in the country.

Next walk west along the river a block and turn right on **Dušní Street**; you will pass the dismal concrete-block pile of the **Intercontinental Hotel**, built by the Communists in 1970 on the site of a large apartment building called the Ship, one of the first with an elevator, in which the Kafka family lived from 1907 to 1913. Construction on the Svatopluk Čech Bridge started soon after the Kafkas moved in, almost directly at their doorstep. The Ship stood here until 1945, when it was destroyed by retreating Nazis. The apartment was said to be more spacious than the previous one but still a tight fit for the eight-member household. Kafka, infamously sensitive, complained of the constant noise yet, as ever, stayed pretty much close to home, and managed to write *The Judgment*, the unfinished novel *Amerika*, and *The Metamorphosis*.

On Dušní Street turn right and right again on **Bílkova**. Kafka lived at **no. 10** in his sister's apartment during the early weeks of World War I and started work on *The Trial*, possibly his most Praguelike, charismatic work, though in the novel the city is more anonymous than even its main character, the unfortunate Joseph K. Also on this street, between Eliška Krásnohorská Street and Dušní, on the south side, stood the baroque Gypsy Synagogue (the street was then named Zigeunerstrasse, or Gypsy Street) of Kafka's youth, site of his bar mitzvah in 1896. The Gypsy and another large baroque synagogue, the Great Court, which stood almost directly across the street, were destroyed along with several other important community buildings in 1906.

Now go back to Dušní and continue walking south to the **Spanish Synagogue** on your left. Unfortunately, as of this writing it is shut down and appears in a deplorable state of disrepair; it is said to be used for furniture storage, no doubt moldering, of the Nazi confiscations of Jewish property from Bohemia. A comparatively recent (1868) structure of imposing, richly detailed Moorish style inside and out, it is the latest synagogue to be added to the Old Jewish Quarter; the Spanish was built on the foundations of the very first Prague synagogue, the Altshul. (Note the Ten Commandments tablets carved into the upper facade.) This neighborhood was the nucleus of the earliest tenth-century Jewish settlement of Sephardic Jews, and later the destination of those fleeing the Spanish Inquisition in the fifteenth century. The height of Jewish prosperity in Rudolfine Prague closely parallels the culmination of Catholic fanaticism in Phillip II's Spain. Opposite is the fourteenth-century Gothic **Church of the Holy Ghost**. A Benedictine monastery also used to stand here.

Now turn left on **Vězeňská Street** and walk to the corner of **Kozí Street**, with its elevated sidewalk on one side. The corner establishment, a new and inexpensive restaurant, used to be the **Café Savoy** (later called Hermann's Café-Savoy), thought to be a bit sleazy. In 1911 Kafka attended more performances of an itinerant Yiddish theater troupe here than any other theatrical events of his life. They were said to have influenced his later writing. Around that time began his lifelong interest in Jewish history and literature and the sources of Judaism, to him subjects of considerable ambivalence that eventually helped clarify his struggle for an identity.

Let's detour for a moment to a charming, out-of-the-way corner of the Old Town: turn left and follow the lane, Kozí, to **U milosrdných Street (At the Merciful Brethren)**, and note on one side the beguiling pseudo-baroque and art nouveau apartment buildings stuccoed in shades of yellow (circa 1900). On the corner is the baroque **Church of Saints Simon and Jude**, which is being used for concerts again (chiefly by the Prague Symphony, which has restored it), as it was in Mozart's and Haydn's day, when the two composers played riffs on the organ. From 1615 to 1620 the church was renovated by the Unity of Czech Brethren, the most important Protestant sect in the fight for religious freedom from Catholic domination. Their sixteenth-century translation into Czech of the Bible, called the Kralice Bible, became the standard edition, equivalent to the King James Version for English speakers. Saints Simon and Jude is a part-Gothic, part-Renaissance church with a pre-fourteenth-century core, its tall Gothic windows and late Gothic vaulting remodeled in 1615; the baroque facade was added later. Running the length of the block is the former convent and hospital of the Order of the Merciful Brethren, connected to a contemporary hospital on the riverfront, Na Františku. The streetside facade here is Dientzenhofer-style baroque (1753).

Now let's go back to Vězeňská, turn right, and walk to **Dlouhá**: note the promontory **no. 16, The House of the Golden Pike**, a pension where Kafka rented (a first) a corner room on the top floor from 1915 to 1917. Then it had a stunning view of the Castle but was, as usual, too noisy. From here we proceed to **Masná Street**, called **Fleischmarktgasse** when street names were in German (as they were until 1891). The word means "meat market," though even in Kafka's day a wholesale fish trade had largely replaced the butchers' offerings. The concomitant odors were said to pervade even the classrooms of the severe-looking, four-story building where from 1889 to 1893 Kafka reluctantly attended the German National and Civic Elementary School for Boys, now defunct—it stood near the corner on the right.

This was a particularly agonizing time in Kafka's agonized life. He had to be literally dragged, flailing, to the dreaded institution every day by the family cook, a "small, desiccated, thin, with pointed nose, hollow cheeks, yellowish but firm, resolute and superior" person who terrorized him by threatening to report his behavior to his parents. Their route from the apartment on the Old Town Square was probably ours. Turn right on Masná and right again on **Týnská**; follow it, staying on your left at **Týnská Ulička (Týn Lane)**, behind Týn Cathedral until you reach **Štupartská Street**, and stay on the right as far as **Celetná**. Follow it in the direction of the Old Town Square to your right. (An alternative route via Malá Štupartská Street from Masná, then right on Štupartská as far as Celetná, will take you past **St. James**, one of the Old Town's finest baroque churches, founded in 1339, with art by Reiner, Brandl, Brokoff, and others, which Kafka used to visit. He was influenced by both secular and sacred applications of the baroque, fascinated by the exactness and incan-

Saint James Church, Old Town

descence of the style, as well as by the revelation of the roots of mannerism, which showed an affinity of the baroque age to his time.)

On Celetná, note **no. 3**, the **House of the Three Kings**, where the Kafka family lived from 1896 to 1907. Here Franz first had a room to himself, completed his university studies, and wrote one of his first stories, "Description of a Struggle." His father had a wholesale business in this building. The city directory entry for Herrmann Kafka read: merchant in decorative goods, fashionable knitware, parasols, umbrellas, walking sticks and cotton goods, authorized consultant to Commercial Court (tel. 141). Ironically, during the Communist period there used to be a vegetarian restaurant on the first floor; it was a steam-table type of cafeteria, and not strict about meatless dishes. Kafka, who was an ultra-finicky, Fletcherizing (that is, he chewed his food slowly) vegetarian, would not likely have approved.

As you near the Old Town Square, notice **no. 2** Celetna, called **Sixtův Dům** or Sixt's House, another Kafka family address (1888 to 1889). The building, from 1737, is haute baroque, ditto the roof statuary. It has had some distinguished owners, for example Sixtus of Ottersdorf (1567), a participant in the 1547 revolt of Bohemian nobles against Ferdinand of Hapsburg. For his role he earned the extremely mild punishment of expulsion from his magisterial duties, and turned to writing an eyewitness account of the events.

Later, after Sixtus's son went into exile with all the other anti-Catholic Czech patriots in 1626, the house was acquired by court secretary Filip Fabricius. This gentleman goes down in history as a survivor of the ignominious defenestration (exit via window) from Prague Castle, along with the two Hapsburg governors from whom he took dictation. A group of conspiring Protestant Bohemian nobles, afraid of losing the rights of their class and religion against Catholic imperial rule, barged in and tossed out the emperor's men. Protected by their thick clothing, they landed on the sloping ground below badly shaken but largely unscathed. Though Fabricius's presence at this most crucial moment is merely of incidental importance—he just happened to be there when the rebels entered the Council chamber—the Defenestration of Prague of May 23, 1618 (the third in the city's history), was the signal event that ignited the Thirty Years' War. (More about this peculiar Bohemian political modus operandi in Walks 3 and 5.)

A couple of doors down note **no. 17** Old Town Square, the **House of the Unicorn**, where Kafka used to attend (sporadically) Prague's only known literary salon of the period. The Tuesday evenings-at-home were hosted by the cosmopolitan Berta Fanta, wife of a rich pharmacist who owned the medieval Unicorn *lékárna* (pharmacy) on the square. Berta devoted herself to eclectic, though serious, cultural activism. Her agendas featured broad discussion programs—everything from Franz Brentano's philosophy (a force in the development of Gestalt psychology), to Rudolf Steiner's anthroposophy, to spiritualism, to early idealization of Wagner and Nietzsche (Kant was a two-year focus). Among the Prague illuminati then in residence who attended were Albert Einstein, Max Brod, and Franz Werfel.

Let's turn now to the **Church of Our Lady of Týn (Kostel Panny Marie před Týnem)**, or **Týn Cathedral**, one of the emblems of the city, instantly recognizable for its stabbing twin Gothic towers, and a key player in the city's history. Access is via the arcade and the small courtyard of the Týn parsonage school, čp. 604/14, the fourteenth-century building that hides the entrance of the cathedral from the Old Town Square. The rounded, ascending gables of the Venetian Renaissance facade here are unusual (for Prague); they were added two hundred years later, when the structure was enlarged and heightened. The early-Gothic vaulted arcade is shared by the six-hundred-year-old building next door, At the White Unicorn, no. 603/15, but its foundation is even older—a turn-of-the-thirteenth-century Romanesque room was uncovered here not long ago. Though the square looks largely eighteenth century, the majority of its buildings are considerably older. And now through the great oak doors (1677) of the cathedral. (It is usually open from 4:00 P.M. to 5:00 P.M., longer in the summer and on holidays).

When the Kafka family lived at no. 3 Celetná Street, which backs into the Týn, Kafka's room had a window that looked directly into the sanctuary. It was placed there by a former very religious tenant who wanted unusual proximity—perhaps it was the next-best thing to inhabiting the prohibited chancel itself. The window is up on the right side wall. A memorial plaque (on the right-hand wall of the rear chapel on the far left side) tells the story, once the sensation of baroque Prague, of how the aisle on the right side wall is said to have contained the remains of a twelve-year-old Jewish boy, Simon Abeles, murdered by his father after Simon, seeking out the Jesuits, converted to Catholicism in 1693. According to mythical sources, when the body was discovered some days later, it appeared healthy rather than deathly. What is known for sure is that the boy's father strung himself up with his prayer cord in the Old Town Hall prison, but this did not prevent the authorities from dragging the body to the Old Town fortification wall and making a public spectacle, as was then customary, of cutting out the heart and stuffing it in the mouth—apparently in retaliation for the mercilessness he had displayed to his own child.

Since for Kafka Prague was the measure of most things, the Týn was what he undoubtedly had in mind in *The Trial* when he described a cathedral that was so big it "bordered on the limits of scale that human beings could bear." But the Týn's origins were on a much smaller scale in the twelfth century, when it was a small Romanesque church serving foreign merchants, who flocked here to conduct their affairs at the central marketplace and nearby customs-house complex (called *Ungelt* in German, meaning customs duties). The original church was replaced in the thirteenth century by an early-Gothic structure, which in turn was rebuilt in 1385 into the three-naved church you're looking at, minus the steepled towers.

If you look closely, you'll see that the tower on the right, supposedly male, is considerably wider than its so-called female opposite. Was this a medieval form of sexism, that the larger should tower over the weaker (to shelter her, naturally)? The towers were added in the late fifteenth century. This was when the homegrown Hussite bishop Jan Rokycana presided and the Týn was *the* church: the sanctuary was packed with *tout* protesting Prague, and a sculptured, gilded chalice, symbol of the Hussite (Utraquist) movement, as well as a statue of King George of Poděbrady, the Hussite hero-king of Bohemia, adorned the facade. The chalice was later melted down to make up the crown, rays, and sceptre of the Madonna that now rests in the niche, but the king's spot remains vacant. (It is said that George's heart is entombed here, while the body rests in the royal crypts at the Castle.) It was a proud chapter in Czech history, overturned in the dawn of night after the Battle of White Mountain in 1620, a seminally tragic episode that started the militant re-Catholization of Bohemia. Counterrevolutionary forces took over and, with their new dramatic, emotional, hyperelaborated, and symbolism-loaded imagery, "baroqued" every church in sight including the inside of this one, particularly the altars, though Gothic and Renaissance architectural elements remain strong.

For example, note the Gothic portal on the north, Týnská Lane side. The splendid tympanum shows scenes from the Passion of Christ, sculpted by Peter Parler's workshop in 1390. What you see here is a copy; the original was fading in Prague's corrosive air and now resides at the National Gallery (St. George's Convent at the Castle). A number of the altar paintings, including the high-altar 1649 Ascension of the Virgin and of the Holy Trinity, are the work of the Czech baroque master Karel Škréta, who lived across from the Cathedral on Týnská, At the Black Stag. In front of the Gothic stone pulpit is an altar with an interesting Renaissance wooden ark containing a very fine late-Gothic carving of the baptism of Christ by Master I.P., a student of Dürer, from the early sixteenth century. And behind the fourth altar on the right of the central nave depicting Christ on the Mount of Olives, note the red marble tomb of the Danish emmigrant Tycho Brahe, astronomer to Rudolf II's court, who was buried here in 1601. The goateed and luxuriantly mustachioed likeness in ruffed period elegance shows a nose almost intact—Brahe lost his in a duel and wore a gold and silver nosepiece. (He collapsed at a banquet when his bladder burst and he expired shortly thereafter.) It is also said that the heads of the executed Protestant patriots, after hanging from the Old Town Bridge Tower for ten years, were secretly brought to the Týn for burial.

Though no longer in situ, St. Mary's Column (*Mariansky sloup*), a principal symbol of the anti-Reformist cult of the virgin, stood on the square from 1648 (Treaty of Westphalia, end of the Thirty Years' War) to 1918, strategically placed in front of the Týn—no doubt meant as an antidote to Hussite heresy. Columns of this type were erected all over Europe, the first one in Munich to commemorate the Catholic victory at the Battle of White Mountain. For Kafka and his friends it was a popular rendezvous spot, and they may have set their watches by the fall of its shadow, the so-called Prague noon, or meridian. (Look for the column in old photographs and art.) In 1918 the column was toppled in a wild melee by Czech nationalists celebrating the birth of the independent republic of Czechoslovakia. To maintain the meridian marking there is a bronze indicator set into the cobblestones in front of the Jan Hus Memorial.

Exiting the Týn, notice next to it on your right **At the Stone Bell (U kamenného zvonu)**, čp. 605, whose present early-Gothic configuration is due to a remarkable, though controversial, architectural reconstruction and preservation. Built in the thirteenth century along the Gothic lines of medieval French palace structures, it was given a baroque facade and an additional floor in the 1600s; then, in the nineteenth century, it was replastered and remodeled again in neobaroque style. It was only in 1961 that restorers discovered the extensive murals and architectural detailing—ribbed vaults, Gothic doorways, frescoes, and two chapels—of what must have been an aristocrat's dwelling of the highest order. Some speculate that it was an early home of Emperor Charles IV, who found an uninhabitable Castle when he returned to Prague from his European sojourns in his teens and started rebuilding immediately on ascending the throne. It took twenty-two years, but the fragments were finally assembled, the inauthentic pieces chipped away, and a new roof created; despite some dissenting views, the consensus seems to be that the results were worth the effort. The Bell House is now a public space for concerts and an exhibition hall for contemporary art.

Next door, projecting into the square, stands one of Prague's most comely buildings, the **Golz-Kinský Palace**. It is very late baroque with confectionary rococo pastel coloring and stuccowork, built in 1755–65, and was designed by Anselmo Lurago (possibly with Kilián Ignác Dientzenhofer) for Count Jan Golz and subsequently acquired by Count Oldřich Kinský. Franz Kafka studied here from 1893 to 1901, when the upper floors were a German gymnasium known for its harsh pedagogy—a cross between a monastery and a reform school, according to Kafka biographer Ernst Pawel. The administration was proud that 75 percent of its students failed, dropping out before graduation (Kafka passed). The front staircase of the building was for teachers only; students went up the back way. A few years later, Kafka's father moved his haberdashery business into a ground-floor corner location on the right side. The Kinský Palace balcony has a more nefarious claim to fame as the staging platform—at another loaded moment in Czechoslovak history—from which Communist (Stalin-directed) leader Klement Gottwald and his henchmen proclaimed the Party's takeover to the cheering masses in February 1948. The invidious event memorably opens Milan Kundera's *The Book of Laughter and Forgetting*, with the soon-to-be cannibalized Foreign Minister Clementis thoughtfully taking off his own hat in the February cold and setting it on Gottwald's head. After 1952 and the culmination of the horrific show trials and Communist purges, photographs of the event included the hat, but Gottwald stood alone—Clementis had been airbrushed out.

On our way across the almost always thronged square to **Pařížská Street**, we can't avoid Ladislav Šaloun's secessionist **monument to Jan Hus**. The colossal stone-and-bronze allegory is an expansive expression of Czech national feeling and a review of some tragically fissured Czech history. Hus stands serenely, silently commanding the turmoil below him: highest-placed figures are the Fighters for God (the Hussites) on one side; the Exiles (turned to the 1621 scaffold site) at the nadir. The mother and child represent national rebirth and the future. The words *Pravda vítězí*, carved into the base, mean "Truth prevails," which was also Václav Havel's rallying cry more recently, and Tomáš Masaryk's, the founder of the Czechoslovak state in 1918, before him. The work's horizontal shape was meant to contrast with the verticality of St. Mary's Column, which still stood when Šaloun started thinking about the monument; it was intended to confront the cult's ideological provocation. The unveiling in 1915, on the five hundredth anniversary of the death of Hus, was controversial; it was seen as an outdated failure by some critics. Even today some architects think it deforms the square, but it stands as a proud symbol of Czech patriotism and a favorite squatting and draping perch for young Praguers and tourists in pursuit of a better view or a respite.

At the corner of Pařížská Street, **no. 6**, the **Oppelt House**, is yet another Kafka family address, from 1913 on, where they had a top-floor apartment. Now we'll walk over to the **Old Town Hall** on the western side of the square and note the memorial tablets on the wall dedicated to the twenty-seven Bohemian nationalists, leaders of the Protestant rebellion against the Hapsburgs, who were executed at this spot in 1621. Among them is the name of Jan Jessenius (Jesenský in Czech), indirectly connected to Kafka via Kafka's close friend and translator, the writer Milena Jesenská, to whom he entrusted his diaries and wrote some of his most passionate letters. She died at Ravensbrück concentration camp during World War II. Her ancestor Jessenius was a distinguished scholar, physician, diplomat, orator, and rector of Charles University. A pioneer of modern anatomy, he performed at the square the first known public anatomical dissection, and spoke at Tycho Brahe's funeral—of the famous astronomer's ill-fated bladder and lost nose. Also at the square, with regiments, citizens, and officiators in attendance, Jessenius met a hideous death: before he was beheaded, his tongue was torn out and nailed to the black-clad scaffold, and then he was quartered. It was the expert, no doubt anatomically correct work of Mydlář the Executioner, previously mentioned near the start of our walk, who also made quite a name for himself.

One side of the Old Town Hall is a truncated version of what it looked like in Kafka's day. It had an eastern wing, a large, rather gloomy-looking Neo-Gothic section with a triple-arched main portico built in the mid nineteenth century. You can see what remains of it in the deep coral wall fragment, which is all that was salvaged from one of the last vicious acts of retreating Nazis, who struck on May 5, 1945, the day Praguers rose up to drive them out at the end of World War II. The Nazis did the same to the **Orloj**, the fifteenth-century astronomical clock on the other side, firing at point-blank range; miraculously, it was resurrected. Numerous proposals over

Art nouveau on Pařížská Street

the years to rebuild have been scotched in favor of the green space, which sometimes serves as a site for temporary concert stages. More than the building was lost, however; the historic, irreplaceable archives of the city also sustained heavy damage.

Now turn right at the Old Town Hall tower and walk past the Orloj (faces south), where tourists congregate to hear the clock strike the hour, and watch a mechanical parade of biblical and allegorical figures. Note the **Minuta House, čp. 3**, the handsome, richly sgraffitoed building in the far western corner. The young Franz Kafka lived there from 1889 to 1896 while attending primary school on Masná Street. He must have crisscrossed the square almost every day of his life—when he wasn't traveling or somewhere at a country sanatorium, taking a nature cure. The Minuta's early-fifteenth-century Gothic beginnings were remodeled to the present Renaissance facade beginning in 1564. A prominent lunette cornice with figurative sgraffitowork depicting allegories and scenes from Greek mythology, ancient battles and bacchanals, and a triumphal march was mostly done after 1600, but apparently covered up at some point, because it was not discovered (accidentally) until 1905. It was restored fourteen years later. The interior rooms have original beamed ceilings and frescoed Gothic vaulting. Set into the corner wall is a sculpted stone lion, left over from the late eighteenth century, when there used to be an apothecary here, At the White Lion. Today the building is part of the Old Town Hall complex.

Now we'll turn off the square and walk down **Želez-ná Street** to the **Karolinum**, the latinized name of **Charles University**, founded by the Holy Roman Emperor Charles IV in 1348, the oldest university in Central Europe. Kafka enrolled here in 1901 for eight semesters at the law school of the Imperial and Royal Karls-Ferdinand University. This Austro-German institution

Minuta House, Old Town Square

Karolinum oriel window detail

originated in Charles University, and in 1882 it was split into parallel Czech and German faculties, a concession to growing Czech nationalism. Students shared the same medieval buildings but little else. In a microcosmic hotbed of the ultranationalist ethnic conflict in the greater society, it was militant Czechs versus reactionary Germans (who also hated foreigners and Jews). Kafka graduated, or was "promoted," to Doctor of Law in 1906.

The main building of the original Karolinum—its other

buildings are spread around various parts of Prague—occupies a block on the left side of Železná, just before the Estates (formerly Tyl, formerly Nostic, forever associated with Mozart) Theater. *Železná*, by the way, means "iron," after the ironmongers who lived and worked here since the fourteenth century. Architecturally not much remains of Charles IV's original Gothic structure except the ornate oriel window on the lane it shares with the Estates Theater, and a chapel, part of the original palace belonging to a wealthy master of the mint, that served as the university's first home. There's a courtyard with a statue of one-time rector Jan Hus, from a baroque remodeling. Notice the beautiful portal (1718) on Železná, which used to be the main entrance, and the earlier baroque window above it. The university's student body was a churning center of Protestant Hussite activity for two hundred years; the Hapsburgs got their revenge when the Jesuits established their own college, the Klementinum, in 1556. After the Battle of White Mountain and the defeat of the anti-Catholic forces, the Jesuits took over and consolidated both institutions.

Now turn left and walk past the current unprepossessing front entrance of the Karolinum with the round fountain and lions, a post–World War II adaptation; head down Celetná Street to the wide expanse of Ovocný trh (the Fruit Market). **No. 15 Ovocný trh, At the Bohemian Eagle**, a charming, picture-book example of Czech Neo-Renaissance architecture, was designed by Friedrich Ohmann in 1897. The wooden bay windows and floral decoration express the roots of the style in local folk history, but it was a passing phase already being overtaken by the new world of art nouveau.

Celetná Street stretches west, away from the direction in which we're going, but take a look—it's one of the oldest streets in Prague. Even in Roman times (though the Romans never made it to the Czech lands) it was a major communications artery traversed by traders from the eastern part of the country headed to market in the

Old Town Square. Back in those days it was bordered by stone buildings, whose foundations are preserved in the cellars of numerous existing structures. The name, Celetná, refers to *calty*, a type of braided roll baked by a proliferation of local bakers. There are many fine buildings; one of the more unusual is at the corner of **Ovocný trh**, čp. 569, **House at the Black Mother of God** (1911–12), a classic work of Czech cubism designed by Josef Gocar. The name is from the seventeenth-century baroque Black Madonna in a gold cage that you can see on the corner of the building, a bit of statuary left over from the site's previous tenant.

Continue along Celetná to the **Powder Tower (Prašná brána)**, which marks the end of the street. The massive Gothic curiosity dates from 1475, when the foundation stone for it was laid. The Old Town was then surrounded by a fortified wall—in those days if you were not so fortified you did not qualify as a real town—with eight gate towers interspersed. Later the tower was used to store gunpowder, and in 1757 it was damaged by Frederick the Great's troops during the Prussian anti-Hapsburg assaults. The facade's ornamental reliefs are Neo-Gothic, the 1875–86 work of Josef Mocker, of whose modifications many purists are critical. The Powder Tower was also a frequent rendezvous spot for Kafka and his devoted friend Max Brod, who used to wait for him in the afternoon when Kafka quit work. Then they would stroll over to the Cafe Arco. Now walk through the tower arch in Republic Square and head for Na poříčí.

At **no. 7 Na poříčí**, you will find yourself in front of the Workmen's Accident Insurance Institute for the Kingdom of Bohemia (the name still runs across the building in German and Czech), a department of the Austrian government where Kafka was employed on the top floor as an insurance executive from 1908 until just a couple of years before he died, in 1924, at the age of forty-one. He had retired early because of his tubercular condition. Though inwardly tortured in his private and literary life, he was highly respected by his employer and colleagues, and immediately hailed as "a superb administrative talent."

Depending on how your feet are holding out, and how zealous a Kafka fan you are, you may wish to walk down Hybernská Street (corner of Dlážděná) and briefly glance at the **Café Arco**, where the famous "Arconauts," of which Kafka was one, used to sip and saw. Max Brod described it as "scurrilous, frivolous/inquisitive, and youthfully lecherous, but also free and open to new ideas, people crowded in four rooms where the air was thick with smoke and the aroma of strong coffee." I say "glance" because the once brilliant, literary Café Arco is dead—the haunt of no one except the sorriest breed of café rat. (Is it Kafkaesque to imagine that someone will resurrect it somehow?) And so our walk ends.

Walk·3

Castle and Monastery

HRADČANY AND STRAHOV

Stairs from Malá Strana to Hradčany

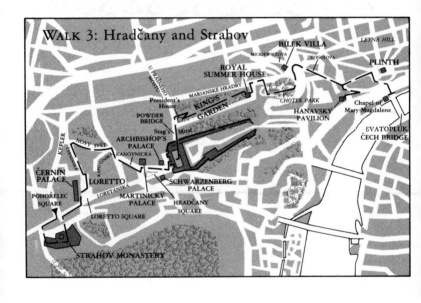

WALK 3: Hradčany and Strahov

LETNA HILL

BÍLEK VILLA

PLINTH

MICKIEWICZOVA

GOGOLOVA

ROYAL
SUMMER HOUSE

U PRAŠNÉHO MOSTU

MARIANSKÉ HRADBY

CHOTEK PARK

President's
House

KING'S
GARDEN

HANAVSKY
PAVILION

Chapel of
Mary Magdalene

POWDER
BRIDGE

Moat

SVATOPLUK
ČECH BRIDGE

Stag's

KEPLER

NOVÝ SVĚT

ARCHBISHOP'S
PALACE

KANOVNICKÁ

ČERNÍN
PALACE

KAPUCÍNSKÁ

LORETTO

SCHWARZENBERG
PALACE

LORETÁNSKÁ

POHOŘELEC
SQUARE

MARTINICKÝ
PALACE

HRADČANY
SQUARE

LORETTO SQUARE

STRAHOV MONASTERY

Starting Point: Pohořelec Square in the Hradčany district. This walk is best done on any day but Monday.
Metro/Tram Lines: Tram 22 from the center
Length of Walk: Two and half to three hours.

Away from the urban hubbub, high in the rarefied atmosphere of an ancient, relatively tranquil zone of trees and green expanses of parks and gardens, you might call this our most pastoral walk, heavenly in spring, summer, and fall. It is also probably the shortest and easiest walk in the book. For one thing, it's all downhill, starting at the top of Hradčany, the Castle district, and descending gradually to the Vltava riverbank opposite the Old Town. Along the way we'll visit, among many other sights, a famous medieval monastery and view one of the largest palaces in Central Europe, a dazzling diamond trove, a king's lavish garden, a queen's summer palace, and the city from some singular angles. It's best to skip Mondays, when most open-to-the-public attractions here close, even though Strahov promises to open its doors seven days a week.

First stop is the square in Hradčany called Pohořelec. Arrive by tram No. 22 from the center of the city—for example, from Národní Street in front of the National Theater (Národní Divadlo), or from Malostranské Square in Malá Strana. Get off at the stop called Památník národního písemnictví (Museum of National Literature) (not Pohořelec, which would be less confusing). The streetcar deposits you right at the feet of Tycho Brahe and Johannes Kepler, a 1980s statue of the two astronomers who made Rudolfine Prague a center of innovative stargazing. Near this spot once stood a house occupied by Brahe in 1601, bought for him by Emperor Rudolf II; the astronomer died not long after moving in. Kepler, too, once lived here, hence the street name, Keplerova.

We'll come back to Pohořelec a little later. For now, let's cross over and head for the **Strahov Monastery (Strahovský klášter)**, up along the narrow, handrailed sidewalk, turning left through the imposing baroque gateway into the grounds of the abbey. Before you enter, note the ruins of a very old wall, sprouting weeds on your right. That's what's left of the so-called Hunger Wall (Hladová zeď), a fortification built by Emperor Charles IV around 1360 to fence in the left bank of the city. The remnants of the wall can still be seen zigzagging across the slopes of Petřín Hill. It is said to have been a public make-work project for the unemployed, following a bad harvest. Dense, wolf-harboring forests once extended all the way west from here to the White Mountain, scene of the first crucial battle of the Thirty Years' War. Strahov sat directly on the critical western approach to Prague Castle (*Pražský hrad*) about a mile away; during the twelfth century the monastery was a key sentry post. Though formidably secure against invasion from the river to the east, the Castle was vulnerable from the side facing the woods; hence the name Strahov, which comes from the Czech word *stráž*, for "guard."

The ancient Premonstratensian (from Prémontré in France, where the order began) abbey of Strahov and its priceless libraries rank among the wealthiest, most prominent religious complexes of their kind. In the Middle

Ages religious institutions were all-encompassing social, cultural, even economic and political forces, and Strahov played a significant role in the internal and foreign affairs of the Czech feudal state. One of its influential abbots, Archbishop Lohelius of Prague and Questenberg, was an advisor to Emperor Ferdinand II. In 1624, a few years after the executions of the Czech Protestant noblemen in front of the Old Town Hall, Archbishop Lohelius advised the emperor that the time was right for launching the massive re-Catholicization of the Bohemian "heretics," which meant nearly everyone who had not already fled the country. Thus Strahov became a hub of the Counter-Reformation while making a name for itself as an educational center, producing exemplary scholars, teachers, and scientists.

From its earliest days, when it was called Mount Zion, the abbey was well connected. Its origins were in an 1140 joint venture between Prince Vladislav II, who later became king, and the progressive, well-traveled (he first ran into the Premonstratensians in Palestine) statesman-priest and Bishop of Olomouc, Jindřich Zdik, who tried to raise the then fairly primitive standards of Czech religious life. Rampant debauchery among the clergy had reached shocking heights, and the time was ripe for disciplinary reforms, especially celibacy of the priesthood, which was mandated only after a long and strenuous struggle during the late twelfth century. The highly structured rigor of monastic life, its cloistered asceticism and self-sustaining community spirit, had always appeared impenetrable and mysterious, if not forbidding, to the outside world. Yet the Strahov community was also exceedingly industrious. However, on the orders of Emperor Joseph II in 1782, all institutions in the Hapsburg Empire not engaged in teaching or nursing were to be dissolved. An extraordinarily resourceful religious leader, Václav Mayer, quickly decided to convert Strahov and its libraries into a research institute, opening it to scholars, and so it was spared by the rationally minded monarch.

At one time Strahov's architecture was said to have surpassed the royal residence, but that only encouraged the marauding hordes: in 1420 Hussites stormed through, in 1648 Finns and Swedes looted it, the French attacked in 1742, and in 1757 it was besieged by the Prussian army. Over the centuries reconstruction was carried out in timely architectural styles—Renaissance, Gothic, classicist, and baroque on top of its Romanesque beginnings, the extent of which were not discovered until the advent of archaeological probes in the early 1950s. That was when the Communist government banished the last of the monks—there were said to be only nine left—and turned the convent into the National Museum of Czech Literature. During the forty-plus years of Communist rule, monastery life almost disappeared, and Strahov fell into desuetude, like most of the rest of the country's treasures; only the most urgent repairs were made. But the Premonstratensians are now back in force if not in numbers, and they have renovated and restored the whole property. In their order's tradition of adept administration and enterprising, businesslike conduct, they have provided tourist facilities unimagined previously, including a restaurant on the site of the old beer brewery—no self-respecting monastery was without one in the Middle Ages—and various concessions, including a confectionary. And they have expanded their hours to seven days a week to accommodate visitors. There's even a popular discotheque called Peklo (meaning "Hell") deep in the Romanesque catacombs; Peklo also serves Italian food.

Pass through the imposing baroque western gate (by Antonio Lurago) with the statue of St. Norbert, founder of the Premonstratensian order to whom the monastery is dedicated, atop the center arch. At Strahov's central square, the rare Gothic-Renaissance, or mannerist, Church of St. Roch on your left is a 1602–12 construction built on orders of Emperor Rudolf II in gratitude for escaping the plague of 1599. (Mannerism tilted toward novelty: deeper decoration and distortion, away from the harmony of the by then antique High Renaissance.) At this point, Prague's architectural Renaissance period was in its waning days, and this church is one of the last pre–White Mountain religious buildings, a reminder of the strong Gothic tradition that had prevailed in the land. After this the baroque pretty much took over. St. Roch was Strahov's parish church until 1784, when it was de-sanctified (Joseph II again); it was restored in 1882, the year the three altars with terra-cotta statuary were placed in situ. These days the small church is used by the Museum of National Literature for changing exhibitions, so you may want to enter and look around.

We meet St. Norbert again on top of the seventeenth-century column at the center of the courtyard green. Straight ahead is the **Church of the Virgin Mary**, originally built as a triple-nave Romanesque basilica with two towers. Its present haute-baroque facade (1743–51) is by Anselmo Lurago. If your timing is lucky, a visiting choir might be in rehearsal for a concert and you may be able to sit and listen for a while. Inside are newly laid marble floors (1993) and a baroque vaulted ceiling covered with stucco cartouches (1743) by Ignác Palliardi containing eight large paintings of the legend of the Virgin and thirty-two Marian symbols. St. Norbert's remains are in the altar of St. Ursula Chapel, entrance from the left rear nave; the martyrdom of St. Ursula is depicted in the ceiling fresco by Strahov monk and painter Siard Nosecký.

To see the **Museum of National Literature (Památ-ník narodního písemnictví)**, exit the church, walk to its northern end, and buy your ticket at the window on the right, under the passage through the building. Just before the inner courtyard you'll find the entrance; your ticket should admit you to both the museum and its libraries. A large lion sculpture in front announces your destination. Inside, walk through the baroque lobby straight ahead and you'll find yourself in the monastery building's glassed-in cloister, with the so-called Paradise Courtyard pool in the center. A Romanesque remnant, the pool was recently restored. Perhaps it will once again be stocked with fish—it's a fair guess that the monks served the freshest and tastiest food around, as many a medieval traveler, lucky enough to be admitted, well knew. Walking around the arcade, you can't miss the Romanesque architectural fragments—pillars, masonry, doorways, several heavily restored—all around.

Turning left from the door and walking straight ahead down the arcade will take you into one of the museum's central exhibition rooms, the former summer refectory of the monastery. Notice the richly stuccoed and frescoed vaulted ceiling (1690) by the Burgundian architect and artist Jean-Baptiste Mathey. The west wing has a narrow Romanesque stairway and two well-preserved rooms supported by the thick, round pillars typical of the period: one of these rooms exhibits material from Hussite times, and the other Gothic literature. Though you may not be able to read Czech and many of the authors represented here have not been translated into English, you should know that the library collections number about 900,000 volumes. They comprise the original Strahov library holdings and contemporary additions, with religious works in the minority. Also here are the more recently installed (since 1953) literary archives of celebrated Czech writers and scholars. The latter add up to about five million individual pieces, according to officials of the museum, who also claim that this is the only library in the world where such literary and biographical legacies are centrally maintained.

To see the pride of Strahov, the libraries, and they are musts, return to the church; the entrance is right next to it. Looking up at the handsome, anodyne classicist facade of 1783 by Ignác Palliardi, you will see a medallion with Joseph II's profile in gilded relief, evidently in obsequious homage to the imperious destroyer of monasteries and a well-established way of life. The first room we want to see, at the top of the stairs on the first floor, is the Theological Hall (1671–79), a splendid architectural expression of the earliest flowering of the baroque. Built by Jan Dominik Orsi, the fairly low, barrel-vaulted ceiling combines richly plastic cartouche stucco with frescoes by Nosecký on subjects relating to books and education; the furniture and globes are original, as are the bookcases. One of the oldest, most valuable manuscripts kept here is the ninth-century Strahov New Testament written in gold on parchment, in an elaborate early-seventeenth-century binding and ostentatiously ornamented with much older Romanesque and Gothic elements. It is sometimes on display in a glass case in the hallway. Behind an ornate iron grille set into the wall is a compartment where books indexed by the Vatican—*libri prohibiti*—were kept, available for the monks' research purposes. Unauthorized random browsing was not permitted, though the monks here were known to be fairly freethinking for their day and occupation.

Two corridor turns around the courtyard will take you to the stunning Philosophical Hall, a later addition (1782–84), where the grand baroque softly shines forth at its most mature and polished, a diverse display of artistry in one extraordinary soaring space. The design incorporates classicist elements for their "spirit of rationality" approach most likely to impress the Austrian emperor, whose portrait is prominently displayed here. This hall is also the work of Palliardi. The heavenly ceiling frescoes (1794) depicting the History of Mankind (or the Struggle of Mankind to Know Real Wisdom) are by Antonin Franz Maulbertsch, the greatest painter of the Viennese rococo; they were his culminating achievement before his death. The inlaid interior doors are from an abolished Cistercian monastery in Prague's Old Town, and the richly gilded rococo walnut bookcases reaching up through two levels are from the disbanded Premonstratensian abbey at Znojmo in Moravia. Forty thousand books grace this hall.

On leaving the library building, prepare to walk back toward the east wall of the monastery grounds, turning left to descend the tunnel-like staircase that runs through the building to the north. But before you do, take a look through the open gate in the wall. On a clear day this is one of the lovely vistas of Prague. You may want to walk down the path a bit. To the right of the path you can see the large, lush monastery orchards and gardens sloping down Petřín Hill all the way to the old hospital complex at the top of Vlašská Street, the city below, and, far beyond that, the countryside fading into the distance, a view not much changed from Strahov's early days (barring the space-age television tower on the horizon).

At the bottom of the stairs you will find yourself once more in Pohořelec Square—*pohořelec*, by the way, means "after the fire." Three times devastating conflagrations reduced this square and the surrounding streets to ashes, the last one lit by the French Army in 1742. The square's proximity to the Castle gave the district of Hradčany a distinct municipal standing from the other Prague towns. Its citizens were subject to feudal obligations imposed by the burgrave, or manager, of the fortress. One such obligation was guard duty at the Daliborka Tower prison on the Castle grounds. Founded around 1350 (though settled at least three hundred years earlier) as the third town to be established on Prague territory (after Vyšehrad and the Old Town), it was not until the sixteenth century that Hradčany was granted official royal status. After Charles IV was crowned, it grew dramatically, becoming a magnet for the aristocratic and religious communities, which established bases here.

Still, for all its royal associations, Hradčany, and this square in particular, retain the character of a typical small baroque town, following a pattern often repeated in village squares around the country. Most of the buildings are baroque, but here, as elsewhere in Prague, scratch many a baroque house and a Renaissance one appears underneath. In the middle of Pohořelec stands a smallish monument to St. John Nepomuk (the stars around his head are a dead giveaway), which once stood lower down on Hradčany Square. To counter the cult of Jan Hus, the churchman was elevated to sainthood in 1729, three centuries after meeting a watery martyrdom in the Vltava; statues in his honor subsequently sprang up all over Bohemia. (A solid silver 3,700-pound extravaganza of a St. John Nepomuk tomb by the illustrious Viennese architect Fischer von Erlach is one of the astonishments of St. Vitus Cathedral.) One of the most attractive houses on the square, with a rococo facade and statuary ornamentation, is the Kučerův Palace, čp. 114, on the corner of **Kepler Street**.

Proceed down from the square now and take the street on your left called **Loretánská**; on the near left corner looms part of the colossal hulk of **Černín Palace**, which takes up the whole western side of Loretto Square. This baroque behemoth—five hundred feet long, adorned by thirty soaring Doric half-columns spaced the length of its uniformly redundant facade, its ground-floor masonry an aggressive nail-head armature—was easily the largest private palace in Prague and was said to be the largest in Central Europe. It was the brainchild and obsession of one Humprecht Jan Černín from Chudenice, descended from a very old (twelfth-century) though penniless and undistinguished Czech family—until they were ennobled and enormously enriched by the victorious Hapsburgs, to whom they had switched allegiance just in time. (Another Černín, Humprecht's great-uncle Divis, was executed for being on the wrong side.) Černín's personal fortune was founded on vast inherited estates which he enlarged even more. He also served as royal governor and later as ambassador to Venice and Constantinople.

Černín's dream palace has an exhaustive and calamitous architectural and social history. Possibly, as a rare survivor of the old Bohemian nobility and chafing at the presence of foreign arrivistes, he sought to surpass them in residential grandiosity. It was in Venice that Černín, dabbling in architecture himself, apparently met with the great Roman architect Bernini, who may have

Černín Palace, Loretto Square

sketched a preliminary plan for the intended project. Starting in 1669, generations of Černíns and an army of architects, contractors, artists, sculptors, and master craftsmen, including some of the biggest names of the Prague baroque, worked on the building—it took at least a quarter century to complete. Architect Francesco Caratti, a Comasque (meaning he was from one of the Italian villages of the Lago di Como area, traditionally strong in masonry and stone masonry and which exported the stuccadors' expertise), died on the job in 1677. Černín himself departed this world a few years later. Caratti had begun with a monumentalized idea of the Palladian Renaissance. Though manifestly an early-baroque building, it's more idiomatic of the sixteenth than the seventeenth century. What you see now is the result of various restorations necessitated by French bombardment, Prussian shelling, and Czech neglect: in 1779 the Černín family decamped because they could no longer afford their palace and couldn't sell. The hapless white elephant, with its grand salons, arcades, and staircases, its exquisite stuccowork, imposing statuary, and frescoes—including a major (perhaps prophetic) work by the superlative Václav Vavřinec Reiner, *Fall of the Titans*—was overrun by hundreds of homeless people, who turned it into a palatial slum. For years these unfortunate dregs squatted and starved and sickened and perished in the periodic epidemics of the unhygienic times until finally, in 1851, the government stepped in and converted the building into an Austrian Army barracks—a fate hardly better, of course, and the results were ruinous. It took six years of reverent restoration, undertaken in 1928 by the Czech Ministry of Foreign Affairs, to correct the horrors. The ministry now rules, which is why, regretfully, you may not enter the palace and look around. You can, however, visit the beautiful garden on the north side—if it's open on the day you choose to be here (as of this writing there is no fixed schedule). Failing that, you might have to settle for peering through the gates. We'll walk by there later and see.

But wait, there's more. In March 1948 the windowsills of the Černín Palace joined the list of Prague landmarks (mostly town halls) from which politically urged defenestrations were staged. The fourth of these, and to date the last, was the fate of the much cherished foreign minister, the affable Jan Masaryk, only son of Czechoslovakia's founder and first president, Tomáš Masaryk; Jan was probably "suicided" from a fourth-floor window of the palace. No one can prove conclusively that this hap-

pened, but his crushed body was found in a rear courtyard under his bathroom window. (Masaryk had been
living in the palace, near his office.) Few believe he actually pushed himself out, though he was depressed and
under excruciating pressure at the time. Who would have
wanted to kill him? The country by then had fallen into
Communist hands—Czech Communists to be sure, but
manipulated directly by Stalin. Masaryk was the only remaining democrat in the government, a symbol of the
First Republic: he fiercely, helplessly opposed the Communists, and his presence was a threat; he also had
friends in the West. It's doubtful that we'll ever know
what really happened because the evidence has vanished, as have all the people who were around at the
time and in a position to know. As for the other defenestrations—a peculiar Prague custom, to be sure—we'll
cover those in other walks.

As you can see, **Loretto Square** (**Loretanské náměstí**) is on two levels. Černín's contracters dug up an
extensive pagan burial site here; at least a thousand graves
with headless remains were found, dating the site to
ninth-century settlements. The graves were finally entombed for good when the ground was raised and the
pavement laid out for the ministry's parking needs by the
palace's last architect, Pavel Janák, in the 1920s.

Now let's walk down to the frothy-looking baroque
Loretto (1721–23) opposite, with its onion-shaped bell
tower, cheerful yellow pilastered walls, and cherubic phalanxes arrayed in front. (If you're ready for a break, there's
a restaurant right next to it; the terrace is pleasant enough
in this nearly traffic-free spot, but the kitchen is ordinary,
so it's probably better for a drink.) The Loretto's facade
is a Dientzenhofer *pere et fils* design, started by Christoph.
Inside the courtyard is the boxlike **Sancta Casa** (**Holy
House**), a shrine that is about one hundred years older
than the Loretto. The Loretto is not just another house of

Loretto

149

Sancta Casa, Loretto Shrine

worship but a major pilgrimage destination in the manner of Lourdes in France and the original Loretto in Italy. As such, the Prague Loretto was an important strategic addition to the antiheretical propaganda contrived by the militant Catholics in their drive to win back souls after the definitive defeat of the Protestant forces at the Battle of White Mountain. About fifty of these chapels were built in Bohemia to promote the miraculous powers of, and further the emotions associated with, the newly introduced cult of the Virgin Mary, the Prague Loretto becoming the most famous. The legend goes like this: The Italian Sancta Casa was transferred to Italy on angels' wings from Nazareth; it was the humble cottage where Mary's family lived and where the archangel Gabriel told her of the coming happy event. The Prague Sancta Casa is a replica of the Italian, outfitted like a modest chapel with somber brick walls, in humble contrast to the elaborately detailed baroque reliefs of the exterior, though the altar, with grinning cherubim, is silver. The shrine's principal benefactress was one Benigna Kateřina Lobkowicz, a pious member of the extremely wealthy Lobkowicz family, which achieved its prominence post–White Mountain. She was also related to the fanatical Spanish branch of the Catholic Hapsburgs.

Around the Sancta Casa are cloisters calculated to shelter the beseeching pilgrims who frequented—and still frequent—the shrine. The cloisters were built in 1664; the functional decoration includes analgesic saints painted in wooden cabinets along the sides. All the saints were specialists in one or more illness or misfortune. (Saint Apollonia was in charge of toothaches.) Apparently pain and discomfort without solace were not deemed as marketable as tortured ecstasy. In the corners and in the center of each arcade are chapels, one of which, the Chapel of the Sorrowing Mary, in the southwest corner, contains a twisted curiosity you shouldn't miss. On one of the rococo altars hangs an un-Christlike crucifix with the figure of Saint Starosta—dark beard, silver-brocaded blue dress, and all. On the story of how she got that way hangs a grotesquely gothic father-daughter tale, yet another variation on the cold, cruel heart of Counter-Reformation Catholicism.

Saint Starosta was a Portuguese princess who converted to Christianity; her tyrannical father arranged a marriage with a pagan he deemed worthy (perhaps the pagan was rich) despite her protestations and refusal to marry him. Prison did not change her mind; she prayed instead for a miracle to make her too unappetizing to marry. She got her wish. Overnight she grew a beard, for which her furious father had her nailed to the cross. It is said that the powers that be at the Loretto tried to make her the official patron saint of unhappily married women, but that did not catch on.

In the center of the eastern side of the cloister is the Church of the Nativity, built in 1734; its furnishings verge on the rococo, though with conservative vaults probably by Kilián Ignác Dientzenhofer and frescoes by Reiner over the presbytery. A depiction of the whimsical angels' holy cargo and heavenly flight is at the back. On the right, however, is a painting of the martyred St. Agatha that will probably fail to make your day. As the patron saint of female breast problems, she is shown serving up her own sundered appendages on a plate to an angel—another example of the violence and mutilation to be found in religious art of the period. But passionists of horror may thrill to the imaginatively conceived forms of death that were so mercilessly glorified.

Turning right from the entrance, take the stairway to the first-floor **Loretto Treasure** gallery, where you will see a glittering spectacle of extravagant jeweled monstrances. They are displayed behind specially secured glass cases, along with a valuable collection of energetically contrived liturgical dishes, utensils, and altar pieces from the sixteenth to the eighteenth centuries. Among them are a superior late-Gothic golden chalice from 1510 with enameled figures, and the Wallenstein monstrance, stud-

ded with extraordinary amethysts. The most obviously
brilliant of the monstrances is the Diamond, encrusted
with 6,500 diamonds shooting quill-like out from a thick
gold center. Amazing enough, but the piece is also admired by some for its haute elegance—a bit chilling, mind
you—designed by Jan Bernard Fischer von Erlach, the
prodigious Viennese whose name is synonymous with
the imperial Austrian baroque. The diamonds are said to
have decorated the wedding gown of Ludmilla Eva Fran-
ziska, a Kolovrat—old Bohemian nobility—who be-
queathed her estate to the Virgin of the Sancta Casa. Her
portrait hangs in the hall. The precious collection here
vanished during World War II, presumed to be stolen by
Germans. It was not until 1961 that workmen found numerous packages wrapped in old newspapers walled in
behind masonry in the Loretto. Inside the cache was the
treasure, hidden for twenty years according to the dates
on the newspapers. No one has ever stepped forward to
take credit for rescuing the trove, however; the hero was
possibly a victim of the war, so his or her identity will
probably remain a mystery.

The bells in the onion-domed carillon tower have
been playing on the hour for three hundred years, usually
from spring through fall. They are known for their sen-
timental mechanical "singing" chime, though "sugary" is
more like it. Numerous doleful stories recount how the
bells started to sing. One of them, by Czech poet and
spinner of tall tales Jan Neruda, is about a poor widow
who lived in the nearby hamlet of Nový Svět with her
twenty-seven children, as many as there are bells in the
Loretto tower. She called her children her Loretto bells.
In those days the bells merely tolled the time: the largest
the hour, and the smallest the quarter hour. The widow
used to say it was the same at home: the oldest child
could wait; the youngest wanted something every quarter
hour. The widow's only fortune was a string of twenty-
seven silver coins; she was saving them for her children.
One day her oldest child came down with the plague and

she couldn't afford medical help, so the widow toiled up the hill to the Loretto and despairingly traded in one of the coins in hopes of divine intercession. The largest bell rang out and the child died. The same thing happened with the rest of her children, the bells sounding according to the child's age, the smallest bell for the smallest child. Finally, her family gone, she herself sickened, wondering who would make the bells chime for her. Then suddenly, just before she breathed her last, a great chorus of pealing bells rang out, as if the angels themselves were singing.

Leaving the Loretto, turn right and head for **Černín-ská Street** across the square. On the way, turn left, walk up to the Černín Palace gate, and note that the garden is visible from here, as is the northern facade with its two loggias, the most Palladian part of the structure. If you're lucky, you may be able to enter and look around. The corner building at Černínská, hardly noticeable in its nondescript simplicity, is the Church of our Angelic Lady, part of the **Capuchin Monastery**, vintage 1600, whose order runs the Loretto. The Capuchins were the poorest sons of saint *par excellence* St. Francis of Assisi, utterly committed to strict vows of poverty. Their leader in Bohemia was the Spanish St. Lawrence of Brindisi, invited to Prague at the behest of Rome. He is said to have helped rout the Turks, bearing only his crucifix into the fray.

Proceed down Černínská and turn right at the bottom of the incline, onto **Nový Svět**, meaning **New World**. And what a world apart it is from the palatial quarters above. In any case, now you know from where the poor widow trudged up the hill. The plain, small-scale houses, straight from a seventeenth-century medieval village, were occupied mostly by those who labored at the Castle and, to intone a cliché of the Communists who ruled here for forty-odd years, "lived on crumbs from the tables of the rich." Fortunately, the quaint neighborhood still looks relatively unspoiled, with its narrow meandering cobbled lanes and two-story cottages, mercifully preserved from the scourges of bulldozers, overrestoration, and urban renewal. The neighborhood's former social status explains the house names, almost all of which invoke something golden. Besides a few (negligible) art galleries and a fine restaurant, **U Zlaté Hrušky (At the Golden Pear)** in the bright lemon-yellow and white-trimmed baroque house at **no. 3**, this is quiet strolling territory. Nový Svět was also a 1600 temporary address of Tycho Brahe, **At the Golden Foot, no. 1**; he used to complain that the Capuchins' post-midnight bells summoning the flock to early-morning worship disturbed his work.

The first street on your right, winding uphill, is **Kapucínská**, site of some of the more unpleasant events of Czechoslovakia's twentieth-century history. Up the street, behind the wall on your right at **no. 2**, was once a Communist military prison (probably a holdover from the former Austrian garrisons at the Černín) in whose courtyard a meager-looking, plain building was used by a counter-intelligence unit, known ominously as the Fifth Department, for interrogations. Starting in 1948, when the army was purged, "enemies of the state" were tortured here by a staff of uniformed sadists. There's not much to see today; the rows of barbed wire strung across the top of the wall may well be gone by the time you read this. If you look through the gate, you should still be able to catch sight of the Small House, where all the nasty work was done—if you care to.

Follow **Kanovnická Street** as it turns up, noting the compelling baroque church on your right, **St. John Nepomuk** (1720), Kilián Ignác Dientzenhofer's first religious commission in Prague sans the collaboration of his father, Christoph. Originally connected to a convent of Ursuline nuns, the church has been under scaffolding for years but should be open by now. Besides being a military hospital, it suffered a few acute misfortunes over the years: in 1784 the sisters departed when the monasteries were abolished, and the army turned it into a warehouse. Then in 1815 a further calamity of uncertain origin resulted in the disfigured tower, marring the otherwise opulent and well-proportioned facade. Inside, splendid frescoes by Reiner (1727) tell the story of St. John's life and miracles, as do the altar paintings by other artists. Back on the street, the Austrian ambassador's residence (1683) is on the left corner, with tennis courts visible deep in the rear gardens below; and opposite is a meticulously restored and sgrafittoed building, originally the 1357 headquarters of the local canonical authorities, as reflected in the name of the street, Kanovnická, today offices of the city of Prague's architects.

On the corner and sharply curving into Hradčany Square stands the sixteenth-century **Martinický Palace**, čp. 67, a splendidly sgraffitoed Renaissance structure. The facade's drawings are scored through the white stucco onto a dark brown ground. They show scenes from the Old Testament's tales of Joseph, while in the courtyard Samson and Hercules disport themselves. The sgraffito was a surprise uncovered during a 1967–72 restoration, when the palace was converted from an overcrowded, ramshackle apartment building to offices for the chief architect of Prague. The Martinic family heraldic emblem is above the door: vine leaves and star. Its most colorful member was Jaroslav Borita from Martinic, rabid enemy of Church reforms, especially the Protestant kind—it is said he once turned his hunting hounds on his serfs, trapping them and driving them into a church during communion services, where he ordered the priests to force-feed them holy wafers. But he is best known for landing in one piece under the second-story windows of Prague Castle, from where, as a Hapsburg governor, he was tossed in 1618 by Protestant nobles and knights. This most famous defenestration of all was the signal for the start of the Thirty Years' War. Farther down, at **čp. 62**, is where Prague's Ur-architect, Peter Parler, lived from 1372, when the building was in its original Gothic state, until his death. Next door is **U labutí (At the Swan's)**, a more than agreeable wine and snack bar with sidewalk tables, weather permitting. The small, tree-shaded green,

Town of Hradčany coat of arms

opposite, on this placid, pleasant spot—the square is closed to traffic—features a 1726 plague column with the Virgin Mary on top and statuary by Ferdinand Brokoff. (The artist's work is among the most valuable of the Prague baroque sculptors and vulnerable to air-pollution erosion, so it's been replaced by a copy). The Hradčany coat of arms is prominently displayed at eye level. These columns were created and commonly centered in town squares as offerings to thank the unearthly powers for

157

sparing them from plagues. This one, however, appears to have been a pitiful failure. The pestilence took its toll despite everything, felling large numbers of people twice in fifty years. Building another costly church, à la St. Roch at Strahov, must have been thought futile because there were enough by then, especially in the oldest districts.

Proceeding along on the left side of the street takes us to the late baroque, really rococo (Renaissance underneath) **Archbishop's Palace**, which you are unlikely to enter because it's open only once a year, on Maundy Thursday (the Thursday before Good Friday). If yours is the lucky hole in one, you'll see a superb grouping of eight Gobelin tapestries, along with other suitably palatial decorations and furnishings. Through the archway on the far left side of the Archbishop's Palace, down a short cobbled driveway, is the entrance to the National Gallery of European Art in Sternberk Palace, not visible from here. The collection is worth a return trip for its supernal painting by Albrecht Dürer, *Feast of the Rose Garlands*—hand-carried across the Alps to Prague in 1606 on orders of Emperor Rudolf II—among six centuries' worth of art. Standing in the center of the opposite side of this spacious square is the **Schwarzenberg Palace**, the second most important (we're getting to the most important) Czech Renaissance structure in Prague. The lunette cornices, the graduated gables, and the thoroughly sgraffitoed facade are thematically northern Italian, especially the Venetian-type black-and-white graphics. Built in 1545–67 by a Lobkowicz, the palace later passed into Schwarzenberg family hands. (The Lobkowiczes and the Schwarzenbergs intermarried through much of their history. The Schwarzenbergs, of German origin, are one of the oldest, most distinguished aristocratic families of Bohemia, owners of numerous great estates throughout this country and Austria.) In 1945 the palace became a military museum. The implements of war here are worth a look, but again, you'll have to return for a couple of extra hours. Footnote: the Nazis plotted to adapt the collection to their

Hradčany Square and Archbishop's Palace

peculiar Weltanschauung and set up a Wehrmacht museum. For "air defense reasons," or some such, during the war they carted the weaponry around Germany, whence it was later returned. Since there is no historical justification for the palace's present use, plans are afoot to turn it into something else. Just what is uncertain as of this writing.

Now let's go on, through the far-left Castle courtyard gate, which will give you a view of the Garden on the Bastion. There's a good place for lunch, **Café Poet**, up the stairs on your left; its outdoor seating is particularly agreeable. Via the archway through the wing on your left, enter the next courtyard, then exit it via the **Powder Bridge (Prašný most)**. The bridge divides a ravine, **Stag's Moat (Jelení příkop)**, into upper and lower parts; it's named for the wild animals that used to cavort there, stocked until the mid eighteenth century by hunting-mad Hapsburgs for handy target practice. The bridge was once a sturdy covered wooden structure standing on five stone pillars; today the valley underneath is filled in with earth. On your left is the late-seventeenth-century **Riding School (Jízdárna)** of Prague Castle, where court tournaments and horseback riding festivals were held. The L-shaped early-baroque building's slender wing facing the road is where the ladies sat and watched the competitions. These days it's part of the National Gallery's Contemporary Art exhibition space. The adjoining Lumbe Gardens are said to have produced unexpected treasure when they were first dug up in the early fifties and in 1971—at least three hundred graves, full of gold jewelry and artifacts from the ninth-century Slavic period, were found. Archaeologists think they are the remains of Prince Bořivoj's personal retinue, which accompanied him back to Bohemia from banishment in Moravia. The Greater Moravian Empire, though expiring, dominated the Slavs of the region in those days, when Bohemia was not yet a kingdom.

From the Riding School, diagonally across the road

on the left, is a small restaurant called **Lví Dvůr** (**Lion Court**, or **Bear Court**), with hearty, generally well-prepared steaks and an outdoor café in the courtyard. Just as nearby St. Vitus Cathedral is encrusted with the bizarre wild creatures of a Gothic bestiary, this spot was once the monarch's private zoo, a de facto living bestiary in which the lion ruled. The double-tailed lion is one of the oldest symbols of royal authority and appears on all heraldic emblems of the nation: Czech historians point to the Vyšehrad codex of 1085, which includes an illuminated miniature of Prince Václav on a lion-claw-footed folding chair with carved lion heads, to prove that wild felines were kept here from the kingdom's earliest days, though leopards, orangutangs, tigers, bears, and peacocks took up residence much later. Lions were a special passion of Emperor Rudolf II; knowing that, his fellow despots often sought favor by gifting him with exotic animals: Czar Feodor I, son of Ivan the Terrible, sent him three leopards in 1585, and in 1602 a couple of leopards and tigers from the Florentine Francesco de Medici were intercepted by Rudolf's valet, who sold them and pocketed the proceeds. It is said that when Tycho Brahe read the stars and foretold that favorite lion Mohamed's fate was tied to the emperor's, it came to pass: Rudolf died the day after Mohamed called it quits. There was also banter about ladies tossing their gloves into the cages to test the chivalrous reflexes of their suitors.

Now let's turn through the ornate wrought-iron gold-laced gates into the **Royal Garden** (**Královská zahrada**) opposite, lying north of Stag's Moat. Our freedom to stroll through this English-style formal park is owed entirely to the demise of the Communist government in 1989 and the installation of Václav Havel as president, who acted quickly to open up the Castle grounds to the public. Before then, the garden—a colorful, vibrant refuge—was not only strictly off-limits during the forty-year Communist occupation of the country, it was hermetically sealed off from the outside world. The reason: what's known as the

Presidents' House (turn right past the gatekeeper's post), previously inhabited by justifiably paranoid and security-obsessed Communist presidents. Nearby, overlooking Castle windows reportedly were heavily screened to block views of the garden and residence, and an iron-reinforced concrete slab was installed above the ceiling of Gustáv Husák's study, presumably in case of air raids. The ghosts of these dubious tenants everyone wants to forget are the major reason the Havels remained in their old, unpresidential apartment across the river. Olga Havel, mindful of ghosts, once told me she didn't care to be reminded of first Communist President Klement Gottwald's drinking sprees, and figured she slept better at home. So the building, originally just the center baroque pavilion designed by Kilián Ignác Dientzenhofer in 1731, with the neoclassical wings added more than two centuries later—in 1947, by architect Pavel Janák—is used mostly for official conferences these days. Dientzenhofer also had a hand in designing the French phase of the garden, though it was originally laid out in Italian Renaissance garden style in 1535 for the first Hapsburg emperor (and king of Bohemia) Ferdinand I. The stone balustrades, lion statuary, and cherubs are from the baroque master Matthias Braun's studio.

When Ferdinand I decided to move his court and household to Prague, he not only made the neglected Gothic medieval Castle livable, he gave it a then-modern Renaissance facelift, and went all out in his garden, built on the site of five vineyards. Greenhouses and an orangerie, farther down, were also built and stocked with imported horticultural exoticisms, all tended by a squadron of Italian gardeners. Along with local varieties of cherry, apple, pear, and plum trees, they cultivated previously unknown imports—apricot, peach, almond, fig, quince, pomegranate, lemon, orange, and pineapple trees. Another happy first, a floral one, took root here in 1563 when the Archduke Ferdinand's personal physician and herbalist, Peter Ondřej Mattioli, author of a famous treatise on herbs, received some mysterious bulbs from the Hapsburg ambassador, Busbeq. They turned out to be tulips (originally from Turkey), and created a sensation, flourishing here, in full view of St. Vitus Cathedral, almost before they reached the rest of Europe.

Farther down on the right, glimpsed behind the giant fir trees, is the **Ball Game Hall** (**Velká Míčovna**), once an indoor royal disporting court echoing with thwacking rackets, thumping balls, and the pounding of pivoting, dodging, running feet. A High Renaissance type of pavilion, it was built between 1567 and 1569 and breathes an air of refined, though solid, Roman antiquity. At the end of World War II the retreating Germans lit a fire that swept through the interior of the hall, collapsing the vaulted ceiling. But the remarkable sgraffitoed facade, scratched with feminine allegories symbolizing Astronomy, Geometry, Agriculture, Industry, Virtue, and the Elements, was not totally destroyed. In a 1952 restoration, a timely addition was made to the design, so skillfully worked in you could easily miss it, but that's what this book is for. To the right of one of the Ionic half-pillars (also originally sgraffitoed) note the hammer-and-sickle Communist emblem above the unscrolling five-year plan on Industry's lap. Amid the raging debates about leaving it there or removing it, the truth-telling preservationists are so far winning. Nowadays, large-scale art exhibitions are held in and around the Ball Game Hall.

Down the center of the garden, at the end of the geometrically ordered alley of trees, is a strikingly handsome baroque niche designed by Caratti, with a fountain and statue of Hercules by Jan Bendl from 1670. (The *L* stands for Emperor Leopold I.) Then, elegantly situated in the garden's eastern end, the only section that was ever open to the public under Communism, one of Prague's great architectural monuments comes into focus, the illustrious **Royal Summer House** (**Kralovský letohrádek**, also known as the **Belvedere**, or **Queen Anne's Summer Pavilion**). It is always presented as the most pristine example of the Italian Renaissance outside Italy, certainly the first north of the Alps, and has been compared to Palladio's celebrated 1546 basilica in Vicenza. Surrounded by a spacious loggia of graceful Tuscan columns as slender as horses' legs and topped with a rare verdigrised (weathered-copper) roof usually described as looking like a ship's upended keel, the pavilion's clean lines present a restful vision of beautiful proportion. The architect was Paolo della Stella, who began it in 1538 for Ferdinand I and his wife Anne, a Jagellon from Poland; neither of them lived to see it completed twenty-five years later. The couple are carved into a relief above the third column from the left: in a courtly gesture Ferdinand is presenting his consort with a flower. Though he died in the building, it was the emperor Rudolf II who seemed to benefit most from its pleasures, which included a ballroom and art gallery. He furnished it royally, providing palatial booty for the marauding Swedes to come. Their armies stormed the city in 1648 and pillaged Rudolf's sublime art collection, up to that time the greatest assembled by one (very strange) individual. As for an oft-told story about the Summer Palace, our ubiquitous star searchers Brahe and Kepler apparently did not peer at the heavens from its gallery; they merely kept some of their astronomer's instruments there. Much later, the spiritually disinclined army man Emperor Joseph II used it as an artillery lab— you can guess at the repairs that necessitated. Today, major temporary exhibitions are held in its spacious interior, which is always worth a visit.

The upper gallery of the Summer Palace offers a comprehensive view of the northern medieval side of Prague Castle. Starting from the left are the ancient fortress towers, frequently used as dungeons: the prismatic twelfth-century Black Tower; under it the Daliborka (1496); then the semicircular White Tower, from the end of the fifteenth century; behind it the northern rump of St. George's monastery (today the National Gallery); and finally, the rotund fifteenth-century Powder Tower.

In front of the Summer Palace, actually in the middle of the *giardinetto*, is another vivid piece of the Renaissance, the sonorous **Singing Fountain** (**Zpívající Fontána**). Designed by Francesco Terzio and incisively sculpted and cast in bronze by bell maker Tomáš Jaroš in 1562, the singing voices issue from the vibrations of water trickling onto the edges of the two bowls, with tonal fluctuations according to the quantity of running water and the whims of wind gusts. So bend your ear to the resonant pulsing and thrumming. On a sultry day you will swear by its soothing, freshening charms.

Now let's exit the Royal Garden via **Marianské Hradby Street**. From here we'll walk down to **Chotek Park** (**Chotkovy Sady**), contiguous to the Royal Garden. This is an easy stroll through a tranquil park full of towering trees, much favored by Franz Kafka. The park features a Neo-Romantic memorial (to the right, shrouded by trees) to the great Czech poet and playwright Julius Zeyer (greatly admired by Rilke), who died in 1901. Created by sculptor Josef Mauder to resemble a grandiose grotto, the bust of the poet stands above marble statuary symbolizing the heroes of his poetic oeuvre, somewhat typical of the secessionist urge to monumentalize. It forms a mysterious backdrop for an even more romantic and evocative (of Japan?) small arching bridge over a meandering artificial pond. When Kafka used to escape to this verdant space, it was one of the few public parks in the city, and the first to be created with public funds—in 1833. All other parklands originally belonged to the Crown, to the nobility, or to the Church. Today Prague has an impressive number of green spaces for a city of 1.2 million-plus people: 20,000 acres in 250 public parks.

From here we'll cross over to **Mickiewiczova Street**, čp. 234, at the end of Marianské Hradby, and leap from the classic, calming Renaissance to the fermenting fin de siècle by visiting the self-designed villa of a buddy of Zeyer's, the multifaceted artist František Bílek. What Bílek had in mind when he conceived this darkened red-brick

Singing Fountain, Royal Garden

house-cum-studio in 1911, the first flat-roofed dwelling in Prague, was a cornfield; perhaps the pillars were stylized sheaves of corn. At the top of the stairs in the front garden is a sculptural grouping called *Comenius Saying Good-bye to his Country*, which refers to the great educator on his way to permanent exile. Inside you will find yourself in Bílek's stone-walled atelier with several works on view. (To see one of the artist's masterpieces, the *Crucifixion*, however, you will have to go to St. Vitus Cathedral.) Though Bílek was the key personality of the Czech secession at the turn of the century, his work was revived here only in the 1960s, when the whole movement was rehabilitated. The most recently opened section of the villa, the uncluttered ground-floor private living quarters of Bílek and his family, throws light on the sculptor's deep spiritual concerns and reveals his immersion in the conceptualization of the house. This is clear in the myriad details of the furniture and hardware, for example, which he also designed. Note the altarlike element set into the corner *archyr* wall, near Mrs. Bílek's dressing table. In the back, which used to be the front entrance, note also the sculpture garden shared by his friend and neighbor Dr. Procházka.

Exiting the villa, let's dip farther down by crossing straight ahead to the park called **Letná Hill** on the other side, keeping, more or less, to your right. Look for the fanciful green-and-white roof of the **Hanavský Pavilion** protruding through the trees and head for that. The pavilion was originally built for Prague's Jubilee Exhibition of 1891 to show off the achievements of Duke Vilém Hanavský's iron foundry. The major exhibition buildings, which still stand on their Holešovice district site, were a bravura display of innovative steel-and-glass construction spotlighting Czech economic, cultural, and industrial accomplishments. The baroque/mannerist revival pavilion, befrilled and studded with ornamental cast-iron elements, was moved to this spot later. It is certainly a dream setting for a restaurant with dance floor and café, though I can't vouch for the comestibles. More important, here is one of Prague's best overlooks, especially the wraparound view of the photogenic Vltava River and of the bridges in the near distance under the terrace. Now you know where some of those postcards were shot from.

When you're ready to tear yourself away, we'll find our path down to that river. Follow the wider path up a bit from the Hanavský—don't be tempted to take the immediate narrow path going down or you'll miss the divided stone staircase we're aiming for. At the top, now a kind of lookout platform, you'll see the plinth from which a gigantic, 14,000-ton granite **statue of Joseph Stalin** towered like a deathly shadow over Prague from 1955 to 1962. (Just before the vernissage the chief sculptor, one Otakar Švec, committed suicide; his adored wife had done the same three years earlier.) When the Russian Communists discredited the dictator, their Czech subservients didn't know what to do with the monster they'd created on their masters' orders. But eventually a mighty struggle with explosives ensued, detonating the dreadful eyesore into enough pieces to cart away, though some debris remains underneath. Some Praguers, when arranging a rendezvous, still haven't lost the habit of referring to the spot as U Stalina—At Stalin's. As of this writing, rumor has it that the inner storage area will become a nightclub. In the meantime, modern sculpture and graffiti (the circled letter *A* stands for anarchy) decorate the parapets.

Before we complete our walk at the bottom of the stairs, note the tiny round early baroque **Chapel of Mary Magdalene** across the street at the corner of the bridge. The 450-ton chapel used to stand lower down on the riverbank before it was moved to its present spot in 1955. In the seventeenth century it was attached to a Cistercian monastery and served the spiritual needs of vineyard workers on the Letná plain and along the Vltava. But the chapel was pressed into wartime service in 1648, the final year of the Thirty Years' War, when the Swedes took Malá Strana and Hradčany. Their next move was to blast the Old Town and the New Town, but the entire right bank was so ably defended by Praguers, students, and imperial soldiers that the Prussians failed to breach the river and the barricades. Firepower, however, inflicted plenty of damage across the Vltava-turned-moat, much of it coming from the chapel, which became a sharp-shooting gallery. It is said that student forces on the opposite bank countered by throwing up blockhouses from which to pick off Swedes, and eventually they captured the chapel in a bold night raid.

And so ends Walk 3. If you're going to the Old Town, you might want to cross the **Svatopluk Čech Bridge**, now at your feet.

Walk · 4

Modernism and Art Nouveau

VYŠEHRAD AND THE VLTAVA

Princess Libuše's Bath at Vyšehrad

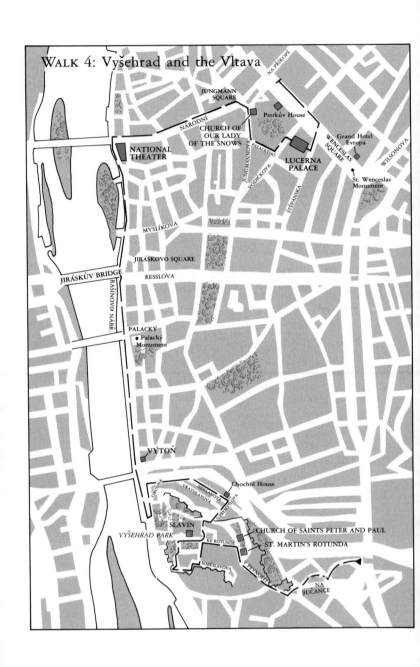

WALK 4: Vyšehrad and the Vltava

NA PŘÍKOPĚ

JUNGMANN
SQUARE

Petrkův House

NÁRODNÍ

CHURCH OF
OUR LADY
OF THE SNOWS

Grand Hotel
Evropa

WENCESLAS SQUARE

WILSONOVA

NATIONAL
THEATER

JUNGMANNOVA

PALACKÉHO

VODIČKOVA

LUCERNA
PALACE

ŠTĚPÁNSKÁ

St. Wenceslas
Monument

MYSLÍKOVA

JIRÁSKOVO SQUARE

JIRÁSKŮV BRIDGE

RESSLOVA

RAŠÍNOVO NÁBŘ.

PALACKÝ

Palacký
Monument

VÝTOŇ

Chochol House

LIBUŠINA

VRATISLAVOVA

NEKLANOVA

PLUKOVA

SLAVÍN

VYŠEHRAD PARK

KE ROTUNDĚ

CHURCH OF SAINTS PETER AND PAUL

ST. MARTIN'S ROTUNDA

SOBĚSLAVOVA

V PEVNOSTI

NA
BUČANCE

Starting Point: The former fortress of Vyšehrad. If you prefer lots of company and wish to mingle with Czech families—children, grannies, dogs, and assorted paraphernalia—on time-off outings, this walk is recommended for an early weekend afternoon, even in winter, and especially on holidays. (You might also run into a wedding party or two.) Otherwise, weekdays, except Monday, when museums are closed, are best. You will not be surrounded by crowds of your fellow visitors, as this is not an attraction much frequented by them.

Metro/Tram Lines: Trams 17 or 21 will drop you off at the base of the steep rocky hill, where there is a stairway to the top, but the most convenient approach is via the metro, Red Line C in the direction of Háje, getting off at the stop called Vyšehrad.

Length of Walk: Three and a half hours. It ends at the bottom of Wenceslas Square.

"Modern" in Prague means from around 1890, though more broadly the Modern Age started much earlier, with the end of the Middle Ages. But this walk will take us even further back than that, to the ninth century. From the remnants of the Prague acropolis, Vyšehrad, a mythic place for a mythic city, we'll leap forward through the centuries and watch as the architectural focus changes to the exotic flourishes of the art nouveau, of which there is an extravagant stock in this city. And, along the captivating Vltava riverbank, we'll look at some of the most important examples of Prague's unique cubist style, with a bit of nineteenth-century revival—Neo-Renaissance and neoclassicism—and some constructivism tossed in for extra flavor and variety. So this is definitely a walk for architecture and design buffs—as so much of Prague is—as well as for river rats. The first half will also take us out of the congestion of the teeming center to an oasis of elegiac tranquillity.

Exiting the metro station, you will find yourself in front of the **Palace of Culture**, an incongruous 1970s-built complex of public facilities (the pride of the Communist regime) that won't remind you a bit of Prague. Best to walk straight past this chrome-and-smoked-glass spread as quickly as possible, going west, while noting the view of the Nusle Valley on your right, particularly the three red spires and domes of the church on Ke Karlovu Street steepling through the trees on the opposite, southeast side, which we will visit on Walk 5. Keep going straight ahead in a westerly direction down a few steps and up along a path—toward the twin Gothic towers of Sts. Peter and Paul Church, then along the street called **V pevnosti** to the first gate, Táborská, of Vyšehrad Park. On the way you will notice that Vyšehrad is also a residential suburb of Prague.

While **Vyšehrad** is not older than the Hrad (Prague Castle), and after 1140 the kingdom's seat of power moved permanently downstream, it is eternally tied to the oldest period of Czech history, when it was the other center of nationhood. Mythically, mystically steeped in ancient ruins and memories of the Ur-ancestor, Vyšehrad is a symbolic aerie, a visual and spiritual embodiment of Czech nationalism. (The Czechs pioneered the idea of nationalism in Europe in the nineteenth century, long before it became a dirty word. Later Hitler and others

St. Martin's Rotunda, Vyšehrad

made nationalism the key political and social phenomenon of the twentieth century, of which Czechoslovakia itself became a victim, when Slovakia decided to go its own way in 1993.) It is safe to say that just as you cannot understand the history of Europe without knowing the history of its heart, the former Czechoslovakia, so you have to register the meaning of Vyšehrad to understand the history of this city.

The name Vyšehrad means "higher castle," and indeed, this former fortress towers dramatically enough above the river that the choice of settlement was an obvious and naturally strategic one. Just as naturally Vyšehrad could only amplify and embellish the library of legends. The most famous stars Princess Libuše and the Czech composer Bedřich Smetana, who wrote an opera about her in which he telescopes six hundred years of history into one excitable libretto. Libuše was the favorite daughter, wise and beautiful and gifted with clairvoyance, who founded a dynasty by marrying the plowman Přemysl. He famously wore shoes of bast (a woody plant fiber used to make rope) and gave his name to the all-powerful Přemyslid clan, which ruled the country until 1360. According to legend, Libuše stood on the craggy Vyšehrad promontory and pointed at the mist-shrouded city in the distance, foretelling the eminence of Prague and the nation. Chronicle after chronicle milked these family sagas and embroidered them, starting with Cosmas in 1117 and continuing right up to the sixteenth century. Later came the period of reawakening, called the national revival, when Czechs rediscovered their language and culture, long suppressed by Austrian domination. (German was the official language of the Holy Roman Empire.) This process, a critical prelude to all nationalist movements, started in the early nineteenth century and finally culminated in the achievement of Czechoslovak sovereignty in 1918. In the nineteenth-century age of Romanticism, the mythology of Vyšehrad played a vitally important role in inspiring a virtual epidemic of patriotic glorification by a new generation of historians, artists, poets, and writers.

Aside from documented Stone Age settlements, the historical facts about Vyšehrad begin in the second half of the tenth century, when, during the rule of Prince Boleslav II (The Pious), coins were minted here. Though this was clear evidence of Vyšehrad's importance, at no time does it appear to have eclipsed that of Prague Castle. Between them, the two strongholds kept watch over the territory of Prague. Vyšehrad later came in handy for Prince Vratislav II, who became the first king of Bohemia (therefore also Vratislav I, 1061–92) when he had a rivalrous falling out with his brother Jaromír, Bishop of Prague. Deciding that the Hrad was too small for both of them, Vratislav moved out, establishing himself upstream. His walled royal palace was said to be spacious enough to accommodate three thousand people. In this early medieval period Vyšehrad became the power center of three generations of Přemyslids, but thereafter its significance declined, though Emperor Charles IV, son of a Přemyslid mother, had the fortifications rebuilt along with much of the rest of Prague. Then in 1420, the garrison at Vyšehrad threatened the revolutionary legions of warrior Hussites but surrendered to them just as the crusading King Zigumund and his imperial Catholic forces were riding to its rescue. But it was too late: the Hussite sympathizers of Prague overran the fortress and demolished its churches, buildings, and all reminders of the nobility.

Since that time little has happened up here except a reconstruction of the fortress walls beginning in 1654, when the two baroque gates were built. Defeat at the hands of the Prussians in 1866 abolished Vyšehrad the citadel for good. Shortly thereafter came the dawning of a symbolic renaissance: Vyšehrad became the keeper of the patriotic flame as the rush of nationalistic furor brought it back into public consciousness. And on November 17, 1989, this is where 5,000 students gathered to begin their momentous march on Prague, thus setting in motion the Velvet Revolution.

Back on our walk, past the first gate, the Táborská Gate, you'll see what's left—not enough to give us much idea of what it looked like—of the Gothic Špička Gate, built in 1360 by Charles IV. Next is another gate, Leopold's, a handsome baroque construction by Carlo Lurago. Now we're in the inner core of the fortified area: to your right is the oldest fully preserved monument on Vyšehrad, **St. Martin's rotunda**, a chapel that is also the oldest (eleventh century) of the three Romanesque rotundas extant in Prague. Heavily restored though it may be with its pseudo-Romanesque portal, it evokes nearly primeval antiquity, particularly strange to most visitors because this style of construction is said to be unknown outside the Czech lands. Reconsecrated in 1880, the cozy chapel is still used for religious services. The original stamped-clay floor tiles were apparently found during restoration and reproduced. Embedded in the eastern wall is a cannonball from the 1757 Prussian assault on Prague. Just north of the rotunda on the right is a column (1714) of the sort that were erected in thankfulness for deliverance from plagues. Behind it stand the tiny baroque chapel of the Virgin Mary on the Bastion and a fourteenth-century parish church.

From Leopold's Gate, head west to the Church of Sts. Peter and Paul, whose spires you have already seen poking through the trees. Our route is up along **Ke rotundě Street**. On the way we'll pass the Neo-Gothic **Vyšehrad Museum** behind the iron fence; before you pay your entry, you may want to find out if the small permanent exhibition of Vyšehrad history is also in English—it wasn't the last time I looked. On the green opposite, near the edge (closer to the corner), you'll notice three stone pillar stumps kind of slumped against each other, looking like a modern sculpture. This curiosity is known as the **Devil's Column (Čertův Sloup)** and thereby hangs a baroque tale about a devil's wager with a priest, and the devil's losing his bet, throwing the pillar to the ground, and breaking it into three pieces. One theory says it's part of the old village pillory; another holds that it could also have been used to mark the solstice in pagan worship. It could also have been a sun dial. The mystery is bedeviled by the fact that the two and a half tons of stone are not of a locally quarried variety; the stone is much harder than the kind found in the area at the time of the Přemyslid princes.

At the corner, turn left and notice, between Ke Rotundě and Soběslavova streets, that next to the **Old Deanery** (**Staré děkanství**), currently also housing a snack bar, is a pseudo-Romanesque portal in an old stone wall: this is where the foundations and other bits and pieces of the Romanesque **basilica of St. Lawrence** were dug up in 1884. The basilica was built by Vratislav II in 1061, presumably as the parish church of Vyšehrad. The buried body of a man clutching a coin was found here near the south wall. In the 1960s another interesting discovery, of an even older, pre-Romanesque church, was made under these foundations.

Now let's head for the bastions—go south, straight for the open sky, where the river-valley spectacles start in three directions. They are always a knockout but doubly so when the afternoon sun dazzles the water, transforming it into a shining silver sheet. You may want to follow the wall around as far as it goes. From here, in the far corner, facing northwest, there's a splendid view of Prague and the Castle. And below you, on the south side, you can see the Vltava rowing club, crowded with watercrafts. In the winter this protected inlet is sprinkled with ice skaters. On an outcrop down below you will see the ruins of an old wall, probably a sentry post, called **Libuše's Bath**. A nineteenth-century Romantic legend, of the throwaway-punchline type, recounts that this is where Princess Libuše frolicked and bathed with her lovers; when she'd had enough fun, she threw them over the cliff into the river. Above this spot is a baroque-style building, what's left of the fourteenth-century fortress tower; today it's the Vyšehrad art gallery.

From here we'll walk over to the open parklike area with the four massive **Myslbek statues** in the corners. This is the site of the original Romanesque and later Gothic Přemyslid palace, and it was from here that the coronation rituals began, with the ruler donning bast shoes in memory of his peasant origins. The statuary, by the master Czech sculptor of the so-called National Theater school, Josef Václav Myslbek, who won out over

Ctírad and Šárka by Josef Myslbek at Vyšehrad

seven other significant Czech artists in a stiff competition, represents some of the stars of the Vyšehrad legends, for example, Přemysl and Princess Libuše, which happens to be the only copy of the lot. The heroically scaled and draped sculptures, works of imposing lyricism in the new romantic spirit of the mid-1880s, stood on the Palacký Bridge (farther along on our walk), but were moved here following World War II air-raid damage. On the north side of this area, near the church, are the remains of a Romanesque bridge that once spanned a ravine and joined the acropolis with the Vyšehrad settlement.

Now, continuing west, let's proceed to the front of the Neo-Gothic facade of **Sts. Peter and Paul**, the parish church. Its history reaches back through seven building stages—including the obligatory seventeenth-century "baroquization," complete with dome and an earlier baroque bell tower. The oldest construction is early Romanesque, from the time of King Vratislav, 1070. What you see is a late-nineteenth-century reconstruction by Josef Mocker, who attempted to re-create the Gothic period of Charles IV's time. Interior furnishings are largely Neo-Gothic and secessionist, with some much older elements, such as an early Romanesque stone sarcophagus attributed to St. Longinus (it's in the first chapel on the right) from the Přemyslid's crypt. The most valuable art here has been moved to the National Gallery's St. George's Convent at the Castle.

There's a restaurant in front of the church, closed on Mondays, serving moderately priced meals. During the summer, Sunday afternoon concerts are held in the Vyšehrad Cultural Theater in the **New Provost's House (Nové Proboštví)**, north of the cemetery; programs vary from jazz to classical music and usually start at 3:30 P.M. Schedules are posted on the grounds.

Local seekers, some perhaps looking for a bit more than just a verdant setting for an afternoon stroll, often fall into a meditative mood here, speak in hushed tones, and tread softly out of respect for the pulse of history and proximity to the celebrated deceased. For Vyšehrad smolders with symbolism for another reason: the **National Cemetery**, adjoining the Church of Sts. Peter and Paul, and **Slavín**, its common burial ground or pantheon, are the final resting places of many of the country's most distinguished personalities in the arts and sciences, representing two centuries of cultural history. But this graveyard will surprise you; it is also an outdoor sculpture exhibition of remarkable, much of it not necessarily tombstone-style, art. A lot of the occupants here clearly wanted to be remembered for their aesthetic sensibilities and achievements. Established in 1869 on the site of the old parish church cemetery (1660), Slavín, and the Italian-inspired, sandstone arcades on three sides, is largely the design of Antonin Wiehl, whose Neo-Renaissance architecture we'll see again on Wenceslas Square. Dominating Slavín is the monumental symbolic sculpture by Josef Mauder (a young associate of Myslbek's) of **Winged Genius** poised over a sarcophagus carved with Italian Renaissance motif reliefs and flanked below by female allegories of Motherland in Mourning and Motherland Victorious. Under Genius it says, "As they died, so they still live." In the right-front area of the graveyard is František Bílek's immediately identifiable—for its style, if you've done Walk 3—Grief headstone sculpture for novelist Beneš Trebizsky's grave. This work of baroque pathos, straining (for some) at spiritual truth, was criticized in the conservative press of Bílek's day as "a monster in a theatrical pose of despair."

The internationally famous cultural lights buried here (there's room for six hundred) include composers Antonin Dvořák and Bedřich Smetana, writer Karel Čapek (author of *R.U.R.*, the play that gave the world the word "robot"), opera singer Emmy Destinn (she sang with Enrico Caruso at the Metropolitan Opera in New York), poet Julius Zeyer (Rilke's muse), artist Alfons Mucha (some mistakenly think he was French), sculptor Josef Václav Myslbek, and nineteenth-century physiologist Jan Pur-

kyně. Another headstone to note is that of Karel Hynek
Mácha, intense young lyric poet of the Romantic movement, often called the Czech Byron. His premature death
at age twenty-six made him eternally popular with students of all ages. His birthday, November 16, was the
target date and his grave the assembly point for the massive November 17, 1989, Wenceslas Square student
demonstration, thwarted on Národní Street. The date was
also chosen because it was the fiftieth anniversary of the
funeral of Jan Opletal, a young man murdered by the
Nazis during student protests in 1939.

One of the oldest graves here, not far from the right
of the gate entrance near the front of the church, is that
of Václav Hanka (1791–1861), a collector of popular poetry, translator, and forger whose "discoveries" of manuscripts of ancient Czech poetry, though controversial,
became the stuff of legend and were accepted as authentic
for most of the nineteenth century. The uproar over their
exposure as fakes by Tomáš Masaryk, the future first
Czech president, then a professor of philosophy, riveted
and outraged many Romantically minded patriots who
preferred to believe in the texts. Their genuineness would
have changed the focus of Czech literary history by plac-
ing the manuscripts among the earliest epics in all European literature, but Masaryk, the consumate moralist
and idealist who was also a realist, was not about to
establish renewed national identity on a falsehood—a
willed fantasy, no matter how ingenious.

We'll leave Vyšehrad via the **Prague** or **Vyšehrad
Gate** (**Cihelná/Pražská Brána**), north of the cemetery
enclave; another way to find it is to go back to Ke rotundě Street and turn left. This empire-style brick gate
was built in 1841 and reminds some people of Piranesi
engravings. Walk down the hairpin curve of **Vratislavova
Street**, part of the former King's Road (Královská cesta)
laid down in the eleventh century. We're headed for the
Vltava riverbank and the foot of Vyšehrad, for a look at
an outstanding cluster of Prague cubism.

Turn right on **Přemyslova Street** and walk down to **Neklanova Street**, where you can't miss the five-floor apartment building, the bold **Chocol House**, projecting acutely at the corner. The site must have been preordained for architect Josef Chochol's 1913 cubist dreams; it has been called the least adulterated cubist building in the city. Among the other influences on cubist architects such as Chochol, critics point not only to late Gothic architecture but also to the spectacular, peculiarly Czech hybrid of baroque Gothic church design invented and perfected by Jan Santini-Aichel in the early eighteenth century. Some architecture critics believe that modernism was clearly not an assault on history, on historical styles. It was, rather, a response to history's assault on civilization, and the so-called cubo-expressionist phenomenon is almost as multidimensional and complex.

Nowhere else will you find a fully developed cubist architectural movement but in Bohemia, and Prague, the cubist, multiangled city of memorable sharp-edged polemics, has several prismatic examples. Not even in Paris, where cubism started, do these buildings exist, nor the energetic cubist furniture, cubist lampposts, and cubist decorative objects designed for them. Though it lasted only from about 1910 to 1920, the movement's artistic ideas motivated a key group of Czech architects and designers, who absorbed the artistic freedom represented by the French avant-garde and soon turned it to their own Central European (though anti-Viennese) spiritual and geopolitical agenda. The years preceding World War I were a time of great global cultural and technological turbulence; seismic explosions were splitting the foundations of society here as elsewhere, and the writing was on the wall for the gasping Austro-Hungarian Empire. Time and space were on a dismembering collision course; the map of Europe was about to be rearranged again. All of this created a charged atmosphere of sudden change, which is reflected in the dynamic planes, pyramids, convexities and concavities, and geometric configurations of Czech cubist applied art and architecture.

Turn left on Neklanova: you will pass an exceedingly seedy pub called **U Karla Čtvrtého** (**At Charles IV's**), not exactly a tribute to its namesake. I mention it not because I recommend the place (though they do stay open late—3:00 P.M. to 3:00 A.M.—and serve food) but because of a story associated with it. On the fateful night of November 17, 1989, a group of students, on their way with thousands of others to the planned demonstration on Wenceslas Square, tore themselves away and dropped into this pub. The question is still debated over foaming glass mugs of the golden-hued local brew in the depths of Karla Čtvrtého: Did the laggard group stay on, imbibing and gabbing, and forget their mission, thus losing out on their chance to be enshrined in history, or did they join the march later and get their heads bashed in? Of such conundrums is pub lore sometimes made. . . .

Now walk to the end of Neklanova, staying on your left, and then cut across to **Libušina Street**, where on the corner of **Rašín Embankment** (**Rašínovo nábřeží**) there is another Chochol building at no. 3, a handsome three-story villa with a cubist fenced wall around it, unfortunately untidily overgrown by weeds. (Maybe the occupants prefer it that way for privacy.) The last Chochol building, a bit farther along the river at no. 6–10, near the tunnel cut through the Vyšehrad rock, is a triple structure best viewed from across the street.

From here we'll turn around and walk up the Rašín Embankment on our way back to the center of the city. In case you were wondering, Alois Rašín was the first finance minister of the newly born Czechoslovak state; he stabilized the currency but was assassinated in 1923 by a Communist fanatic. First stop on this route is across the street from the Railroad Bridge, at a small, sunken, late-Gothic building, surrounded by a green, called **Vý-toň**. The prominent, colorful coat of arms above the former front door is that of the New Town district of Prague. (Each of the city's medieval towns had its own insignia.) For almost three hundred years, until 1828, this was the customs house of a fishing and lumber community called

Podskalí—the name means Under the Rock Cliff. If Vy-šehrad was a long lost world, Výtoň is all that's left of this more recently extinguished and slightly less legendary, but perhaps more thoroughly obliterated, one. It flourished here from the late-twelfth to the nineteenth century, extending from Vyšehrad to the Palacký Bridge farther up the riverbank as one of Prague's poorest but, oddly enough, more exclusive neighborhoods, distinguished by an independent and robust lifestyle and a livelihood drawn from the unruly river. Logs were floated downstream and sold here, and the lumbermen carefully guarded their franchise on each journey. By the fifteenth century they had set up their own raftsmen's guild and a hundred years later were granted jurisdiction over their own community. Some of the liveliest hubs of the national independence movement sprang up in the taverns right under the rocky face of Vyšehrad. Podskalí folk prided themselves on standing in the very spot of the former graveyard of the first pagan Přemyslid princes, and the sturdy, good-humored shore dwellers became part of the national mythology. Popular songs and novels were written about them, and a film was made by a celebrated local storyteller. Podskalí folklore entered the literature as a typical pre–World War I Prague phenomenon.

To imagine what this maritime community looked like, close your eyes and picture disheveled rows, village-style, of two-story cottages—no grid patterns in those days—with high red clay-tiled roofs and pointed gables, surrounded by picket fences enclosing spacious yards stacked with piles of fragrant, freshly cut lumber. No high stone embankments cut the lumbermen's yards off from the river's gently sloping shore; flooding was frequent, but the logs floated conveniently at hand. (That's why Výtoň is so obviously below street level—the ground was later raised.) In summer fishermen sit on crude wooden benches outside their cottages repairing fishing nets and barefoot children play nearby.

With only a small number of exceptional late-baroque

buildings, including the town hall, that's what Podskalí looked like until the 1870s, when fewer fish were squirming in the nets and sprawling big-city syndrome and unstoppable urban renewal started to encroach; by 1924 the remaining traces of Podskalí had been demolished—all except Výtoň, now looking utterly stranded. You may want to drop in on the exhibition in the small, log-walled Výtoň Museum, which also records the history of steamship transport on the Vltava. It's open from April to October, on Wednesdays, Saturdays, and Sundays, from 9:00 A.M. to 12:00 noon and from 1:00 P.M. to 5:00 P.M. Walking two blocks north along the riverbank, stop a moment at the corner of Plavecká, and look up the street a few blocks to the left: you will see a lone red-roofed, high-gabled house, looking rather oddball in the surroundings, a suggestion of the area's former Podskalí profile.

If the castles were built to protect the burgeoning trade center of Prague, the city owes its existence to the river, and so it is appropriately said that the Vltava founded Prague. Watching the river traffic and the sea gulls wheeling and dipping overhead hundreds of miles from the sea brings to mind a little-known fact about this waterway: it runs to the North Sea via the Elbe River, arriving at the port of Hamburg in Germany. (Of course, this would *also* have been news to Shakespeare, who called Bohemia a seacoast in *A Winter's Tale.* . . .) The Czech Republic maintains a large berth in the port of Hamburg, said to be a prominent space, that dates back to the First Republic, one of the deals President Masaryk negotiated when he was in office. Alas, it's hardly ever used—some cynics say that Vltava water is too dirty to empty into the sea. Another little-known, surprising seafaring fact: the Czech Republic has the biggest seagoing merchant fleet of all the world's landlocked countries, with eighteen vessels plying the oceans.

Before reaching our next stop along the riverbank, the Palacký Bridge, you can't fail to notice the striking and

Staircase to lower Vltava embankment

unusual—for Prague—contemporary spires of the church high on a bluff between Trojická and Dřevná streets. We will examine this church more closely on another walk, but you won't get this view; for now, suffice it to say that the spires belong to the partially restored Church of the Virgin Mary Na Slovanech. They replace the original conventionally Gothic towers destroyed early in 1945, when they were strafed by Allied bombers trying to ferret out German troops, one of the blessedly few examples of war destruction sustained by the city. The same calamity almost befell the four giant Myslbek statues illustrating ancient Czech myths that we saw on Vyšehrad. It was on the four corners of our next stop, the **Palacký Bridge**, that they were designed to stand, and there they did, on top of the octagonal toll collector's booths, from 1889–97 until the end of World War II. Damage caused by the bombers was restorable for all but one statue, which exists now as a copy.

Opposite the bridge is the **Palacký Monument**, a major art nouveau sculpture, created to commemorate the great Czech historian—also philologist, grammarian, poet, and archaeologist—František Palacký (1798–1876). He is venerated as one of the first champions of the national revival, the father not only of Czech historiography but of his people and of a new age. The memorial is an example of the rage in the country to monumentalize, to anchor Prague's public places with art commemorating national heroes, real and imagined—again, a direct product, politically and emotionally, of the national rebirth movement. The laying of the foundation stone in 1898 was celebrated by 31,000 people, with fourteen musical choirs and representatives from the entire Central European region in a colorful thicket of hundreds of ancient emblazoned standards and flags of local civic groups. The sculptor, Stanislav Sucharda, whose piece was not unveiled until 1912, had to fit it into the probably unsuitable setting of the river, the bridge, and Myslbek's massive figures, so the challenge was daunting. His solution was to situate the dignified, seated figure of Palacký, in granite, as spawner of revolutionary spiritual upheaval, on a lower plinth surrounding him with flamboyantly dramatic groupings, in bronze, symbolizing the Awakener of the Nation, Victory, the Muse, and the Voices of History, Fame, and Oppression, some of which recalled the heathen and Hussite periods of Czech history. The nude represents the defeat at the Battle of White Mountain. In total impact the work's composition proved satisfyingly symmetrical and compelling—a daring synthesis of con-

Memorial to František Palacký (detail)

Feeding the ducks and swans on the Vltava

structive considerations and flights of the imagination. It also shows the dynamic influence of Auguste Rodin, who visited Prague and left his mark on several Czech sculptors of the period.

Starting in the 1890s and peaking around 1910, the modernist art nouveau movement convulsed the worlds of art and architecture in Prague as much as anywhere else in Europe; it was known as *fin-de-siècle* in France; *Jungendstil* in Germany; *stile floreale*, *Inglese*, or *liberty* in Italy; and the wavy line, the erotic, or neo-floral style in England. In Prague (and Vienna) the word was secession (*secese*)—a parting of the ways with the past that unknowingly turned into an unforeseen prelude to the cataclysmic events of World War I. It was cultural evidence of converging social, artistic, and philosophical currents—something more than just another design trend. As critics have noted, Czech secessionist fervor, in its juxtapositions of the fantastic and the real, the ordinary and the extraordinary, manifested a metamorphosis of the national mentality.

From here we will continue our walk north along the

waterfront, passing art nouveau and historicist buildings and curiosities, remarkable for a world of different reasons. Scattered formations of wild ducks and swans with giant webbed feet litter the quays performing their toilette, the swans acting very nervy and ducklike rather than graceful and swanlike. They hobnob on the lower embankments in any weather, in and out of the water, as long as someone's feeding them. Parked alongside the fowl are the passenger boats, called *parníks*, that cruise the wide river flowing through the entire length of Bohemia; it's a beautiful, stately ride through lush countryside. Also on the water is a rustic restaurant called Vltava that's very popular for its decent Czech food, fresh fish dishes, and very reasonable prices.

Just before the next bridge, **Jiráskův**, named after a popular nineteenth-century Czech author of historical novels, Alois Jirásek, whose statue stands in the small green square named after him, is a battered-looking, sadly chipped and worn art nouveau apartment building, **no. 78**. Its most famous resident was Václav Havel, the first president of the post-Communist revolutionary government, playwright, essayist, and much-jailed human rights activist, the most famous ex-dissident in the land. The structure was built by Havel's grandfather, a prominent contractor in the First Republic, in 1905. Soon after the Velvet Revolution the lobby wall became a target for Havel enthusiasts from all over the world to scrawl admiring messages to him in several languages. Others strummed guitars and serenaded the windows. These days the building occupants more fittingly lock the door, though Havel now lives elsewhere. From the apartment the view of Prague Castle where he presides over the government is forever captivating, but during his outlaw days and the acid reign of Communist secret police, agents erected a watch booth opposite the building from which they directed his personal surveillance. The currently empty lot next door will have a new tenant by the time you read this: controversial and profusely admired

American architect Frank Gehry has designed an ultramodern building inspired by Ginger Rogers and Fred Astaire (of its two towers, one looks like a dancing skirt) for the site, which was bombed out in the last war. It's one of the last waterfront lots left inside Prague's historical center.

Past the bridge the street changes names and becomes **Masaryk Embankment** (**Masarykovo nábřeží**). Tomáš Garrigue Masaryk, founder and first president of the Czechoslovak state, widely acclaimed as one of the most remarkable statesmen of the European century, was a professor of philosophy whose earliest published work was "About Hypnotism (Animal Magnetism)," and who twenty-four years later wrote "Suicide as a Social Mass Phenomenon." During the Communist period every effort was made to eradicate his name and image: Masarykovo nábřeží became Gottwaldov nábřeží, named for the first Communist president. You might think the renaming of streets was a favorite pasttime here, but it merely reflects the city's stormy history.

Walking along, traffic streaming past, you may have company, for, as you might expect, the waterfront is a favorite strolling area. The rather dour-looking onion-domed water tower on your left, called **Sitkovská věž**, is a relic from the fifteenth century, when its construction was a technical advancement because the water collected under the roof entered the wooden pipe network by means of its own weight; from there the water was distributed to the fountains and breweries of the New Town. Up to 1847 the tower was still in use, and of all six leaning towers in Prague, this one is said to lean the most—sixty-eight centimeters. Next to the tower stands a low constructivist-style building called **Mánes** (1930), which refers to that hotbed of artistic turmoil the influential Union of Artists, established in 1887 and named after painter Josef Mánes, a Romanticist of the national revival movement. The Mánes Union played a key role in the development of Czech art. Once headquartered in an art nouveau pavilion designed and built for it in 1902 on the other side of the river, this association of young artists was the site of a critical Rodin exhibition that electrified the art community of the time. In its present-day manifestation here you will find art exhibitions, an art gallery, and a casual restaurant in the back.

Farther up the riverbank, amid all the neobaroque and pseudo-Gothic apartment structures stands the **Hlahol House** at **čp. 248**, a restrained art nouveau building arresting in its colorful and sculptural details despite the relative simplicity of the whole. It was designed by Josef Fanta for the Hlahol choir, a nineteenth-century singing group (the verb *hlaholit* means "to resound"), one of whose choirmasters was composer Bedřich Smetana, according to one of the bronze wall plaques. A favorite outstanding secessionist building is no. 26 (čp. 234), actually Gothic-secessionist, with its fine, elaborately wrought, plant-motif stuccowork by architect Kamil Hilbert, a devotee of art nouveau naturalism. If the front door is open, be sure to stick your head in and take a look at the lobby courtyard window's marvelous stained glass, and more romantic stuccowork on the stair landing. Farther up, projecting formidably like a ship's prow on the corner of Na struze Street (čp. 224), is another exceptional secessionist building, today Goethe House, previously the East German embassy, originally built for a bank. The excitement here is on the roof: note, between two chimney stacks, the exuberant, whimsical, triumphantly winged freestanding eagle and globe by Ladislav Šaloun, one of the era's top monumentalist sculptors.

Opposite these buildings is a short bridge to **Slovanský Island**, which used to be called Žofín. Liszt, Berlioz, and Wagner were among the composers who directed concerts in the Neo-Renaissance building, which became a social and cultural center in the nineteenth century and was also known for its grand and festive balls. You can rent rowboats from the island's docks on the river side and feast on new perspectives of Prague from the water.

Slovanský Island

The **National Theater**, on the corner of **Národní Street**, is not just a grand and ornate historical Neo-Renaissance building for opera, ballet, and dramatic performances. Not here in Prague. In the superheated atmosphere of the national revival, the drive to the ultimate realization of this theater and its house was as much political as cultural. Czechs believe that what distinguishes this building, with its regulation architectural period features—pillars, pilasters, cornices, vaults, arches, and grandiose statuary—from all the other European public cultural emporiums of the day was the spirit in which it was conceived and in which it materialized. Not coincidentally was it called the cathedral of the renaissance, and the story of how it came to be built is a saga of heroic proportions and aspirations. Since theaters had long been a privilege of the ruling German-speaking nobility and wealthy city-dwelling class, frustration and resentment at not having their own stage lay deep among the Czech people, just then awakening to their identity, language, and history. Efforts to raise money for construction began in 1851 with a successful nationwide public subscription drive, but it still took thirty years. In the meantime, a so-called Temporary Theater was quickly built to satisfy demand and later incorporated into the final structure. In 1868 the first cornerstone, inspirationally inscribed, arrived in Prague from the countryside, followed by cornerstones from at least twenty towns and regions tied to Czech history, including two from Vyšehrad (and one that took a year to arrive from the Czech community in Chicago). This lapidaria can be seen in a subterranean exhibition area of the theater. Palacký himself helped lay the foundation. The building, designed by Josef Zítek, who won a hotly contested competition for the project, was almost complete when a huge fire broke out, leaving only the seriously scorched walls standing. Amid the national mourning was equal resolve to rebuild. Two years later, on November 14, 1883, the National Theater rose from the ashes with an opening production of Smetana's opera *Libuše*. Architect Zítek, undoubtedly influenced by Vienna's Staatsoper, created a Northern Italian–style example of academic historicism, a milestone in the development of Czech architecture that just caught the peak of the Neo-Renaissance wave. Naturally, the biggest names in Czech painting and sculpture worked on the superb interior and exterior decorations, including Myslbek, Šaloun, and Aleš, all of whom came to be known as artists of the National Theater generation.

Next to the theater is a more recent structure, **Nová scéna**, built in the early 1980s, which houses performance facilities with diverse production capabilities, as well as a restaurant and a café. The blocky, glass-brick facades, said to be necessary acoustical additions, are in extremely odd partnership with the older, dominant theater. Across the street, on the corner of the riverfront, is the famous **Slavia Café**, with its rows of great windows, a popular meeting place of the intelligentsia since the hectic days of the First Republic. Czech avant-gardist and Nobel Prize–winning poet Jaroslav Seifert immortalized this establishment in his "Slavia" poems. Under Communism the service waxed as abysmal as the food and the maintenance, but tables were scarce because everybody went anyway—it was *the* place. Its next incarnation remains to be seen, as the new owner, who has also spiffed up the restaurant next door on the waterfront side, Parnas, renovates.

Parnas is one of Prague's better eateries, with a classic view of the Castle from its elegantly *echt* 1930s dining room; at night the illuminated, floating ship of state glows in shades of blue and green tinged with pale gold. The composer Bedřich Smetana, eternally associated with the river and the embankment and churned by the mythology and the genius loci, lived on the first floor from 1863 to 1869, when the former palace of the counts of Lázeňský was a brand-new building. No doubt the expansive riverscape under his windows soon found vivid expression in his music. A few years later, in 1874, the composer, an intensely patriotic nationalist, conceived his masterpiece, *Má Vlást* (*My Country*), a cycle of six symphonic poems of which "The Moldau," as the Vltava was called in German, is universally celebrated. Smetana went stone deaf the very day the lyrical theme sounded in his brain, and he never actually heard the piece performed. Though he died in an insane asylum, mentally and physically broken, he had managed to rise, at least temporarily, above the tragedy of his affliction and write unforgettable music. There's a museum devoted to Smetana farther up the embankment, which changes names now in his honor, just before the Charles Bridge.

Walking along Národní on the right side of the street—in order to better see the opposite side—we next come to two superior and colorful examples of art nouveau by the influential Prague architect Osvald Polívka, who was awarded several important institutional commissions and seems to have designed more secessionist buildings than any other architect in the city. Across the street, at čp. 1/011 is the **Prague Insurance building**, probably Polívka's most successfully composed and harmonious facade; certainly it's his most whimsical, with its ceramic-relief window frames under a protruding cornice spelling out the word "Praha." Notice the splendid symmetry of the details: balconies, windows, flag holders, painted murals of the first floor, and Šaloun sculptures on the roof. The mosaic lettering above the windows refers to types of insurance: *život*, life, *důchod*, pension, *vena*, dowry. For the contiguous **Topič** publishing house, built at the same time as its neighbor, Polívka created rich, finely wrought relief decorations but kept them comparatively simple and nonpictorial; the juxtaposition of the two buildings works beautifully.

Continuing along Národní Street, our next stop is the arcade on the right, between Mikulandská and Spálená streets. The building, **čp. 118**, is the baroque **Kaňka house** (circa 1740). Kaňka was one of the few native architects of the baroque period (see Walk 1). On the wall of the arcade you will see a small, poignant memorial of outstretched fingers appealing for help, with the date in gold lettering, November 17, 1989. This was the day and this was the place that riot police and dogs attacked the marching students on their way from Vyšehrad to Wenceslas Square to stage their demonstration. On the wall is a tattered didactic display of photographs of that seminal event and underneath are the puddles of melted candle wax from the eternal flames that keep vigil.

At the end of Národní and the intersection of ulice 28 října (28 of October Street) is **Jungmann Square** (**Jungmannovo náměstí**), with the bronze figure of its namesake, another hero of the Czech national rebirth, prominently seated high up on his marble pedestal. The translator Josef Jungmann was an important figure for his contributions to the revival of the Czech language in a country where German was the official, despotic tongue in the arts and sciences and in business. He spent forty years, under conditions of censorship and police surveillance, on his dictionary, five volumes and 4,500 pages, which appeared between 1835 and 1839. He also published the encyclopedic *History of Czech Literature* (1825), the first of its kind.

Walking north, past Jungmann (in the direction of Wenceslas Square), notice the cubo-expressionist lamppost placed here in 1913. Some people think its base resembles a palm tree. It stands in front of a Gothic tympanum atop the gate of a Franciscan monastery graveyard, which belongs to a fourteenth-century Gothic church, **Our Lady of the Snows** (**Panny Marie Sněžné**), founded by the emperor Charles IV immediately following his coronation in 1347. Though a detour from our major theme, it's worth a quick peek inside: enter through the open courtyard opposite Jungmann. Despite the abnormal height (one hundred feet) of its gracefully ribbed Gothic vault—it was actually lowered during restoration—this church is today so hemmed in by the modern buildings of the New Town you'd never know it was there; if you look at old engravings of the area, however, you'll see it formerly towered above all else. What you see now is a partial, unfinished structure (funds ran out): Charles IV's plans had called for the largest and tallest church in Prague, a church fit to hold coronations in—an ambition achieved only by the early-baroque main altar, said to be the highest in the country. The radical Hussite priest Jan Želivský, key demagogue of the revolutionary movement, preached here, but we'll save his story for Walk 5.

Back on the square, a striking art nouveau building, **no. 1/761**, stands opposite the church courtyard entrance; note the elaborate, leafy reliefs of the impressive circular portal. From this, we'll move to the post–World War I phenomenon of rondocubism and consider the example of the **Adria Palace** (built for Reunione Adriatica di Sicurtá, an Italian insurance company), opposite on Národní. Designed in 1923–25 by Pavel Janák, the future chief architect of Prague Castle, and Josef Zasche, it was said to be have been inspired by Venetian Renaissance architecture. Also called the National Style, rondocubism has been described as the union of crystallized forms with the decorative curves of art deco. It was definitely the end of the cubist era, and the heavy relief and dark stone found few adherents, as there are only three other examples of rondocubism in Prague. Inside the Adria Palace there's a restaurant with a terrace facing Národní; the bronze sculpture grouping under the main cornice is called *Sea-crossing* and is by Jan Štursa. The modern theater in the bowels of the building secured its place in history as the venue for early meetings of Václav Havel's fledgling dissident party, Civic Forum, during the heady days following November 17, 1989; Civic Forum also held its postelection press conference—following the first free elections since the overthrow of Communism—here seven months later.

Now let's proceed down **Jungmannova**, a bustling area of shops and hurrying Praguers bent on their missions. At **no. 30** (čp. 748), you'll find a modernist building known as the **Mozarteum**, designed by Prague's first art nouveau master, Jan Kotěra, in 1912. This extremely restrained building, ultramodern for its time, reflects the architect's interest in exposed masonry such as raw, unvarnished brick. With his romantic play on Czech cubism evident in the triangular gable, the whole is a major departure from his earlier decorative style. He was probably also influenced by Frank Lloyd Wright's work, which he saw during a visit to the United States seven years earlier. The two half-figure sculptures of Orpheus and Eurydice on the ground-floor facade are by Štursa, who had a keen sense of architectural form and frequently collaborated with Kotěra. The Mozarteum was built for a famous music publisher and housed the avant-garde theater group of E. F. Burian. From here turn left onto the short stretch

František Palacký above his portal

of **Palacký Street** (**Ulice Palackého**), whose best-known resident's sculpted likeness sits elegantly on the portal of the house in the center of the block where he lived and died. The bust of František Palacký is by Myslbek.

This brings us to **Vodičkova Street**, where we will turn left and view the most exotically adorned, painted, and festooned art nouveau building yet, **U Novaku**, Prague's first department store when it was built in 1902. Designed by Polívka, it displays all the classic ornamental art nouveau features: stained glass, an expansive mosaic mural of an idyllic spring celebration in soft pastels (by Jan Preisler, a key Czech symbolist in the vanguard of the modern art movement), and fanciful stucco and metalwork urged into naturalistic motifs and shapes. At the moment the restaurant and nightclub on the premises are negligible attractions, as is the interior decoration, which, except for the stained-glass elements, bears no resemblance to the exterior.

A few doors down the street, heading toward Wenceslas Square, is the rear of the **Lucerna Palace**, the first steel-and-concrete building erected in Prague—you can get a better view from the corner of Wenceslas Square and Štěpánská Street, čp. 704, so let's enter here and walk through the *pasáž*, an interior passage. Its architect, contractor, and jack-of-all-building-trades was Václav Havel's paternal grandfather of the same name. A statue of the elder Havel has been returned to its original spot on the landing in the center of the *pasáž*; the Communists had removed it in an effort to obliterate the "bourgeois" element. Built 1913–17, the Lucerna was one of the first mixed-use complexes. In addition to offices, it housed a variety of cultural facilities including an enormous Great Hall, among the largest in Bohemia (seating capacity 2,500), used for concerts and large gatherings; a restaurant; a cinema; and a cabaret theater that drew some of the most famous Central European vaudeville acts, including the extremely popular prewar comedy team of Voskovec and Werich. The name Lucerna comes from the architect's wife, who remarked that the complex resembled a lantern. The Havel family plans to restore the Lucerna to its former prominence in due course.

And so here we are on **Wenceslas Square**, a very wide boulevard rather than a traditional European square, historically a convergence point of national, political, and social life, its broad sidewalks, shops, hotels, and entertainment emporiums ever the place to be seen and heard. When the Communist government ran the show, these sidewalks were prime black market currency exchange territory; fortunes were made by the scofflaws thus engaged. It was here that all the mass demonstrations were held during the Velvet Revolution of 1989, where Václav Havel and Alexander Dubček addressed the crowds from the balcony of **no. 36**, **Melantrich**, the oldtime publishing house on the west side of the street. (Jiří Melantrich started the first Czech printing press in the sixteenth century.) The Neo-Renaissance National Museum at the top may be a bit of a pompous pile, but it certainly has more *gravitas* than the old triple-arched Horse Gate that used to stand there before 1875, when Wenceslas Square was called Horse Market, because it was. The square's lower part, which intersects Na příkopě and 28 října streets, is known as the Golden Cross. (The name Na příkopě, or On the Moat, comes from the watery ditch and fortified wall that used to divide the Old Town from the New Town in the Middle Ages.)

There are too many interesting buildings and stories here, so we'll just focus on a few of the significant art nouveau landmarks, and include **Saint Wenceslas's equestrian statue** near the upper part of the square. The patron saint of the land was sculpted by Myslbek, the top traditionalist of Czech public monuments, yet not wholly uninfluenced by Rodin and the French school. Starting in 1887, the statue took fourteen years of the artist's life, and the four figures, representing Czech saints, surrounding the pedestal were still incomplete (though he actually executed a number of models for the work) when he died in 1922. Wenceslas (Václav)—yes, of the Christmas carol—is also honored as the patron saint and founder of the Czech state, which he ruled until his murder in 935 by his brother Boleslav the Cruel, whose men trapped Wenceslas in a church where he had sought sanctuary. The manner of his departure undoubtedly contributed to the vivid sacred and nationalist mythology in which his name is forever wreathed. The hero's statue has long been a witness to the victories and tragedies of the nation, and many of the victims of the Communist period are remembered in the makeshift memorial area a bit farther down from the monument. This is where stunned Praguers vented their outrage during the 1968 invasion of Warsaw Pact troops, where tanks and weapons mowed some of them down, and where the student Jan Palách set himself on fire six months later to protest the crackdown. Prague Spring, the short-lived though intoxicating period that sparked these horrors, was an experiment in democratic reforms that strove to create a new socialist model along the lines of Czech humanist traditions. It was led by the sympathetic Alexander Dubček, who, though a lifelong Communist, valiantly defied the Soviets but couldn't stop them from intervening. (In Moscow they perceived not a reform program but a revolution, which of course it was.) A nation and its people were demoralized for another twenty years. Then, at a rally commemorating the twentieth anniversary of Palách's self-immolation, Václav Havel, the gentle rebel armed with the terrifying power of the word, was arrested—again. It was not until November 1989, when the writing was on almost all the walls of Central and Eastern Europe, that the Communists finally read it, folded their tents, and snuck away.

Today the statue is a favorite soapbox and rallying point for scores of Praguers who have things they need to get off their chest. Layabouts, retirees, exhibitionists, and serious activists alike come here to act out, argue about the state of their world, and simply opine. Since these people were silenced for fifty-odd years and isolated from the outside world and from one another, you can imagine the traffic and the heat that is generated here on some days.

Returning to fin-de-siecle Prague, the **Grand Hotel Evropa** on the eastern side of the square, near Saint Wenceslas, is the most irresistibly charming art nouveau confection in the metropolis, besides being the most captivating, fundamentally unrestored, and therefore slightly rundown hostelry. And as interesting as it looks on the outside, it's the luxuriously embellished interior that justifies the "jewel box" cliché so often used to describe it, and that warrants your attention. You can give it that and refresh yourself in the café at the same time, a tradition enjoyed by so many people on such a presumably regular basis that on my last visit the management was collecting a (modest) cover charge. Or perhaps that's a ploy to keep out the riffraff. The clientele is a mixed bag of ordinary Praguers and tourists. Vintage 1906, the Evropa is a joining of two hotels, hence its asymmetrical facade, whose coloring and elaboration project the comforting warmth and decoration for their own sake so loved and admired by the human soul. The wooden bow windows, for example, are the modified bay windows of folk architecture, part of a desire to root building styles in intimacy and local history. I recommend walking through the lobby and going upstairs, noting the highly wrought art nouveau details of the polished rosewood walls inlaid with ebony and mother-of-pearl, the stair rails and balustrades, the lighting fixtures (the latter visible close-up from the handsome second-floor café). At the back of the first floor (behind the bar), is the cozy, elegant French Restaurant. Don't miss the rose marble fireplace and, above it, the lurid, backlit, contrastingly kitschy mural of Prague's postcard river-valley setting. In its former incarnation as the Grand Hotel Šroubek, the Evropa was the setting for part of Bohumil Hrabal's coming-of-age novel, *I Served the King of England*. (Hrabal is one of the best Czech writers whose work has been published in English.) The dining room, by the way, is said to be a replica of the one on the Titanic, made for the ship-loving owner Mr. Šroubek in the same Parisian workrooms.

Our final stop will be at Jan Kotěra's **Petrkův House, no. 12**, on the lower left-hand side of the square. Not just another art nouveau building, it was an early (1899) milestone in the evolution of local art nouveau synthesis and innovation and started the ball rolling on further pos-

Jan Kotěra's Petrkův House, Wenceslas Square

sibilities of the style in Prague modernism. Trees all but camouflage the Petrkův, so you'll have to step back and crane upward to view this classic. Though not the first art nouveau building in Prague—that was the Café Corso on Na příkopě, which didn't survive the twenties—Kotěra's first major work achieved the most felicitous equilibrium of ornamentation and function yet seen in the city. The decorative aspects here became secondary, though complementary, to the total work of art, in which Kotěra first considered the building's purpose and organized its space accordingly. For example, the large storefront windows were a novelty, as were the frameless upper-story windows. The stucco detailing is relatively light and subtle and, along with the walls, of subdued coloring; vertical lines and the facade's arrangement into three balanced sections were also important. Unadulterated, lyrical, it seemed an eon from historicism—compare it to Wiehl's 1896 painted Czech renaissance building less than a block away, on the corner of Vodičkova and Wenceslas Square—but less distant from the constructivism to which Kotěra was headed.

Our walk ends here, but if you have time and can't get enough of art nouveau, I recommend walking down Na příkopě to Polívka's **Municipal House** (**Obecní Dům**), an extravagant, exultant space on náměstí Republiky, to see the largest and most complex example of the style in Prague. The café and restaurant are architectural treats, but so is the building as a whole, especially the intricately detailed interior public spaces. And if you haven't already stopped for a meal or a snack, this might be the time and the place.

Walk · 5

From the Emperor's Vineyards to His New Town

VINOHRADY AND NOVÉ MĚSTO

Apollinářská Street, New Town

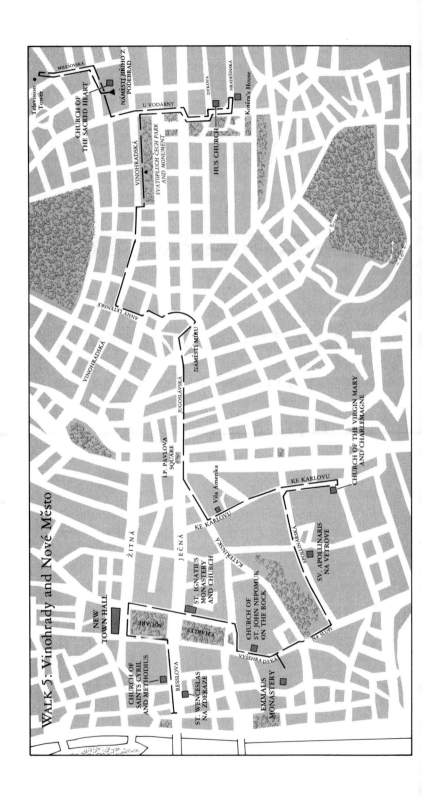

WALK 5: Vinohrady and Nové Město

Starting Point: Jiřího z Poděbrad Square in the Vinohrady district. This walk is best on a Sunday (or any holiday), timed to arrive at the Church of the Virgin Mary and Charlemagne between 2:00 P.M. and 5:15 P.M. (The church is open only on Sundays.) However, the walk can also be profitably done on weekdays, when the neighborhood is most alive.

Metro/Tram Lines: Metro Green Line A or trams 9, 26, or 5.

Length of Walk: As this is the longest walk, where the sights are the most spread out, budget at least three and a half hours to complete it. Otherwise it is a fairly easy walk with only a few (short) ascending stretches.

This is another walk that takes you out of the center of the city—to Vinohrady, a largely middle-class residential neighborhood where the historical associations are of more recent vintage and somewhat more scattered than in the Old Town, but still make for a rich repast, and where I venture you will meet hardly any of your fellow visitors. Yet it's easily accessible from the heart of the city. From Vinohrady we will explore a contiguous district as laminated by history as any other in Prague, the

New Town (Nové Město), which was founded in the 1300s: nothing "new" about it. Also in the interest of crowd avoidance, this is a good walk for a spring or summer weekend, or any good-weather weekend, because many Praguers escape the urban madness for their *chatas* (country cottages), so you will have the tree-shaded streets to yourself. (This is not true in the center, where tourists gravitate.)

At **náměstí Jiřího z Poděbrad** (or **náměstí Jiřího**, as it's known locally), you'll find yourself on a spacious grassy square at the edge of Vinohrady. First, however, we'll cross over briefly into the bordering district of Žižkov, a working-class district with numerous Romany residents, known across Europe as Gypsies. (Originating in India, they have lived on the continent for hundreds of years, and you will see lots of them around town.) Žižkov is named for one Jan Žižka of Trocnov, the one-eyed military genius and rugged warrior second in Czech remembrance only to Jan Hus, in whose name he led ferocious armies of Hussites, often outnumbered but never defeated, against imperial Roman Catholic crusaders bent on eradicating their heresy. Žižkov used to be named Vítkov Hill, a former battleground on which Žižka won two victories; but more about the proud, homegrown Hussites later. Žižkov is also the birthplace of Nobel Prize–winning poet Jaroslav Seifert and was a cauldron of local Communist Party support for much of this century.

But don't worry—it's peaceful enough at the moment, and we won't have to venture far into the neighborhood to visit that awesome anomaly in thousand-year-old Prague that you already see sticking into the stratosphere just north of you, the space-age **Radio and Television Tower**. If you like heights and sweeping panoramic views thrill you, the tower may be of special, if unexpected, interest. So let's head via Milěsovská Street (north of the square) in the direction of the Tower (also known as the **Žižkovska věz**), which stands in Mahlerovy Sady, the green surrounding it. Six hundred eighty-three feet tall, looking like a colossal needle, or something the Soviet space agency might have plotted during its wildest interplanetary-warfare dreams, the tower was not innocently conceived. On the pretext of improving television reception, it was designed (by a Prague Communist Party committee apparatchik) to throw a giant blanket of obstruction over the region, jamming Western airwave transmissions, particularly Austrian and West German television signals.

Entrance to the tower as of this writing is twenty-five crowns for Czechs and twice that for others. The elevators are high speed, of course, and they whisk you up to two different levels with viewing areas on all sides. If the visibility is good (hardly a sure bet in Prague even on sunny days) and you're not afraid of heights, you may be able to pick out some landmarks in the Old Town and Hradčany northwest of here; Žižkov is at your feet to the north and Vinohrady to the south. The tower also has a restaurant and a snack bar; they open at 10:00 A.M., so you could try a late breakfast. What you won't find up here in the pale-blue ether is a lot of other people, since the tower's sinister origins have not endeared it to Praguers and most tourists don't know about it or are attracted only to Prague's historical patina—well, thank God this *is* history.

On terra firma again, retrace your steps back to Vinohrady and the square named for the much-admired king of Bohemia, George of Poděbrady. After Emperor Charles IV, he is probably the most popular monarch in Czech history (along with Wenceslas I, patron saint of the land). But George was a hero foremost because he was king of the Hussites, those indigenous Czech religious rebels whose memory is cherished by Czech nationalists of almost any stripe. They started a revolution when they separated from the Roman Catholic Church, with whom they disagreed about certain ancient practices. One of the big issues, though seemingly a mere technicality to our thinking today, was the taking of communion in both kinds—that is, whether congregants would be allowed to drink the wine, symbol of Christ's blood (then always reserved for the presiding priest), as well as eat the bread. For this the Hussites were also called Utraquists (from *sub specie utraque*, which means "in both kinds") and the (wine) chalice became their symbol. They also believed that the Bible was the final arbiter of the word of God and no intermediaries, including the Roman Church, were necessary. Hardly just a technicality in the eyes of Christendom's most powerful institution, this conviction represented dangerously subversive insubordination. These were some of the key differences for which Jan Hus was burned at the stake in 1415. The pacific King George, under whom the country prospered economically because he reestablished peace and order, also tried to free politics from the influence of religion. Medieval Bohemia became the first country in Europe where religious toleration was guaranteed by law, a whole century before the Edict of Nantes (1598), that thunderously significant decree halting the religious warfare that had been such a staple of French life and death.

So now you know why this square is named after King George. I told you about him because he was an important figure in Czech history and this walk later penetrates deeply into Hussite territory, not because of any associations he has with the square or even the neighborhood. Those belong to Josip Plečnik, the Slovenian architect of the parish **Church of the Sacred Heart of the Lord** (**Kostel Nejsvětejšího Srdce Páně**), which completely commands this simple park. Though Plečnik is better known for his remodeling and design work at Prague Castle—including the graceful, timeless, Greek-inspired furniture of the Gold Salonek that he created for long-stemmed Tomáš Masaryk—this church, designed in 1928 and completed three years later, is arguably the most remarkable example of modern architecture in Prague, one that has held up better over the years for its freshness and stunning boldness than most other structures that fall into the various modernist slots, of which there are many. The idea of the gargantuan glass clock set like a window into the equally dominating tower that extends across the entire breadth of the structure foreshadows plans for the new Staten Island ferry terminal in Manhattan—without the neon. (The clock also brings to mind the regulation rose windows of Gothic cathedrals.) For a sui generis twist on the usual top-of-the-tower vista, you can actually ascend and view from a platform across the window the panorama of Prague Castle framed by the clock face's circumference. (Entrance is around the side.)

Josip Plečnik was the opposite of the typical all-powerful swaggering figure of an architect (the calling does leave a few traces, after all). He is defended by aficionados as a philosopher steeped in history and art and a man of deep faith, admired for his humility and profound respect for the Castle and the challenge posed by restoring a monument so loaded down by age and tradition. Architecture apparently had a more profound meaning for Plečnik: he viewed it as a religious confession whereby he expressed the spiritual essence of his being. Perhaps that is why he never paid much attention to architectural theory but trained intensely in the classical styles of Greece and Rome. His very presence in Prague as chief architect of the Castle (1920–34) was controversial, mainly because he was not Czech. Appointed by President Masaryk at the recommendation of Jan Kotěra, the key figure in Czech modernism, with whom he had studied in Vienna under Otto Wagner, Plečnik endured a steady barrage of nationalist criticism. Eventually he retreated to his native Ljubljana in Slovenia and continued to design and teach. The consecration of Sacred Heart Church has been compared to that of the basilica on Montmartre in Paris—an expression of gratitude for the attainment of the nation's independence. Architecturally, the building gives the impression of having been inspired by the forceful statements of some Italian monastery churches or the classical temples of antiquity—the original plans called for surrounding it with Greek-style columns. A prismatically shaped rectangular structure, with wide open single-chambered sanctuary, the main altar is white marble, and the decor art displays Byzantine motifs.

From the church we will walk to the westernmost end of the square through a stretch of Vinohrady down to the New Town. The district was formerly called the Royal Vineyards because since the days of Charles IV the terrain was planted with rows of grape vines—*vinohrady* means "vineyard"—and was owned by the Crown, the aristocracy, the Church, and a few wealthy burghers. The fortified walls and watchtowers of the medieval city were the frontier, and until the mid–nineteenth century this area was all gardens, farmsteads, and orchards. Some of the streets had names referring to farm produce and barn creatures, like Svinská (Swine Street). Of this vast natural preserve, only two extensive former garden sites remain, converted to public parks. While the architecture is almost entirely nineteenth-century pseudohistorical, based on architectural styles of previous centuries, the development of such a large area of new buildings, outfitted with the latest (nineteenth-century) comforts and conveniences, as compared to the cramped medieval sections of town, made Vinohrady a desirable suburb of the well-to-do. You can see that in the expansive layout of the wide, leafy streets lined with handsome mansion-like apartment houses. Invariably the apartments featured high ceilings, generous, light-spilling windows, and spacious rooms; most apartment buildings came with equally spacious tree-shaded courtyards. It was not unheard of for the wealthiest to own an entire apartment building, live on two floors, rent out a floor or two until a daughter or son married, and then give them a floor—family togetherness being far more common in those days. The owner, if a professional, might have his office under the same roof, along with rooms for the household help, of course.

Of special interest to history-of-architecture buffs will be our next stop, a landmark of Prague modernism, architect Jan Kotěra's own family villa at **no. 6 Hradešínksá Street**. So before we continue down through Vinohrady, let's head south via U Vodarny Street (to your left as you exit Plečnik's church), past the secessionist water tower on the corner of Korunní Street. The Kotěra house stands near the edge of Bezruč Park (Bezručový Sady), a pleasant green refuge on a street of potentially highly attractive, presently shabby, private homes. The founder of Czech modernism's abode was so sadly run down the first time I saw it, I nearly walked right by, even though I knew from published photographs what it looked like. Built on a steep slope, with a terrace to take advantage of the view over the valley below, the house is an early (1908) but already remarkably advanced document of Czech functionalist architecture. All purely decorative elements have been eliminated, replaced by the raw building materials—brick and mortar—that characterized Kotěra's work at the time and that focused all attention on the building's purely structural features. The severe angular lines are softened solely by the semicircular canopy over the covered entrance passageway.

On the way to Hradešínská Street you will have passed another modernist church on the corner of Dykova, the **Hus Congregation of the Czechoslovak Church**. Not most people's idea of a house of worship, it's a factory-drab, typically constructivist creation of strict architectural severity, with a hollow, skeletal bell tower. The church was designed by Pavel Janák in 1930. Notice the verdigrised copper chalice, symbol of the fighting Hussites, atop the tower. The large memorial slab on the wall ("Raise the Barricades—Help Prague") refers to this church's truly sanctuarial role during the final days of the Nazi retreat at the end of World War II, when it riskily harbored radio microphones and broadcasters. On May 5, 1945, the Czechoslovak radio broadcasting organization rallied the whole country to drive out its German oppressors: "Calling all Czechs . . ." Radio technicians concealed their hardware behind the church altar and announcers continued to transmit from what became Studio X. How they linked up their equipment and cables and telephone lines to the church from the government-controlled broadcast building several blocks away on Vinohradská Street, amid street fighting and desperate Nazi artillery barrages, is no small wonder. Wires were strung on tree branches and residents' private phone lines were commandeered. Later the radio men burrowed underground into the church's crypt. Unlike the bombed-out studios, flooded cellars (to flush out German soldiers), and bullet-riddled walls of the main building, for which there was a major battle and many died, this one sustained relatively little damage: no makeshift street barricades had to be dismantled, no bodies carted away. . . . Broadcasts continued for four days, until the end of the uprising; and the clandestine activity was never discovered or betrayed.

Twenty-three years later, on August 21, 1968, the year from hell for revolutions worldwide, it was the turn of the Soviet-led Warsaw Pact armies to train their guns and tanks on the main radio building, wreaking murder and mayhem in the streets. But in vain did the airwaves rally the country this time. The Czechs never had a chance. It's worth noting that Czech radio was among the first on the continent to begin broadcast operations, in 1923. According to a French source, it was just one year after the official inauguration of the London transmission station, when France had only the Eiffel Tower, when the German transmitter at Königswüsterhausen was operating on a trial basis and Vienna was still building its small tower, that Prague was already providing regular daily broadcast services. Soon after, Smetana's opera *The Two Widows* was transmitted from the National Theater, the first opera to be broadcast in Europe; later, the first full program of concerts was broadcast.

Now we'll walk back to **Vinohradská Street** (two

blocks north of the Hus church—you could walk through Bezruč Park near Hradešínská, if you wish) and continue down it via the narrow stretch of **Svatopluch Čech Park**, between Vinohradská and Slezská streets. You will come to a memorial sculpture of the nineteenth-century literary figure, a poet, after whom the park is named. The work is a joint 1924 effort of architect Pavel Janák and sculptor Jan Štursa and has been criticized for its placement in a neighborhood unrelated to the subject. Čech liked to ferret in the philosophical depths of historical themes and wrote an early epic poem based on Žižka's extermination campaign against the Adamites, the most extreme religious cult to sprout from the Hussite movement. The Adamites practiced an early form of communism, believing that everything should be shared, including women, that marriage was sinful and clothes were unnatural.

At **Peace Square** (**náměstí Míru**) you will be in the commercial heart of Vinohrady. To get there, walk straight ahead on Vinohradská, then turn left on **Anny Letenské Street** (you could take the more direct Slezská from the park, but Vinohradská is a far more attractive street). You will arrive at the square via Šubertova Street and the back of the Vinohrady Theater. First we'll stop at the grandiose hulk of the Railway Workers Cultural Center at **no. 9**, which has recently reverted to its original name, **Národní Dům** (**National House**). A number of these municipal buildings were erected near the turn of the century, of which the Obecni Dům (Municipal House) on Na příkopě Street is the largest and most famous, particularly for its restaurant, café, and brilliant art nouveau architecture and decoration. There's an inexpensive restaurant and café and a wine bar at this municipal house too, and you might want to take a rest stop here. Otherwise there's not much to see, unless you're besotted by very late-nineteenth-century Neo-Renaissance architecture, interiors bedecked with elaborate plasterwork, and the mural art of an era already gone by when this building was conceived. In that case you might want to wander up the broad staircase to the top floor and look around. The place is spaciously laid out with grand ballrooms and public meeting facilities. When the government was privatizing and auctioning off small businesses and real estate following the 1989 restoration of democracy, this is where the action was. A few valuable historic properties went under the hammer to the buzz of media attention and busloads of respectful gawkers and budding capitalists who crowded into these upper halls and corridors to witness the proceedings. Otherwise this is a kind of social center where you can also take inexpensive dancing, sewing, exercise, and other classes, with a program of just as reasonably priced concerts and entertainments.

In the center of the square stands the pseudo-Gothic (Northern German–style) **Parish Church of St. Ludmila**, built 1888–93. This dark brick construction is more often cited for its technical architectural qualities than for its artistic success. The tympanum above the main portal, depicting saints Wenceslas and Ludmila, is by Jan Václav Myslbek, a key Prague sculptor of the period whose work we have seen on the previous walk. And the church's twin spires do suitably dominate the square. Depending on the weather, the benches in the park around the building are most likely to be occupied by local pensioners and their grandchildren, chatting and basking in the sun or cooling off under the trees. You might like to join them. On the northern side of the square sits the cream-colored, richly ornamented **Vinohrady Theater** (1904–07), an impressive secessionist creation that has traditionally offered some of the highest-rated Czech productions in town from an eclectic international repertoire that now includes some big Broadway musicals.

From the relatively peaceful square we'll continue our walk straight down **Jugoslávská Street**, which runs off the square's lower center, past náměstí I.P. Pavlova, where the street becomes **Ječná**, often a virtual one-way highway of streaming traffic, and turn left on **Kateřinská**, if it's open, then left again on **Ke Karlovu**. (If Kateřinská is blocked, turn left a bit farther down onto Ke Karlovu.) The street is named after the Church of the Virgin Mary and Charlemagne at its very end. You will find yourself in the secluded, hushed world of Charles University's medical faculties and hospitals. This is a neighborhood that Albert Einstein got to know well when he lived here and taught at the university in 1911 as professor of theoretical physics, taking time off now and then to join friends in Prague's German-Jewish community. In the eighteenth century, however, this area was nothing but country fields and gardens until a wealthy, aristocratic family, the Jan Václav Michnas of Vacínov, built an exquisite summer pavilion here. Rumor has it that for a time Count Michna used the house as a trysting hideaway for his mistress.

Later the house changed hands several times. In 1826 it was a garden restaurant and pub with a German medical student clientele; it was baptized Amerika, because the area was considered so far out it was like the new American frontier. The name stuck, and it's still called the **Vila Amerika**, the baroque gem you see behind the finely wrought iron gates on the left side of the street, at **čp. 462-II**. The house might almost be dwarfed by the taller surrounding structures except for its garden and outstanding beauty. The count had called on Kilián Ignác Dientzenhofer, the most promising young architect of his day, to draw up the plans. It was Dientzenhofer's first secular commission, begun shortly after his return to Prague from Vienna in 1717, following a ten-year study-tour of contemporary European architecture, principally in Vienna. It shows the influence of the esteemed Viennese architect Lucas Hildebrandt, designer of Vienna's Belvedere, with whom Dientzenhofer had trained. (Hildebrandt in turn had picked up in France the flat, delicately executed, ornamental forms he favored.) Faithful to the dictates of baroque symmetry in all elements, the two small pavilions, with the larger center one, form a

Vila Amerika on Ke Karlovu Street

diminutive, open *cour d'honneur*, a kind of staging area for reviewing troops that is common to palatial landscape architecture. But while the decorative architectural features of the house are Hildebrandtian, the whole effect is achieved with Czech motifs, such as the dormer window set in a gallery on the mansard roof. In the lightness and delicacy of the work's decorative forms, you can sense a breath of rococo. The sculptures in the back, representing the four seasons, are from the workshop of Matthias Braun; the two figures in front are of Hercules, by an unknown artist.

The Vila Amerika stands across the street from a psychiatric institute whose residents have been known to wander over and request postcards or selections of Czech composer Antonin Dvořák's music "in stereo, please." From 1953 to 1955 the villa was acquired by the Antonin Dvořák Society, which converted it to a museum honoring the composer. Though neither the house nor the street have any immediate connection with Dvořák, it's a delightful destination not only for lovers of Prague baroque, but for music lovers, who can enjoy the bright and intimate upstairs salon with buoyantly frescoed walls and ceiling (by Jan Ferdinand Schor). You can sit and listen to Dvořák's recorded music or attend the concerts often held there. If you haven't already had a respite, this would be an ideal place to relax. The personal memorabilia on exhibit include the composer's academic cap and gown that he wore when he received an honorary degree from Cambridge University in 1891; furniture from the Dvořák apartment on nearby Žitná Street (which we will pass later); a piano, viola, and assorted smaller items; and facsimiles of some of his most important scores. (Music-lore passionists and pilgrims are also advised to visit Dvořák's hometown of Nelahozeves on the Vltava river, only thirty-three kilometers from Prague; I recommend going by boat along the river, a delightful cruise.)

Antonin Dvořák probably doesn't need much of an

introduction, since he is one of the most popular composers of classical music who ever lived, his works standards of the world repertoire. Perhaps it is only slightly
less well known that he wrote one of his masterpieces,
the "New World Symphony," in New York City when
he lived and taught there from 1892 to 1895, as well as
the extremely tuneful Humoresque in G-flat major, the
famous cello concerto, and several other splendid works.
Dvořák felt that his mission to the New World was not
to interpret Beethoven or Wagner for the public, but, as
he said, to "discover what young Americans had in them
and to help them express it." This was a time when
Americans felt they could boast of few native composers
and themes. Dvořák's New York sponsors, seeing in him
a self-made man and composer of nationalistic music,
hoped he would help them develop some. And so he
did, if indirectly and only to prove that great music could
be written in America and to point out the genuine
sources of American idioms. Though his immediate students didn't see it, among the Negro spirituals and native
themes of America Dvořák discovered "all that is needed
for a great and noble school of music."

As much as Dvořák relished his stays in America,
he was also terribly homesick. It is worth noting that
wherever he was, Dvořák was distinguished by his
homespun family life. Unlike several of the giants of
nineteenth-century European music who were prone to
depression, conflict, solitariness, and even misanthropy,
Dvořák was usually surrounded by a devoted wife,
(ultimately) nine children, and a gaggle of relatives. By
1895 he was back in Prague writing the operas and symphonic poems that spoke so eloquently of his love for
his country.

Music had long been a key cultural export of the
Czechs; it almost made up for whatever may have been
lacking in world stature of the nation's early literary out-
put. Czechs were said to be the most musical people of
Europe, so musical that, according to legend, within reach

Emperor Charles IV at Church of the Virgin
Mary and Charlemagne

of every newborn child was placed a silver spoon and a
fiddle. If the baby lunged for the spoon, his future as a
merchant—or a thief—was assured. If it was the fiddle
that snagged his gaze, well, of course, what else could
any Czech infant overflowing with *amour propre* possibly
want?

From here we'll walk to the very end of unruffled Ke
Karlovu Street (it means To Charles's), lined on both sides

by turn-of-the-century and older medical buildings, and enter, via the wrought-iron gate, the grounds of another Prague landmark seldom visited by tourists, the **Church of the Virgin Mary and Charlemagne** (1377). You saw its red dome and triple spires, all three with the red cupolas, from a distance at the start of Walk 4. With good planning, you will have arrived during the Sunday opening hours. There are a great many churches in Prague, and four founded by Emperor Charles IV, of which this is one of two monastery churches, but none like this. Augustinian, at first, it was designed to be sacred to the memory of Charles IV's patron, Charlemagne, and meant to recall his octagonally shaped burial church in Aachen (Aix-la-Chapelle).

Since no one knows who the original architect of the church was, one of those lugubrious, magic-laced stories arose to fill the vacuum. It's about a young architect, a neophyte named Bohuslav Stanek, known as the Velvet One, whose dreams came crashing down though his creation didn't. To wed the maiden he loved according to her father's wishes that he achieve something of distinction, young Stanek labored long and hard and succeeded in persuading the emperor to let him build a church with a daringly conceived vault. (*Stan*, by the way, means "tent," which was the original shape of the church's soaring late-Gothic roof and later became a popular local style of building.) Meanwhile a rival for the hand of Stanek's sweetheart appeared and was turned down by her. So the rejected suitor hatched a plot to ruin Stanek's budding reputation: he bribed the workmen into declaring the new church vault unsafe, liable to collapse. On the very day the emperor was to arrive for a viewing, they refused to take the scaffolding down. The young architect got so upset, he broke out in a fever; then a fire mysteriously erupted on the scaffolding. In the confusion, and presumably on schedule, the workmen caused an uproar, and the architect, on the verge of heart failure, ran away, sure he'd been disgraced. Though the vault stayed put, its creator vanished, not to reappear for thirty years; meanwhile stories were circulating about how he'd made a pact with the devil to sustain the vault. When an aged and worn-out Stanek learned that his heartbroken betrothed had entered a convent, dying soon after, he found her grave at the church and expired on top of it.

Indeed, the magnificently ribbed, star-shaped vaulted ceiling is the star attraction here: the enormous eight-pointed star is repeatedly divided into smaller areas overlaid with gilded, stuccoed Gothic lilies and two varieties of acanthus leaves. The ceiling, and the structure as a whole, is also a relatively rare example (in Prague, as opposed to other parts of Bohemia) of the new and unique hybrid of Gothic and baroque styles invented by one of the outstanding indigenous Italians, Jan Santini Aichel, who worked on the church in the early eighteenth century, when it became a major pilgrimage destination. Additions were then made to the monastery complex, though the ceiling is attributed to Boniface Wohlmut and the date of its keystone is fairly precisely set at 1575. The softly luminous intricacy of the gold-and-red ceiling undoubtedly recalls the era of Peter Parler, genius of the Prague Gothic, and the decorative elements of St. Wenceslas chapel in St. Vitus Cathedral. A kind of captivating, lavishly conceived sacred Gothic glow emanates from both. The two side altars here are flamboyantly baroque with faux marbling; the Neo-Gothic main altar, on the other hand, is almost austere. Richly theatrical is the life-sized plasticity and animation of the figures on the balconies over the entrance and the staircase on the opposite side. That staircase, an unusual feature in Prague churches, is supposed to be a reference to the so-called "sacred stairs" of St. John Lateran, the cathedral church of Rome, said to have been brought from Jerusalem, where they led to Pilate's judgment table. Under the stairs is one of the early-eighteenth-century additions, a kind of grotto or cave meant to resemble the one the Christ child was born in, though I thought he was supposed to have been born in a manger. You can see this and the subterranean chapel of the Holy Nativity by exiting the sanctuary through a door opposite the main entrance, opening another door in the arcade on your immediate left marked "Bethlehem," and descending a stone staircase. This is particularly popular at Christmastime, of course, but though well lit, the frescoes and illusionist stuccowork have faded considerably.

Once you've seen the church, do walk around the park to the back and view the Nusle Valley to gauge how high up you are on one of Prague's seven hills. This one is actually higher by about ten meters than the one under Vyšehrad, whose twin spires you can spot on the other side. The adjoining monastery buildings now house a Police Museum with exhibitions that I recommend only to the most ardent fans of police work—unless they bring back (it was mothballed after wowing the public in post-revolutionary days) the perversely fascinating display of secret-service surveillance paraphernalia that was used on dissidents during the Communist period. There is, however, a snack bar in the courtyard through the museum entrance hall as well as restroom facilities.

From here we can retrace our steps on Ke Karlovu two blocks and turn left at the mysterious-looking eggplant-colored brick structure on the corner into **Apollinářská Street**. This building, despite the Gothic oriel window, is—guess what? A maternity hospital. You'll hardly pass a soul on this tranquil, tree-lined street as you walk down the hill to **Na slupi Street**. On the way, on the left, obscured behind the trees, stands a large fourteenth-century Gothic church called **Sv. Apollinaris Na Vetrově**. In 1419 a Hussite delegation approached King Wenceslas IV at this church and peacefully presented its demands, but the king wasn't listening and ordered the group leader's arrest and expulsion from Prague. The bland-looking church on the corner of Na Slupi is a rather uncharacteristic Kilián Ignác Dientzenhofer building of minor interest, unlike our next stop farther up on **Vyšehradská Street**, also a Dientzenhofer church, Saint John Nepomuk on the Rock. However, before we talk about that one, we'll go and see the church and monastery complex opposite, **Church of the Virgin Mary Na Slovanech**, also called **Emmaus**.

You've already seen the modern intersecting spires of the fourteenth-century Gothic church from the riverbank on our Walk 4. It's no accident, by the way, that most of these houses of worship are located on or near this street, Vyšehradská, because this is the ancient route from the Old Town to the Vyšehrad fortress, and later became a fixed axis of the New Town. The Benedictine monastery here was strategically placed for its educational mission, formulated by Emperor Charles IV in 1347 with the Pope's blessing, of spreading the liturgy in the old Slavic language, because the population did not understand Latin. Geopolitics were more to the point: the idea was to solidify ecclesiastical bonds with the Eastern Church, as well as relations with states of the Slavic world. Monks were imported from Croatia, Bosnia, and Dalmatia, where the Slavic liturgy existed along with the Latin, and Charles even wrote to the king of Serbia in kinship. The traditions of early Slavic saints, such as the Greek apostles Cyril and Methodius, who arrived in Bohemia around 863 with a Glagolithic (the ancient alphabet of the Western Slavs, also called Cyrillic) Bible, also meant a lot to the emperor. The monastery opened officially in 1372 in his presence, but the name Emmaus arose later; it refers to the day that Christ (following his crucifixion and the empty-tomb event) revealed himself to two of his disciples on the road from Jerusalem to the village of Emmaus. Biblical scholars have pointed out that Emmaus, like Nazareth, was a nondescript location elevated to wondrous meaning.

This monastery has shared more generously than most in the erratic highs and lows of Czech history. Up until the Hussite thunderstorms it was a distinguished nucleus of learning; its famous cloister wall murals (on

our itinerary) were created at the zenith of the Czech
Gothic period. Also from this period is the Glagolithic
section of the so-called Rheims Gospel, a sacred printed
work that, some time after 1546, got into the hands of
the French monarchy and was used to administer the
coronation oath in Rheims Cathedral. In 1419 the Emmaus Benedictines, quickly assessing their proximity to
the fire and knowing they wouldn't have a nanosecond
of peace, didn't miss a beat and went over to the Hussites. In so doing theirs became the one and only Utraquist
(Hussite) monastery in Bohemia. In the seventeenth century, following the disastrous Battle of White Mountain,
a new group of Benedictines from Spain moved in and,
predictably, "baroquicized" the place, wiping out all traces
of the heretical religion. Then in 1880 German Benedictines re-Gothicized it. Not much else to report until February 14, 1945, and this time it was bombers of the Allied
air forces who remodeled. By mistake. Their mission was
to find Nazis. Finally, a few months later, in May, it was
the not-quite-dead Germans who left their unmistakable
mark: prior to their final retreat, they shelled what the
Allies had left. World War II damage in Prague was vicious but minor compared to that sustained by other,
truly razed, European cities, but Emmaus got the cata-
strophic worst of it. The huge church, one of the largest
in the city, was almost entirely bombed out, and interior
restoration remains skeletal. The monastery buildings
were also badly injured, in part irreparably so. And
the Communists? They threw everybody out and filled
the monastery with the offices of a scientific institute. The
latest group of Benedictines, now returned, is, of course,
fixing things up.

Entering the grounds, turn left and walk to the monastery building entrance. As of this writing, and since the
Benedictines' return, policy on visitors and opening hours
is unclear. If you can manage it, it's best not to stop at
the porter's booth—simply walk through as if you know
where you are going. This usually works, possibly be-

cause the place is not typically jammed with visitors. You will quickly find yourself in the glassed-in, Gothic-vaulted cloister. The wall frescoes are the most valuable sights here, in fact the most valuable of the period in the entire country. Unfortunately they were also one of the most grievously hurt victims of the bombing. Of a cycle of eighty-five scenes from the Old and New Testaments painted in 1362 by court artists, who also worked at the royal castle of Karlštejn, that used to cover all four walls nearly from floor to ceiling, a third were destroyed and the rest remain fragmentary. The church itself is used for art exhibitions these days; otherwise its future is uncertain. But you can see what a lavish space it used to be. When the decision was made not to rebuild the formerly Gothic towers, the ruins were removed and the present modern crossed steel-and-concrete wings designed by František M. Černý in 1966 were bravely erected instead. Architects see them as an important precedent for successfully imposing contemporary architectural forms on sacred-cow historical monuments.

Returning to the street from Emmaus, you'll get an arresting view of Kilián Ignác Dientzenhofer's **Church of Saint John Nepomuk on the Rock (Sv. Jan Nepomuckého na skalce)** across the street. You'll see why, to appreciate the imposing symmetry of its superb perch "on the rock," you have to step back and view from a distance this altogether slender, twin-towered baroque structure (1730–39). The effect is dramatized by the grand, crossed double-ramp staircase and the distinctively shaped and complex spires. Notice how, instead of merely flanking the central structure like the usual sentinels, the towers are set diagonally, creating a continuously curved facade. The church was built on the vineyard site of a seventeenth-century wooden chapel that belonged to the senior scribe of the royal revenue office. It's a curious matter of record that the church's layout, despite its sophisticated design, evokes that of the old chapel. The entrance to the church is from Charles Square through

Church of St. John Nepomuk on the Rock

the baroque gate and garden on the corner—if they're open. Chances are you won't be arriving in time for mass on Sundays and holidays at 7:30 A.M. (or 5:00 P.M. and 7:00 P.M. on Mondays and Thursdays), so you may not be able to enter unless the church fathers change their policies about keeping the church closed at other times. If you do get in, it will be worth it, for the interior is expansively frescoed and the art impressive, including on the main altar, for example, a 1682 statue of St. John Nepomuk in gold-plated wood by the celebrated sculptor Jan Brokoff.

At this point you might want to find a bench in the park you are now facing and rest while I tell you about this greened square. It might be said that **Charles Square (Karlovo náměstí)** was to the New Town what the Old Town Square still is to the Old Town, at least in terms of spirit and center of urban gravity. That's because the New Town, though larger and more populous, was politically overshadowed, for the most part, by the Old in feudal times. (As you may remember from Walk 1, the four independent towns, including Malá Strana and Hradčany, were not joined administratively to form the City of Prague until 1784; today they're districts.) The exception was the explosive Hussite period. The New Town's initial glory days were those of its founder, Charles IV (1346–78), but they continued through the Hussite turmoil, for this was the radical center of Hussite activity in Prague until the late fifteenth century. Charles IV's Prague was not only the capital of the Kingdom of Bohemia, but also of the very large Holy Roman Empire—then roughly and loosely the area of modern Germany, Austria, Holland, and Switzerland, besides Bohemia. Charles, as king of Bohemia and Holy Roman Emperor, was one of the most powerful monarchs of his time. Under his wise, pragmatic rule, marked by versatile diplomacy, common sense, and cultural stimulus, Bohemia entered its Golden Age and prospered as never before. The most international of rulers, he had grown up and was educated at the University of Paris and at the court of his uncle, Charles of France, in whose honor his Czech name of Wenceslas was changed. He also spent time in Germany and Italy and spoke all the languages of those lands, including, of course, Latin. On his mother's side he was Czech (she was a Přemyslid princess); as a member of the Luxembourg dynasty on his chivalrous father's side, he was closely tied to France, then the seat of the papacy at Avignon. Perhaps the memory of his mother was one reason he favored Prague as his seat of power, for he was said to be even more Czech in his sentiments than some of his Přemyslid ancestors. Several firsts punctuate the biography of Charles IV; for example, he was the first medieval Western sovereign to write his own biography. In this compelling, innovative document, written in Latin and translated upon his commission into Czech and German, the two vernaculars of his domain, he described personal experiences for their own sake, not in the service of his historical deification. In one episode, for example, he describes his sentiments upon returning to Bohemia after spending most of his childhood in France and having to learn Czech all over again. In another he tells of being awakened by a ghost. And he was the first to order an actual, thought-to-be-true likeness of himself and his family (he had four wives) instead of an idealized portrait symbolizing divine power. The sculpted heads can be seen on the triforium of St. Vitus Cathedral—a little high up, it's true, but copies are in several museums and at the Old Royal Palace on Hradčany.

Charles's appearance, according to an unflattering chronicler, was not one of overwhelming majesty—he was short, possibly hunchbacked, and bald. But his impact was far greater than that of most kings no matter their physical stature, for he started a massive rebuilding program and transformed Prague into a modern city of about 40,000 people, said to be greater than London or Paris at the time. He also made it an intellectual center of the Empire by establishing Central Europe's first university in 1348, which attracted scholars and humanists from all over the continent. The fertile intellectual soil that universities nourish also inevitably encouraged Hussite ferment.

One of the emperor's first decisions on ascending the throne in 1346 was to build a new town, including an improved system of fortified walls and watchtowers extending as far as Vyšehrad. He was particularly interested in creating new marketplaces and in redistributing craftsmen and skilled laborers from the Old Town. They settled here in great numbers, and it was mainly of this element, plus the lower nobility (whose motives had less to do with religious reform than with acquiring Church-owned land) and the poor that the Hussite warrior bands were comprised. It was also the most homogenously Czech of the towns; the others included more German residents. The broad streets and open spaces you see in the area today, as distinct from the narrow, labyrinthine lanes of the Old Town, were part of Charles's urban blueprint. All the Gothic churches and monasteries we've seen were built during those years, and Charles Square, one of Europe's biggest, became a major market center. Called the Cattle Market, it had the appearance of a barnyard—unpaved and uneven, muddy, dusty, debris littered. In the fifteenth century near the New Town Hall stood a huge two-tiered, wood-roofed pickling barn where dried and salted fish were sold. And in the center of the square stood a tower of plain wood, in amazing contrast to its rarified, simultaneously royal and public purpose, which was to annually display the crown jewels of Bohemia, ordered by Charles for his coronation, as well as the saintly relics in whose miraculous powers he believed.

On the second Friday following Easter the coronation jewels, whose centerpiece is the crown, a brilliantly barbaric-looking 22-carat gold creation with 96 bulging, polished, but unfaceted sapphires (one weighs 330 karats and is the world's third largest), plus rubies and other precious gems including 20 pearls, were brought here from their repository at Karlštejn (meaning Charles's Rock) Castle. Today they are housed in a safe in the chapel of St. Wenceslas at St. Vitus Cathedral and displayed on rare state occasions—only eight times this century, the most recent in January 1993, when the Czech Republic split with Slovakia. Seven state officials, starting with the president, hold keys to the seven locks, and all must be assembled to open the safe.

The curious choice of the Cattle Market for such a public exhibition is explained mainly by the size of the square: the annual event became a magnet for tens of thousands of pilgrims from all over the country and neighboring lands. The wooden tower was later replaced by an octagonal Gothic chapel named Body of God that stood until about two hundred years ago. In the mid nineteenth century the square was finally sodded and trees were planted to make the park you see today, partly because at the time it was felt the city didn't have enough green public spaces.

Up until the middle of the nineteenth century the only buildings still standing directly on Charles Square were the Town Hall, Faust House, and the Church of St. Ignác and its monastery. And those are still the most interesting structures today, so let's start our walk around the square at **Faust House** (**Faustův Dům**), turning right onto it next to the garden entrance to St. John Nepomuk on the Rock. (If you've been sitting in the park, retrace your steps to the corner of Vyšehradská Street.) The brass plates on Faust House say "Lékárna" ("Pharmacy") because it's now part of Charles University's medical faculty. Though it looks innocent enough, this comely late-baroque building, whose nucleus is actually Gothic and, later, Renaissance (as you can see by the bay window addition on its right side) is among the most legend-larded and mystically obscured in Prague. It is associated with the old Dr. Faustus story, though it never belonged to anyone by that name. Still, the list of owners and tenants is bizarre enough.

In the fourteenth century a courtier named Prince Wenceslas Opavsky installed in the building an alchemist's lab, which came in handy for the next tenant, one Edward Kelley, a Brit from Lancaster, a charlatan who had persuaded Emperor Rudolf II he could brew gold and caused various sensations around town until he was finally arrested. In 1770 one Mladota of Solopysk took the house over and started tinkering with chemical experiments, which really started the witchcraft stories piling up like ghosts after midnight: it was whispered that he had made a pact with the devil. The building's location at the edge of the square probably fed and elaborated the graveyard myths, for hand in hand with illegal anti-Catholic fervor the square developed the reputation of attracting conjurers and dealers in souls, grave robbers, secret gatherings and executions—perfect pickings for demonic spirits and a perfect spot from which to pick mandrake herbs for the laboratory.

From here we'll stay on the right and walk around the eastern side of the square. Our next stop is the baroque **Church of St. Ignatius (Sv. Ignác)**, named for St. Ignatius of Loyola, founder of the Jesuit order, and located at the end of the former New Town Jesuit College on the corner of Ječná Street. The two-story early-baroque college that borders the whole lower eastern half of the square has a particularly handsome portal. St. Ignatius is a typically elaborated baroque church (1665–71) probably designed by Carlo Lurago, who did a lot of work for the Jesuits, though some sources list Domenico Orsi as architect. Inside, the pink marble and gray colors of the interior are vivid, but the gray shades may actually be ivory white turned dirty, an effect no doubt encouraged by the lighting, for the deeply carved and encrusted moldings look like they've been dusted by a fresh fall of silvery snow. Meant to overwhelm, the furnishings are also baroque but predominantly befrilled rococo from the late 1700s. Particularly fine is the splendidly ornamented pulpit (circa 1765) by the sculptor Jan Antonin Quittainer. Among the artworks here is a seventeenth-century silver-plated statue of St. Václav by Jan Jiří Bendl; it's in one of the chapels on the right, under the tower.

If you're a Dvořák fan, you might want to turn up **Žitná Street**, one block over, and see the apartment building at no. 10 where the composer lived and worked for nearly thirty years. A wall plaque marks the spot.

On the southeast corner of Řeznická Street, at **čp. 672-I**, you'll see a large bronze memorial tablet set into the wall, a typically compelling, highly wrought creation of František Bílek, the remarkable Czech mystical fin-de-siècle artist whose home and atelier we visited on Walk 3. It's a reminder that this site was the birthplace of Jerome of Prague in 1380, the martyred friend and supporter of Jan Hus who followed him into the flames of Roman Catholic–designated heresy when he was burned at the stake at the very spot where Hus died. Though the younger Jerome was of a very different temperament from Hus—Jerome was a sophisticated, spirited product of the boiling medieval student world, educated at Oxford and the Sorbonne, rather than a theoretician—both priests had preached against corruption of the clergy, and especially against such egregious and pervasive practices as the selling of indulgences. These were nothing more than insurance policies assuring a speedy ascent to heaven upon death, with which the Church tried to raise money for its bloody crusades. And both priests believed that the scriptures, not the Church, were the final authority on religious questions. Jerome, in a moment of terror, had at first admitted his master's heresy and recanted, but later withdrew those words and passionately defended his original position. He proved a more eloquent humanist than reformer: reviewing some of the historic cases where men had been killed for their beliefs, such as that of the apostle Stephen, he told his accusers that there could be no greater sin than that priests, as men of God, should wrongly execute a priest.

Reaction to the capital punishments of Hus and Jerome was swift, and brings us right to the Gothic **New Town Hall** across the street. Here the first serious riot broke out, the first volleys were fired in the deathly battle for ideals by the two condemned men's followers, the Hussites you've been hearing so much about. Unable to suffer these martyrdoms, much less the abrading friction of Czech vs. German sentiment they symbolized, the Hussites stirred up a revolution, the most slashing, sensational drama of Czech history. It may have been another first: the nineteenth-century Czech historian František Palacký believed that the Hussite conflict was the first war in history that was fought for intellectual, rather than material, interests, a statement other historians might challenge.

The event known as the (first) Defenestration of Prague took place at these New Town Hall windows on Sunday morning, July 30, 1419. (Unlike at the Castle, it is impossible to say exactly which window.) Lighting the fuse at Our Lady of the Snows church, a radical, fiery priest named Jan Želivský, with monstrance aloft, gathered a huge band of armed sympathizers and led them here to demand the release of cohorts imprisoned in the tower's dungeons. On the way they forcibly took back St. Stephen's, a nearby church that had been theirs for a while, as Želivský conducted mass—bread *and* wine, of course. At the Town Hall, the crowd's demands were met with abuse and rocks thrown from the windows. Next thing you know, the hated Catholic town councillors appointed by King Wenceslas IV (son of Charles IV) were themselves being flung from those windows, impaled on the pikes and halberds and spears below. Those who survived the fall were finished off by the mob. The enigmatic Jan Žižka may or may not have made an appearance at this point; reports conflict. Three hundred mounted soldiers of the king's guard apparently did show up, but fled at the sight of the ferocious-looking people's militia.

It was not to be the last time that Hussite foes would

spin on their heels in fear. A few years later, so formidable a fighting machine had the citizen's army become that, as one version of the story goes, an entire imperial crusading force, spurred by rumor before they spotted even a single Hussite, bolted from the battlefield. Back at the Town Hall, the New Towners chose and voted in their own representatives. When the apoplectic, alcoholic king heard what had happened there, he must have suffered a stroke, because two weeks later he was dead. Before his demise, at the urging of his wife and other sympathizers, he had managed to corroborate the new town council. Žižka's military organization and tactics were ingenious and matchless, chief among them was the novel mobilization of farm-wagon phalanxes. Spirits soared, and by 1431 there wasn't a mercenary or crusading army in Europe that dared to challenge the Hussites. As they continued to pile up victories, they received invitations to lend their expertise to struggles in other countries, and parents all over the continent brandished the word "Hussite" like "bogeyman" to quiet disobedient children. Of course, all these gains were not without their dark side: the raids were extremely destructive to life and property, especially to churches and monasteries, and not always evenhanded; the violence fed on itself and soon the Hussites split into unhappy factions. In 1422 the "leftist" Želivský got too far out of hand for the more conservative Old Towners: they trapped him on the pretext of a meeting in the Old Town Hall and decapitated him. In 1434 the Old Towners marched on the New Town Hall, headquarters of the radicals, and ripped up the town charter. In the same year, the factions fought each other and almost committed suicide at the tragic Battle of Lipany. The contradictions of the strife has led some contemporary historians to condemn the Hussites' methods as fascist, and yet their achievements were real, at least for a time. Astonishingly, the Hussites not only never lost a battle with their enemies, they actually won the war—when a 1436 agreement called the Basel Compactata guaranteed their religious rights and demands. They were substantially the same principles that characterized the Lutheran Reformation a century later. Never before had the authority of the Roman Church been challenged and successfully ruptured. But it was too much too soon for the rest of a traumatized Europe.

The original New Town Hall was built in stages and, like so many Prague buildings, has many architectural layers, the first two dating to 1377–78 and 1411–18; in 1451 the tower we see today was built on top of the older substructure through which there had been an arch, now walled in. Between 1520 and 1526, steep late-Gothic gables were added to the Renaissance south wing facing the square. Then in 1806 the New Town Hall was rebuilt in a classicist style for the purposes of housing a criminal court and prison. About a hundred years later this facade was removed and Antonin Wiehl, one of the foremost architects of the historicist school, reconstructed the wing in mid-sixteenth-century Neo-Renaissance style. Inside is the original Gothic two-chambered main hall, with cross-ribbed vaults on massive cylindrical pillars, vintage 1411; today it's used for weddings. The tower itself has been minimally restored over the years. Note the bit of chain, once used to close off the street, hanging from the side of the east wall. Next to the chain is a measuring rod. Inside the tower is a chapel, and deep down in the Gothic cellars are the dungeons that caused the New Town Hall to be called the Czech Bastille until the turn of the century. The east wing, extending into Vodičkova Street, though well preserved, is being restored at the time of writing; eventually it will hold an art gallery, a library, a reading room, and conference and reception rooms for concerts and theater programs in the arcaded courtyard.

From here we'll head for the west side of Charles Square and down **Resslova Street**, where our walk ends at the **Church of Saints Cyril and Methodius** on the right side of the street. Thus we leap into the twentieth century (via this eighteenth-century baroque church) with

the story of a very differently inspired, though nonethe-less elegiac, martyrdom. Though Kilián Ignác Dientzen-hofer may have participated in the design of this church from 1735 to 1740, and it is admired for the architectural resolution of the unusual forecourt, its place in history is assured by events that took place in the large crypt, which used to be underground in the days before the street was lowered to access the river.

In June of 1942 Czechoslovakia had been occupied by Nazi troops for three years. The population had ca-pitulated; resistance was desultory, because soon after the arrival of Hitler's golden boy and possible successor, Reinhard Heydrich, a reign of terror began in which more than five thousand Czechs died or vanished into concentration camps. Betrayed and abandoned by their allies, many Czechs had caved in to small-defenseless-country syndrome and were reluctant to commit suicide. The president, one Emil Hacha, collaborated further by handing Heydrich the keys to the Castle treasure, where the Nazi tried on the crown of Saint Wenceslas, ignoring the legend that anyone but the rightful anointee who wears the crown will promptly perish. Over in London, the site of a truly active Czech resistance, a plot was hatched to assassinate Heydrich by parachuting several exiled Czechoslovak soldiers into the country. They shot at the Nazi as he rode in his open Mercedes, and he died nine days later. If the Czechs had pulled off another first, it was also a unique act that was not to be repeated dur-ing the course of the war: Heydrich was the sole key Nazi to be eliminated.

Immediate and horrific retaliation followed: German orders were given that one out of every ten citizens was to be shot until the assassins were found, and any town or persons who had connections with Britain's Royal Air Force, which parachuted the men in, became an instant

Memorial at Church of Saints Cyril and Methodius

target. Two entire villages, Lidice and Ležáky, were lev-
eled, the ruins pulverized, the ground planted over, and
the names obliterated from maps and documents. Their
male population was shot. The Nazis were nothing if not
thorough. During the search, the two Czechoslovaks who
had fired the shots were hidden in the church crypt,
whose narrow window you see in front of you from the
sidewalk. Their protectors were the Czech Orthodox
Bishop Gorazd and his colleagues, their surroundings 112
coffined clerics. Before they could be smuggled out of the
country, the men were betrayed by one of their own now-
terrorized plotters. An assault started on the church and
water was pumped in, but rather than be taken alive the
paratroopers killed themselves. The bishop, two priests,
the chaplain, and the chairman of the parish council were
all executed. A parachutist and a priest are the odd couple portrayed on the memorial bronze wall plaque. Inside
the crypt there is a small exhibition of photographs. It's
usually open in the mornings from 9:00 to 11:00, Tuesday through Saturday, or by telephoning 29 55 95 for an
appointment.

Though our walk ends here, you might be wondering
about the severe-looking, black-edged stone church across
the street, at the corner of Dittrichova. **St. Wenceslas na
Zderaze** is a primarily Gothic, particularly old church,
even by Prague standards of antiquity, with the first Romanesque layer originating 1170–81. It takes its name
from a pre–New Town settlement in turn named for one
Zderada, a favorite of Prince Vratislav I, one of the earliest
Bohemian rulers. You can still see how the church's Romanesque tower wall was incorporated into its later
(1380) enlarged Gothic incarnation. A star-shaped vault
frescoed with legends of St. Wenceslas crowns the nave;
the frescoes under the choir are seventeenth-century late
Renaissance. Admirers of František Bílek will fixate on
the altar and crucifix with bench, created by the sculptor
in 1930.

From here you can return to the city center by continuing down Resslova to the riverbank, where there is a streetcar stop; or you can take the tram or metro from Charles Square. Wenceslas Square is just a few of blocks by foot via Vodičkova Street from the New Town Hall.

And so we end our final Prague walk. The somber events connected to the latter portion of this walk might strike some as too woeful for words, but like the eyesore Communist-era structures scattered around the city (though there are few in the historic center), these sad stories are, of course, part and parcel of the omnipresent past that Czechs have always lived with. Somebody once said that geography is destiny, and certainly it has proved disastrous for this city and this country to be situated right in between the maws of Germany and the former Soviet empire. Yet the consequences of this reality only underscore the miracle of survival and beauty that is Prague—they don't call it magic for nothing. There it goes again, reinventing itself before your very eyes. Prepare to be equally amazed when you next return.

Hotels,
Restaurants,
Cafés, Shops, and
Museums

Hotels

This is a select list, by district, of recommended establishments with emphasis on smaller, characterful hostelries, generally omitting ultramodern charmless establishments catering mostly to business travelers.

Malá Strana

There are very few hotels in this district at the time of writing, though a couple of projects are under way.

U Páva (At the Peacock's), U Lužického Semináře 106, Prague 1, tel. 53 22 51. Tiny—three suites, eight

Stairs down to Uvoz Street, Hradčany

doubles—renovated seventeenth-century town house on narrow, winding street near Vojanovy Park. Restaurant, bar. Expensive.

U tři pštrosu (At the Three Ostriches), Dražického Square 12, Prague 1, tel. 53 61 51. Once owned by the feather purveyor to the royal court; small, charming, extraordinarily located immediately off Charles Bridge, so it may not be for light sleepers. Upper rooms feature original painted and beamed ceilings; furnishings need updating. Expensive.

Hradčany

U Raka (At the Lobster), bottom of Černínska 10/93, tel. 351 453. A cozy guest-house (log-cabin) style hotel with only five rooms, just off the villagelike Nový Svět Street, near the Castle. Quiet. Moderately expensive.

Savoy, Keplerova 6, tel. 53 74 50. Following total renovation, promises to provide top-grade service and modernity (Austrian management) behind restored art nouveau facade. Expensive.

New Town

Ambassador, Wenceslas Square 5, Prague 1, tel. 21 43 111. Medium-sized hotel, small bustling lobby, decent food. Expensive.

Grand Hotel Evropa, Wenceslas Square 9, Prague 1, tel. 235 52 74. Charming and old world, a touch seedy, unexceptional service, food. Moderate.

Palace Praha, Panská 12, Prague 1, tel. 236 00 08. Fully renovated, top service, all amenities including CNN, casino, indoor parking, hotel food. Very Expensive.

Esplanade, Washingtonova 19, tel. 22 25 52. Near top of Wenceslas Square/main railway station; comfortable, commendable food, good service. Expensive.

Meteor, Hybernska 6, tel. 235 85 17, fax 22 47 15. Completely renovated, all amenities. Moderately Expensive.

Opera, Tešnov 13, tel. 231 56 09. Decent, not luxurious; close to freeway, so ask for a quiet room or skip it. Inexpensive.

Old Town

Ungelt, Štupartská 1, Prague 1, 232 04 70–71. If you prefer mazelike, medieval streets, nothing beats this location, also for proximity to historic attractions. Eleven suites, fully renovated, parking, summer terrace. No elevator; no room service. Moderately expensive.

Paříž, U obecního domů 1 (at the Municipal House—near náměstí Republiky), Prague 1, tel. 236 0820. Splendid, rich art nouveau exterior and café, rooms more prosaic, service indifferent. Expensive.

Dejvice

Praha, Sušická Street 20, Prague 6, tel. 333 81 11. Large, modern, efficient, out of the center. Expensive.

Botels on the River
(An alternative for the budget minded; all are permanently moored.)

Admiral, hořejší nábřeží (upper embankment), Prague 5, tel. 547 445–9. Moderate.

Albatros, nábřeží Ludvika Svobody, Prague 1, tel. 231 36 00. Clean and rudimentary; nightclub. Inexpensive.

Restaurants

Expensive

U zlaté hrušky (At the Golden Pear), Nový Svět 3, Hradčany, tel. 53 11 33. Refined international with thoughtful variations on old Czech themes. In summer there's garden seating behind the wall across the street, with cut-rate set price and menu.

U Malířu (At the Painter's), Maltézské náměstí, Malá Strana, tel. 53 18 83. Very good French cooking at extraordinary (high) prices; wonderful painted ceilings, elegant yet rustic.

Vinarna V Zátiší (Still Life), Liliová 1, Old Town, tel. 265 107. Considerably better than average cooking on Bethlemské náměstí; local (well-heeled) chocolate-mousse freaks gravitate here.

Parnas, Národní třída, New Town, tel. 26 12 50, 26 57 00. On the riverfront, unbeatable view of the Castle, elegant, authentic thirties decor, more than passable food, champagne brunch on weekends.

Lobkovická vinarna, Vlašská 17, Malá Strana, tel. 53 01 85. Top wine tavern, renovated, better than average eating with tasty appetizers; menu includes fish, chicken, rabbit, and venison in addition to beef.

Peklo—Calafuria Club, Strahovské nádvoří 1/130, Hradčany, tel. 53 32 77. Italian/Czech specialties deep in a spacious cellar on Strahov monastery grounds; lively disco.

Lucullus, Pštrossova 29, Prague 1 (behind National Theater), tel. 29 42 24. Stately dining, excellent service, commendable menu.

Moderately Expensive

David, near American Embassy on Tržište 21/611, Malá Strana, tel. 53 93 25. Small, elegant, white-washed walls, antiques.

U červeného kola (At the Red Wheel), Anežská 2, Old Town, tel. 231 89 41. Tucked away near the old convent of St. Agnes; basic menu, well-prepared food.

Vikarka, Vikarska 6, Hradčany, tel. 535 158, 536 497. Also a pub. Former canteen dive (since 1566) of the vicars and canons of St. Vitus Cathedral, in whose shadow it stands; later haunt of famous writers, musicians, artists, and dissidents; recently thoroughly renovated.

U 7 andělu (At the Seven Angels), Jílská 20, Old Town, tel. 26 01 04. Spacious, somewhat like a refined tavern; satisfying Czech food.

Lví dvůr (Lion's Court), U Prašného mostu 54, Hradčany, tel. 53 53 89. Small, super steaks, often excellent service, reasonable.

Nebozízek, Petřínské sady, Prague 1, tel. 53 79 05 (take funicular from Ujezd Street in Malá Strana to first stop). Decent food (try the garlic soup), but it's the romance and the view from Petřín Hill you come for.

Faros, Šporková 5, Malá Strana, tel. 533 482. Greek-Czech, very cozy, food more Czech than Greek.

Myslivna (The Hunting Lodge), Jagellonská 21, Prague 3 (Vinohrady), tel. 627 02 09. Specializes in well-prepared game: venison, pheasant, quail.

Valdštejnska hospoda, Tomášska 16, Malá Strana, tel. 53 61 95. Czech restaurant whose menu lists no Czech specialties, though they are available. Attractive above-ground wine cellar, caters to tourists, food is evolving.

Florianuv Dvůr (Florian's Court), Ujezd 16, Malá Strana, tel. 53 05 02. Respectable fresh-fish cuisine in an imaginatively artistic setting.

Ali Baba, Vodičkova 5 (near Charles Square), Prague 1, tel. 20 36 36. Authenic Middle Eastern, spicy and well prepared.

I n e x p e n s i v e

Pizzeria Macedonia, Korenského 3, Prague 5 (Smíchov), tel. 54 17 92. Good individual-sized pies, salad bar, satisfying.

Buffet Delicatesse, Palace Hotel, Panská 12, Prague 1. Handy for a quick bite, salad bar varies from acceptable and fresh to yesterday's leftovers mixed anew; also filling but unexceptional hot food. No reservations.

Penguin's, Zborovska 5, Smíchov, tel. 54 56 60. Frequently lauded for fresh vegetables and efficient service; open to midnight.

U Vladaře (At the Sovereign's), Maltežské náměstí 10, Malá Strana, tel. 53 81 28. Very reasonable prices in the vinarna part; try the three-dumplings sampler dessert.

Vltava, on the river at Rašínovo nábřeží (lower embankment), New Town, tel. 29 49 64. Fish, Czech favorites, hearty and rustic; Havel was a customer when he lived in the area.

Na rybarně (The Fishmonger's), Gorázdová 17, New Town. Fresh fish natch, simple and unpretentious but teensy.

Radost (it means "Joy"), Bělehradská 120, Prague 2. Includes vegetarian menu, part of disco, open after midnight.

U Dvou Koček (At the Two Cats), Uhelný trh 10, Old Town. Historic brewery and pub with dining room at the back; typical Czech standards.

U maltézských rytířu (At the Knights of Malta), Prokopská 10, Malá Strana, tel. 53 63 57. Very friendly family-run eatery.

U Cedru, Na Hutích 13, Prague 6, Dejvice, tel. 312 29 74. Excellent Middle Eastern appetizers, Lebanese style—you didn't come to Prague for this? Variety is ever the spice . . .

U Fleku, Kremencova, tel. 29 24 36 (but they don't take reservations). Large noisy beer hall beloved by Germans. Food not the object here: roast beef, pork, or goulash with bread dumplings—cheap and filling. Go for the beer.

Country Life, Jungmannova 1, open 9:00 A.M. to 6:30 P.M., Mon.–Thurs.; 9:00 A.M. to 3:00 P.M. Friday; closed weekends Vegetarian, natural food cafeteria, run by Seventh Day Adventists.

Cafés

Hotel Paříž, Obecní Dům, náměstí Republiky, Prague 1, tel. 236 08 20. Elegant art nouveau surroundings.

Obecní Dům (Municipal House), náměstí Republiky 5, Prague 1. Offers two cafes loaded with art nouveau splendor: Nouveau Café and Café Mozart.

Slavia, across the street from the National Theater on Národní. The dissident literati hot spot since it opened in the First Republic.

Café Evropa, Wenceslas Square 25, Prague 1. Faded but elegant, service reminds of the bad old days, open till midnight.

Café Savoy, Vítězná 5, Prague 5 (across the river from the National Theater). The elaborately painted 1800s ceiling is the main attraction here.

F/X Café F/X, Bělehradská 120, Prague 2. Specializes in coffee concoctions, also vegetarian; open twenty-three hours a day.

U zeleného čaje, Nerudova 19, Malá Strana, open daily to 7:00 P.M. Really a tearoom, intimate, serves Czech herbal teas, a *non-smoking* rarity with piped-in Vivaldi.

Shops

Bookstores

Collet's, inside Československy spisovatel bookstore, Národní 9, Prague 1. Reasonable selection of books in English (fiction, poetry, drama); coffee table and armchairs provided for browsers.

Antiquariat na Janskem vršku, Janský vršek, Malá Strana. Secondhand, rare books, periodicals, old prints, helpful service.

At Charles Bridge, Karlova 2, Old Town. Secondhand, rare books, prints, drawings.

Antikvariat, Celetná 31, Old Town. Old and rare books, prints, photographs.

Antiques

(Shops generally closed on weekends and often for lunch.)

Antikvita, Na hutích 9, Old Town. A favorite of local dealers.

Hodinařství Václav Matouš, Mikulandská 10, Old Town. All manner of timepieces, repairs.

Athena, U Starého hřbitova 4, Old Town. Jumblemania; open weekends.

Rudolf Spičák Vetesník, Ostrovní 24, Old Town. Secondhand stuff, bargain-basement legend.

Folk Art

Česká jizba, Karlova 12, Old Town
Krásna jizba, Národní 36, New Town

Costume Jewelry

Bijoux de Bohème, Old Town Square 6, Prague 1; also Na příkopě 15, Prague 1, and Wenceslas Square 53, Prague 1

Recordings/Music Publishing

Supraphon, Palackého 1, Prague 1, and other locations around town. World repertoire, classical, CDs, international shipments.

Glass, Porcelain, Ceramics, Glass Art

Česky porcelan, Perlova 1, Old Town. Czech porcelain from Dubí only; identified by its slightly bleeding blue dye on blue-onion (trade name Rokoko) pattern.

Bohemia Moser, Na příkopě 12, New Town. Most famous name in Czech glass and crystal; also porcelain. Especially reliable for color, style, and quality.

Galerie Bohm, Anglická 1 (enter Legerova), Prague 2, open Tuesday–Friday, 2:00–6:00 P.M., Saturday/Sunday, 10:00 A.M.–6:00 P.M. Best selection of glass art in town.

Gloves

Rukavice, Železna Street (on the left side of the street en route from Old Town Square to the Karolinum). Great ivory chamois styles.

Rukavice, Vinohradská 38, Vinohrady. Also suede, fur-lined slippers. Very reasonable.

Department Stores
Hours (generally): 8:00 A.M. to 7:00 P.M.

Kotva, Republic Square, Prague 1. Also has a good bakery.

Maj, Národní třída, Prague 1.

Družba, Wenceslas Square 21, Prague 1.

Bíla Labut, Na pořičí 3, Prague 1.

Diamant, Wenceslas Square 3.

Selected Museums and Galleries

Museum of the City of Prague, Na poříčí 52, Prague 1. Local lore. Most important exhibit is Langweil's painstakingly handmade early 1800s model of Prague. Closed Mondays.

National Museum, top of Wenceslas Square. Natural history—save this for the kids. Includes a pantheon of Czech heroes. Closed Tuesdays.

Golz-Kinský Palace (National Gallery), Old Town Square 12. Changing exhibitions of graphic art. Closed Mondays.

Lobkowicz Palace, Prague Castle area. General Czech history up to 1848, third-rate facsimile of crown jewels. Also special exhibitions, for instance on the delightful Czech puppetry tradition. Closed Mondays.

Troja, outside the center in Prague 8, near the zoo, tel. 84 51 33. Baroque chateau with permanent and changing nineteenth-century Czech art exhibitions; spectacular trompe l'oeil frescoed ballroom and formal gardens.

Zbraslav Collection of 19th–20th Century Sculpture, in a former Cistercian monastery thirty minutes outside Prague. Get there by buses 129, 241, 243, 255 from Smíchov railway station to Zbraslavské náměstí; or by boat cruise from an east bank pier under the Palacký bridge. Tel. 293 803. A must for lovers of the plastic arts. Open May–October. Closed Mondays.

Museum of Decorative Arts (Uměleckoprumyslové muzeum), 17 listopadu 2, Old Town. Tops in its class—arts, crafts, applied art, furniture, from the late sixteenth to the nineteenth century; also contemporary glass art, prominent art history library. Open 10:00 A.M.–6:00 P.M. Closed Mondays.

National Technical Museum, Kostelní 42, Prague 7. Fascinating, required viewing for old-car buffs; also transport, astronomy, metallurgy, mining, aviation. Closed Mondays.

Bertramka (Mozart Museum), Mozartova 169, Smíchov. Villa and gardens; Mozart stayed here with his hosts, the Dušeks, and wrote the *Don Giovanni* overture. Closed Tuesdays.

Bílek Villa (see Walk 3), Mickewiczova 1, Hradčany, Prague 1. Private home and studio of the great Czech symbolist sculptor František Bílek; designed entirely by him in 1911. Open May 15–October 15. Closed Mondays and between 12:00 noon and 1:00 P.M.

House of the Lords of Kunštat and Poděbrady, end of Řetězová, off Husova street, Old Town. The best place to see what thirteenth-century Romanesque Prague interiors looked like. Once the home of King George of Poděbrady (see Walk 5), it's a series of chambers buried under the Old Town, only discovered at the turn of this century. Open May to October. Closed Mondays.

Břevnov Monastery, at 22 tram Břevnovský klaster terminus. Though not technically a museum or gallery, this Benedictine abbey celebrated its thousandth anniversary in 1993 and is likely the outstanding high baroque structure (both Dientzenhofers worked on it) of its kind in Prague. See the church, prelature, Romanesque crypt, and grounds.

Index

Index

Index

Index

Index

Index

RUSSIAWALKS by David and Valeria Matlock
Seven intimate tours—four in Moscow and three in St. Petersburg—that explore the hidden treasures of these enigmatic cities.
304 pages, photos, maps $12.95 Paper

NEW YORKWALKS by The 92nd Street Y, edited by Batia Plotch
One of the city's most visible cultural and literary institutions guides you through six historic neighborhoods in New York.
336 pages, photos, maps $12.95 Paper

BARCELONAWALKS by George Semler
Five walking tours through Spain's cultural and artistic center—synonymous with such names as Gaudí, Miró, and Picasso.
272 pages, photos, maps $12.95 Paper

JERUSALEMWALKS, Revised Edition, by Nitza Rosovsky
Six intimate walks that allow the mystery and magic of this city to unfold.
304 pages, photos, maps $14.95 Paper

BEIJINGWALKS by Don J. Cohn and Zhang Jingqing
Six intimate walking tours of the most historic quarters of this politically and culturally complex city.
272 pages, photos, maps $15.95 Paper

MADRIDWALKS by George Semler
Five extraordinary walking tours that uncover the many architectural and historical secrets of this glorious city.
272 pages, photos, maps $14.95 Paper

BERLINWALKS by Peter Fritzsche and Karen Hewitt
Four intimate walking tours of Berlin's most enchanting quarters.
288 pages, photos, maps $14.95 Paper

Available at your local bookseller or from Special Sales Department, Henry Holt and Company, 115 West 18th Street,

New York, New York 10011, (212) 886-9200. Please add $2.00 for postage and handling, plus $.50 for each additional item ordered. (New York residents, please add applicable state and local sales tax.) Please allow 4–6 weeks for delivery. Prices and availability are subject to change.